D0436180

JEWISH WRITING IN THE CONTEMPORARY WORLD

Series Editor:

Sander L. Gilman, University of Illinois at Chicago

Contemporary Jewish Writing in Germany

An Anthology

Edited by Leslie Morris & Karen Remmler

University of Nebraska Press : Lincoln & London

Acknowledgments for the use of copyrighted material appear on p. 247, which constitutes an extension of the copyright page. Publication of this book was assisted by a grant from the National Endowment for the Arts. ∞ Manufactured in the United States of America.

Library of Congress Cataloging-in-Publication Data
Contemporary Jewish writing in Germany:
an anthology / edited by Leslie Morris and Karen Remmler.
p.cm. Includes bibliographical references.
ISBN 0-8032-3940-8 (cloth: alkaline paper)
1. German fiction – 20th century – Translations into English.
2. German fiction – Jewish authors – Translations into English. 3. Short stories, German – Translations into English.
4. Jews – Germany – Fiction. 5. Jews – Fiction.
6. Holocaust, Jewish (1939-1945) – Fiction. I. Morris, Leslie, 1958- II. Remmler, Karen.
PT1327 .C68 2002 833'.9140808924–dc21 2001056850

Contents

Preface

Our intention with this volume is to present the English-speaking reader with a range of texts that express the complexity and diversity of contemporary Jewish writing in Germany. Unlike Elena Lappin's or Susan Stern's previously published collections of Jewish writing from the German-speaking countries, this volume includes longer works and fewer authors. Instead of aiming for a 'representative' overview, we have chosen the works of four authors whose contribution to Jewish writing in Germany today is significant and, we feel, merits a wider audience. The experimental, at times even cryptic, style of Esther Dischereit's work, for example, poses certain challenges for the translator, editor, and reader. We have opted to rework substantially the initial translation of the texts included in this volume and have striven for accuracy while taking some liberties to convey the disparate styles and literary experimentation of the original texts. Our work as editors and translators is informed by the belief that the goal of translation is not to produce transparency but rather to maintain the ambiguity of meaning and, in the case of these texts in particular, a deep-seated skepticism about the viability of representation after the Shoah. In the texts by Biller and Dischereit, in particular, we have preserved the gaps and empty spaces on the printed page, as they are intrinsic to the voice of fragmentation and dispersion found within these texts. The pitfalls of translation were at times a direct consequence of the nonstandard syntax found in many of these works, and yet we would hope that whatever gaps might still exist in the translation are consonant with the defamiliarization that characterizes the original. Our one regret is that we were unable to include Honigmann's *Soharas Reise* (Sohara's journey) in its entirety.

As an additional guide for readers unfamiliar with German Jewish or German culture and history, we include occasional notes and a glossary of names, terms, and organizations.

We are grateful for the generous support of Mount Holyoke College, the Alexander Humboldt Foundation, and the Jewish Studies program at the University of Minnesota. For his careful and skillful reading of an earlier draft of the translation, we would like to thank Don Eric Levine. Karin Obermeier contributed her critical eye to the final translation of Esther Dischereit's *Joëmis Tisch* ('Joemi's Table') and translated the original glossary that appeared with the German version of this novel into English. Blythe Inners deserves special mention for her assistance in this project. Our involvement in this project would not have come about without the support and encouragement of the series editor, Sander Gilman, and the editorial support of the staff at the University of Nebraska Press. Finally, we would like to thank Katja Behrens, Maxim Biller, Esther Dischereit, Barbara Honigmann, and their publishers for their generosity in granting us the rights to translate their work.

Leslie Morris and Karen Remmler

Introduction

Any volume on Jewish writing in Germany published more than a half-century after the Third Reich will inevitably raise the specter of the Shoah and its impact on present-day life in Germany.[1] Katja Behrens, Maxim Biller, Esther Dischereit, and Barbara Honigmann are only four of a growing number of second-generation and, more recently, third-generation writers for whom the remembrance of the Shoah plays a major role in their self-understanding as Jewish writers living in Germany. While the life stories in this volume may speak again and again of Auschwitz, these four writers embrace a multitude of identities not defined solely by post-Holocaust Jewishness.

With the exception of Maxim Biller, all were born in West or East Germany, and all but Honigmann live in Germany today. Although their lives have not been disrupted by forced exile, a distinctively diasporic consciousness marks their writing. Unlike the first generation of German Jewish writers, who either survived the concentration and extermination camps, escaped Germany, or lived there in hiding under an assumed identity, the writers in this volume draw from imagination and 'postmemory' rather than firsthand experience of the Shoah. Postmemory circulates in the aftermath of the Shoah, no longer as lived, experienced memory but rather as memory that is mediated through existing representations—linguistic and visual—of the Shoah.[2] Most significantly, these four writers all refuse to be confined to the role of victim by Germans seeking absolution; instead, their lives and their work complicate the monolithic German Jewish dichotomy of perpetrator and victim. The subject of their writing is not the Shoah per se—they have no firsthand memories—but the meaning of its remembrance (and forgetting) in contemporary Germany and its impact on relations among Germans, Jews, and others living in the now unified nation. Although these writers are not engaged in the act of bearing witness, as was the previous generation of German Jewish writers, such as

Grete Weil (1906–), Paul Celan (1920–1970), Nelly Sachs (1891–1970), and Jurek Becker (1937–1997), they nevertheless testify to the psychological and historical trauma of the Shoah and its impact on the children of both survivors and perpetrators.

Yet even as the remembrance of the Shoah in contemporary Germany is a common thread in their writing, these authors have a distinct approach to incorporating its presence. They write of the strangeness of living in a country where the absence of Jews drives political decisions, cultural identities, and social interactions, and where unencumbered relationships between Germans and Jews are rare. The authors do not promote a facile reconciliation between Germans and Jews but rather dissect the mechanisms and attitudes that shape contemporary German-Jewish relations. In fact, the literature of contemporary Jewish writers in Germany could be called German writing since the characters and the circumstances depicted are often mired in national icons and histories particular to non-Jewish German experience. The texts by Behrens, Biller, Dischereit, and Honigmann seek to break down monolithic images of 'the Jew' as victim yet question the continued sense of alienation that many Jews feel in Germany. These authors question the possibility of reestablishing a Jewish culture in Germany; however, the diversity of their writing reminds readers of the heterogeneity of Jewish life in Germany today. This writing deals not only with the question of Jewish identity but with the vicissitudes of Jewish male and female identities in the context of emigration, intergenerational conflict, and sexuality.

Behrens, Biller, Dischereit, and Honigmann all touch on the cultural and social issues that are raised by inhabiting a hyphenated identity. A central question that emerges in these texts is how they, as writers and public intellectuals, can establish themselves in the public realm as Jews *and* Germans. Are Jews by definition outsiders in German society regardless of their 'Germanness'? As Honigmann wrote in a 1992 essay entitled 'Selbstporträt als Jüdin' (Self-portrait of a Jewish woman), 'I am also a writer, and one can say lightly, a Jewish one. But I am not so sure about that, because what I have said does not make me into a Jewish writer. It means that I belong existentially more to Jewish culture than to the German one, but culturally I belong to Germany and to nothing else.' Honigmann sums up the dilemma by saying that the so-called German-Jewish symbiosis, this 'inability to come free of one another,' had finally come about 'because the Germans and the Jews had now become a pair in Auschwitz, whom even death could not separate.' Similarly, Dischereit writes about the tendency of Germans to see themselves as indirect victims of the Shoah, since the remembrance of the Nazi past continues to occupy the German present.

Despite their secular upbringing, these German Jewish writers nonetheless have strong Jewish identities. Yet this Jewish identity is complex and unstable, shaped and defined by a continuously charged and problematic relationship that persists between German and Jew. On the one hand, German Jewish writers are exoticized, fetishized, and commodified by their non-Jewish reading public, yet at the same time, they are observers of the Germans who are watching and objectifying them. In a recent essay Katja Behrens has noted precisely the instability of what she terms the 'rift' between German and Jew: 'This rift between us, the progeny of both sides, is an unstable thing. It isn't always the same size. Sometimes it closes and becomes a hairline crack, a fracture you can forget, then it suddenly yawns wide and becomes unbridgeable.'[3] In many respects, the texts included in this volume testify to the Morphean quality of the rift between German and Jew as they create, in narrative form, alternative ways of approaching the problem. Most significantly, however, by reclaiming a semblance of subjectivity and agency in their writing, Behrens, Biller, Dischereit, and Honigmann refuse to be co-opted into the Jews that many Germans would have them become—petrified victims.

Yet despite the complexity and ambivalence about their Jewish identities, contemporary German Jewish writers are defined by their publishers and a non-Jewish reading public as *Jewish* and not simply *German* writers. Since Jews comprise only a marginal percent of the German population (official estimates of the total Jewish population in unified Germany is approximately eighty thousand in a total population of approximately eighty-two million), the reception of the work by Jewish writers and journalists is foremost by *Germans*.[4] Yet the diversity of opinion about what constitutes Jewish identity and culture within the specific historical context of Germany's past and present problematizes the possibilities of self-definition among

German Jews. Quite often the marketing of this literature emphasizes the Jewish identity of the authors even when the texts themselves do not concern themselves with 'Jewish' themes or topics. It is, to say the least, ironic that emphasizing the Jewish identity of an author, whether that author accepts this designation or not, has a strong impact on the sale and reception of the book. Often the literary quality of the text itself receives little attention, while the 'Jewish' content or biography of the author is highlighted in the press releases and reviews.

Written in a witty, journalistic idiom stripped of lyrical image and literary metaphor, these texts seem at times to lack the poetic, self-consciously 'literary' qualities of earlier German Jewish writing. Yet the halting speech and staccato rhythm of Dischereit's many 'scenes' in *Joëmis Tisch*, for example, or the dispersal of fictive and nonfictive documents, letters, and interview protocols in Behrens's short story 'Arthur Mayer oder Das Schweigen,' suggest a desire to fuse imaginative and historical writing. Significantly, all the texts in this volume are written in the first-person narrative voice. However, rather than asserting an authoritative, monolithic narrative voice, these authors evoke a sense of the historically provisional while writing in the first person, thus creating new layers of diasporic consciousness even as they seek to insert themselves into German culture. Writing in German necessitates an interrogation of their role in conveying firsthand knowledge of being Jewish within a German context.

By writing in the first person (or a constellation of first-person narrators), the authors in this volume express the complexity of being Jewish in Germany. They deliberately question the tendency of the German public to ascribe autobiographical aspects to their writing. By placing unstable first-person voices at the center of their texts, they complicate all too facile interpretations of a static or monolithic Jewish identity. Inevitably, the rift that Behrens identifies finds its way into the linguistic and narrative structures of these texts. The stylistic rifts express a wariness about the viability of a closed, coherent, straightforward narrative and instead insist on the text as one that, in its sense of incompletion and fragmentation, marks the ongoing presence of the rift. These writers draw on a direct, often anecdotal and less aestheticized, form of speech, what one character in Maxim Biller's 'Harlem Holocaust' calls 'demeaning, insulting transparency' (134). The sacrilegious tone that characterizes Biller's short stories, for example, counters the expectation of a predominantly non-Jewish German readership that stories by Jews about the Shoah should remain pious, respectful, and, above all, devoid of references to sex. These writers, particularly Biller and Dischereit, question the notion of a 'proper' discourse for representing the Shoah and present instead narrative strategies for facing its obscenity.

As part of the current market interest in matters Jewish, it is significant that recent series in Jewish literature by major German publishing companies, such as Suhrkamp, frequently include translations or reprints of texts by Jews who live outside of Germany (Ochse 119) and few works by younger authors living and writing in Germany. As Dischereit comments in her essay 'No Exit from This Jewry' (1994), publishers have a difficult time categorizing her work when the 'Jewish' content is treated in conjunction with other issues of identity or when the images require a differentiated view of 'The Jew.' She calls for a recognition that Jews are contributing to German culture not as outsiders or as *Mitbürger* (fellow citizens) but as Germans. Writing for an audience that is predominantly non-Jewish, Dischereit has even gone so far as to compare this phenomenon to prostitution (Ochse 128 n.27).

Of course, there is no one Jewish 'voice' in Germany but rather a diverse chorus of writers whose work is read by both Jewish and non-Jewish readers. German Jews born after 1945 and writing in the 1980s and 1990s represent a new generation of Jewish Germans whose decision to remain in or to leave Germany is as much a statement about their German identity as it is about their ambivalence toward official, mostly religious, Jewish organizations in Germany. Rafael Seligmann, a German Jewish writer born in Palestine in 1947 who immigrated with his family to Germany in 1957, points out that most of the literature published in Germany by Jewish writers before the 1980s consisted of autobiographical accounts of the Holocaust or of life in exile (Seligmann 173). Not until the mid-1980s did contemporary Jewish writers living in Germany begin to write about their lives in present-day Germany, and their presence in the cultural sphere has increased throughout the 1990s.

The very presence of Jewish voices in public debates about Germany's memory politics and about what constitutes 'German' identity after the unification of East and West Germany, following the collapse of the Berlin Wall in 1989, is itself worth examining.

To readers unfamiliar with contemporary German culture, it might seem strange that Jews would even choose to live in Germany much less participate actively in public discourse. By reading literature by second-generation German Jews, the non-German reader can better grasp the intricacies of German-Jewish relations and its part in defining the role of Germany in the world. The texts included in this volume offer complex portraits of contemporary Germany that invite readers to reassess critically their own assumptions about not only German Jewish but also German culture before, during, and after the Shoah.

How can we define Germanness and Jewishness? What constitutes Jewish writing? How does remembrance of the Shoah shape and form these heterogeneous identities? How are these identities and experiences embodied in the literature written by Jewish writers living in Germany today? Under what circumstances have these writers published their work in the Federal Republic, and how do they perceive their role as Jewish writers in Germany today? How are the bodies of their fictional characters marked as Other?

The answers to these questions lie in part within the political and cultural context of the Federal Republic in the 1980s and in the consequences of those public events that brought about a stronger self-awareness and self-definition of Jewish identity. The fall of the Berlin Wall on 9 November 1989—a date that also marked the fifty-first anniversary of Kristallnacht (the November Pogrom) of 1938—and the subsequent call by major German politicians and many German citizens for a new era free from the burden of the past accentuated previous attempts by both conservative and liberal political factions to establish a positive German national identity throughout the 1980s. In extreme cases, attacks against people who were perceived to be 'foreign' highlighted the tensions that remained in a country that had supposedly dealt with its past through numerous rituals of *Vergangenheitsbewältigung* (coming to terms with the past), a term that itself signals the conflicts and tensions of an impossible task. The fall of the Berlin Wall in 1989 may have been a major turning point in German-Jewish relations, but it followed an already present increase in publications and public statements by Jews during the 1980s. What were the factors that brought about the increased presence of a Jewish voice among writers, journalists, and intellectuals of the postwar generation?

The impact of the controversial events of the 1980s cannot be underestimated: the increase in local and oral history projects encouraged Germans to take an interest in the legacy of Jewish life and death in their villages, towns, and cities; at the same time, several key public events brought about increased tensions between Germans and Jews. Most significant in this regard were the Bitburg affair (1985), the boycott of Rainer Werner Fassbinder's allegedly anti-Semitic play *Garbage, the City, and Death* (1985), the *Historikerstreit* (Historians' debate) (1985–86), and Philip Jenninger's speech to the Bundestag in November 1988 (commemorating the fiftieth anniversary of Kristallnacht) and his subsequent resignation as President of the Bundestag. These events coincided with a growing number of essays and articles on issues affecting the everyday life of Jews in Germany that appeared not only in mainstream German publications but also in journals with a more explicit Jewish readership.[5]

Two journals founded in the 1980s and dedicated to German Jewish life and culture in present-day Germany, *Babylon* and *Semittimes*, contain analyses of the political and cultural structures that both obscure and encourage anti-Semitism. They also contain discussions by Jewish intellectuals about the behavior and policies of the German government toward the commemoration of the victims of the Shoah and the controversial reaction of many self-proclaimed leftists in the German peace movement to the Gulf War. The discussions provoked by the work of Henryk Broder, Dan Diner, or even Marcel Reich-Ranicki bear witness to the living presence of Jews in Germany who have established themselves not only as Jews but also as leading critical voices in contemporary German society. Journalists such as Broder or Lea Fleischmann have written polemical critiques of the hypocrisy and ignorance of the Germans with regard to Jews. Broder's *Fremd im eigenen Land: Juden in der Bundesrepublik* (1979; Foreign in one's own country: Jews in the

Federal Republic of Germany) and Fleischmann's *Dies ist nicht mein Land: Eine Jüdin verläßt die Bundesrepublik* (1980; This is not my country: a Jewish woman leaves the Federal Republic) express not only alienation but also a growing insistence among Jews that non-Jewish Germans learn to accept 'that there were *live* Jews in Germany who wanted to be known for who they were and what they were doing' (Zipes 19). Conversely, the historian Michael Wolffsohn's book *Ewige Schuld?* (1988; Eternal guilt) pleads for a reassessment of the centrality of the Shoah in Germany today and calls for a less polemical relation between Germans and Jews.

As many second-generation Jews living in Germany began to participate more fully in the cultural life and public debates of the 1980s, a parallel generation of non-Jewish Germans sought to break with the past and establish a German national identity that was free from the burden of the Shoah. Consequently, much of the dialogue between Germans and Jews revolves around the difficulty that German society has in dealing with living Jews and with the ambivalence of some Jews toward their German heritage.

As a case in point, the political symbolism of the 1985 commemoration of the German soldiers at Bitburg, where German and American politicians gathered at the Kölmeshöhe military cemetery to commemorate the end of the war, did not go unnoticed. President Reagan's decision to visit the cemetery and his initial refusal to visit a concentration camp drew heavy criticism from Jewish leaders around the world and from U.S. veterans. By laying a wreath at the grave of German soldiers, President Reagan announced his intention to lay the past to rest as well. (Reagan did finally lay a wreath at Bergen-Belsen on 5 May 1985.) In discussing his reasons for visiting the cemetery, Reagan claimed that the German soldiers (some of whom were members of the Waffen SS) were victims of the Holocaust 'just as surely as the victims in the concentration camps' (Hartman xiv).

Two more recent cases have raised the question of how both Germans and Jews can mourn their dead without erasing the different circumstances under which the respective groups were killed during the Second World War. In one case German veteran organizations demanded proper burial of the corpses of German soldiers killed at the battle of Stalingrad in 1943. In another instance the dedication of an enlarged replica of Käthe Kollwitz's sculpture *Pietà*, commemorating all victims of the Second World War at the site of the Neue Wache in Berlin, was perceived by some as an affront to Jews whose ancestors had been killed in concentration camps and whose death was not to be compared with the death of German soldiers fighting on the front.

The increase in acts of blatant anti-Semitism that emerged at the time of these other controversies made it clear to a new generation of Jews living in Germany that the commemoration of Jewish victims in the Nazi death camps continued to be an artificial imperative in German society—more ceremony than deep contemplation or active interaction—and new concerns about the viability of Jewish life in Germany began to take hold. Jewish intellectuals such as Dan Diner and Michael Brumlik analyzed the social and psychological structures of German-Jewish relations in present-day German society and articulated why it is difficult even for Jews active in German public life to feel comfortable in Germany. At the same time, Jewish writers such as Biller, Dischereit, Honigmann, and Seligmann contributed to theoretical and political discussions about Jewish identity by raising questions about the inadequacy of official public policy to express the experience of Jews living in Germany. These writers all reflect upon German Jewish forms of dialogue in their writing, although not all agree on what the value or outcome of a continued dialogue with their non-Jewish German counterparts might be.

The writing in this volume records the tensions between Germans and Jews in the postwar period when both groups found themselves inextricably bound by Auschwitz in what Hannah Arendt (and more recently Diner) termed a 'negative symbiosis.' The attitudes expressed in these works, dating from 1989 to 1998, might seem particularly harsh toward the Germans whose more recent role in the European Union and NATO is a far cry from the fascist dictatorship of the Nazis. Yet the current fascination, perhaps even obsession, with Jewish life and culture has, of course, a flip side where denial and repression of memory are also still operative. As a result, the metaphysical guilt of the *Nachgeborene* (those born after) and the survivor guilt inherited by the children of survivors takes on uncanny parallels. Even those of the second-generation, the sixty-eighters, who demonstrated against U.S. imperialism and fought for educational reform (and promoted anti-Israel sentiment in their support of the Palestinian Liberation Organization) are seen as projecting their own self-absorbing guilt onto their concern with properly commemorating the victims of the Shoah.

The overview of the postwar era suggests that the 'fear of touching' (*Berührungsangst*) has not dissipated but rather has been displaced into symbolic acts of mourning the Jews. (In Behrens's short story 'Salomo und die anderen,' the fear of touching is briefly overcome in an informal soccer game in Israel played by Israelis and German tourists but abruptly reinstated when the touching becomes sexual). Even as the presence of Jews remains relatively small despite the immigration of tens of thousands of former Soviet Jews (Jews are not counted as a minority and do not show up in statistics about foreigners in Germany because, for the most part, they are German citizens), media attention to things Jewish and to the commemoration of the Shoah is immense. Germans live with the 'burden' of mourning not their own but the victims of their parents' and grandparents' criminal acts, a topic that the Jewish character in 'Harlem Holocaust' takes up in an essay entitled 'Zyklon D': 'The Germans of today . . . are of course *not* guilty. But the defeat, the partition of the country, the painful reunification, and above all their perpetrator complex will force upon them again and again a new guilt. For what other nation in the world and in this historic region knows what it means to forever have to water the flowers on other people's graves.'

The ten-year anniversary of the fall of the Wall has come and gone, but the ensuing struggle of former East Germans to assimilate or, conversely, to rebel against assimilation into the western model of the free market has often been accompanied with debates about how Germans in general are to 'work through' the past. Whose past is it anyway? What claims have been made to owning a past fraught with human tragedy and brutality? What are the parallels between the confrontation with Stalinism in the East and the confrontation with Nazism in the West? The writers here, except for Biller, came of age and found their voices long before German unification became a marker for measuring the capacity of Germans to be German in a increasingly globalized world. Biller, Behrens, Dischereit, and Honigmann refuse to be acquiescent *Mitbürger*, to be trotted out as token Jews. Instead, they (and others such as Diner and Brumlik) are often at odds with the official Jewish community and with the German status quo.

Katja Behrens, born in Berlin in 1942, is the only one of the four writers presented in this volume who was born during the war. In addition to translating a number of literary texts from English into German, she has published a number of essays, short stories, and novels, including *Die dreizehnte Fee* (1994; The thirteenth fairy), *Die Vagantin* (1997; The wandering minstrel), *Salomo und die anderen: Jüdische Geschichten* (1995; Solomon and the others Jewish stories), and *Die weiße Frau* (1994; The white woman).

Behrens writes from the concern she shares with other German Jewish writers, such as Honigmann, of the indeterminacy of place and identity in the post-Shoah landscape and of the elision of language in locating these places. In 'Arthur Mayer oder Das Schweigen,' place names and proper names are presented by first letters only ('Mr. A, as in Anders or Anhalt'), thus denying the reader any sense of certainty or knowledge. The veil of 'accuracy' that Behrens places over the narrative not only suggests the impossibility of knowledge of the past or its narratability but also insists on the protean quality of this knowledge. People and places cannot be fixed with signifers but instead are floating endlessly in a sea of possibilities: 'S, as in Schönberg or Schwarzdorf.' The elision of these names reinforces the narrative conceit of the detective story that runs throughout 'Arthur Mayer oder Das Schweigen.' Yet at the same time this is a detective story that presents itself with multiple 'solutions,' as the title of the story suggests, with its own choice of titles within the title, 'Arthur Mayer oder Das Schweigen.'

While Honigmann's novel *Soharas Reise* explores the spatial relationship between France and 'Germany, over there,' Behrens's short story 'Salomo und die Anderen,' on the other hand, examines the spatialized memory of Israel and Germany. The story opens with the narrator musing on the nameability of the Holocaust: 'Only yesterday I was still at home. Here they say *shama*, which means simply *there*, but they don't mean simply *there*. They mean a place that is so terrible it is better not to name it; to call it by its name would be to evoke the memory of it. If one doesn't talk about it, then it isn't real, perhaps not real after all, or at least not quite real. Silence is like a bandage over that which happened *shama*, there in the land where I was born and where I grew up.' The narrator's need to move between languages creates the recognition that knowledge of the past cannot be fixed or contained within one single linguistic structure. This is, perhaps, the narrative embodiment of the rift that Behrens has identified, the rift that is embedded in linguistic and epistemological structures overall. For Behrens, Biller, Dischereit, and Honigmann, this rift is what generates their writing, while their self-critical voices challenge received notions of the value of 'normalcy' and 'reconciliation.' In Behrens's story 'Arthur Mayer oder Das Schweigen,' the narrator, not unlike the protagonist in Michael Verhoeven's film *The Nasty Girl*, experiences curiosity and then hostility in her search for information about a Jewish doctor from a small German town. Her delving into the past makes people suspicious because she is Jewish and doesn't really belong; however an older German man, rumored to have fought in Poland, commands the authority to be the one to possess knowledge of Jewish history and culture in the town. The townspeople readily tell him their stories and leave documents in his mailbox, whereas they refuse to cooperate with the Jewish narrator. By raising the question of who can claim authority over the past, Behrens suggests that the perpetrators create a version of the truth that is inherently fraudulent, even as it ostensibly supports a good cause—the remembering of Jewish neighbors and their fates. This remembering only represses the past and consolidates Jewish stories of the past into the myth that Mayer died of 'homesickness' in Auschwitz.

Of the four writers, Barbara Honigmann is the only one to have left Germany and to have become an observant Jew. Born in 1949 in East Berlin, the daughter of remigrants to the German Democratic Republic (GDR), she joined the small Jewish community in the GDR in 1976. In 1984 she left the GDR and moved to Strasbourg, where she currently resides with her family. Her two previous novels, *Roman von einem Kinde* (1989; Novel of a child) and *Eine Liebe aus*

Nichts (1991; A love made of nothing), and her more recent works, *Soharas Reise* (1996; Sohara's journey), *Am Sonntag spielt der Rabbi Fußball* (1998; On Sunday the Rabbi plays soccer), and *Damals, Dann und Danach* (1999; Back then, then and after), explore her life in France and her growing distance from Germany. In part, this distance is due to the fact that Honigmann's Germany, the former GDR, no longer exists as a political entity, although its presence for many of its former citizens is still palpable.

In an essay that appeared in *Nach der Shoa Geboren* (Born after the Shoah), a collection of essays, fiction, and poetry by Jewish women living in Berlin, Honigmann discusses her complicated status as a German Jew living in the GDR, the daughter of remigrants who identified themselves as socialists, not Jews. The legacy that she carries with her can be shared, she believes, with only those from a similar background. 'I believe that we children of the Jews in my parents' generation have remained our parents' children for an exceptionally long time because it was difficult to free ourselves from the history and stories of our parents. Others [Germans in the GDR] heard other stories, about the front, about Stalingrad, about the flight from Silesia, about prisoner of war camps and about bombs falling on German cities.' Honigmann comments on the dilemma of not belonging to the Jews anymore but of not being able to become German either. 'Realistically, I was in search of a minimum of Jewish identity in my life, of a natural passing of years and a discussion about Jewish culture beyond the incessant discourse about anti-Semitism—but that was asking too much under "German conditions" ' (38).

Honigmann addresses the dilemma of navigating Jewish, German, and female identity. Interestingly, her own search for Jewish identity includes incorporating the experiences of her parents, who did not primarily identify as Jewish. Her collection of short stories, *Roman von einem Kinde*, dissects the ambiguities of Jewish identity from the vantage point of Strasbourg, a city with a thriving Jewish community that stands in contrast to the GDR. In her short story 'Doppeltes Grab' (Double burial), Honigmann describes Gershom Scholem's visit to the site of his family's tomb in the Jewish cemetery in Berlin-Weißensee. After clearing the tombstones of branches and vines, Scholem remarks that 'one needs an ax to cut a path through the overgrowth of time.' Indeed the 'overgrowth of time' that obscures the memorial inscription of the names on the graves of Jewish relatives has an ambiguous connotation in Honigmann's story. It is not the 'natural' passing of time that has obstructed the inscriptions of names but the rapid consolidation of Jewish memory within German culture that leaves little room for the different experiences of Jewish life in Germany.

In her novel *Eine Liebe aus Nichts* Honigmann describes the tenuousness of Jewish existence within the borders of the former GDR and within German culture, a culture in which family ties and language create a semblance of *Heimat* not necessarily bound by national borders. The protagonist in Honigmann's novel seeks to write the life of her past by reconnecting with her father after his death. She retrieves his mostly blank diary from his room in the Belvedere Schloß in Weimar. By filling in the dates of his death, his funeral, and her last encounter with him, the narrator takes leave of her father by updating his autobiography thus making his presence felt even as it has faded. The scenes of railroad stations that symbolize the experience of forced exile under the Nazis (her parents' experience) and her own chosen exile evoke the experience of a Jewish woman in the process of rediscovering her Jewish heritage and coming to terms with her German identity.

The specter of the GDR appears in Honigmann's most recent book, *Damals, Dann und Danach*, a series of autobiographical essays about writing, family history, Jewishness, and German identity. In one of these essays, Honigmann writes of her decision to move to Strasbourg: 'So we sit on the other side of the Rhine and look across at Germany, over there, as it was called for so long in the GDR.' France is, she explains in this recent book, 'the land of freedom,' a foreign place that enables her the necessary critical distance in order to write and in order to be a Jew, with both conditions somehow linked, synonymous. The weight of France's colonial past and the interstices of an ongoing postcolonial present are absent in this recounting of what led her to Strasbourg; rather, she describes the pull of the 'foreign,' a place 'three streets from the border' where the tensions between German and Jew subside.

In this volume, borders are crossed and the locations of exile are charted, as though the nation of Germany itself were more a metaphysical than a physical reality. This is also the case in Honigmann's novel *Soharas Reise* where the narrator has moved to France and refers continually to 'Germany, over there.' *Soharas Reise* explores the oppressive structures of colonialism and its ongoing presence in the postcolonial experiences of subsequent generations. The colonial history of France and the Algerian War for Independence function as a displacement for both the short-lived colonial history of Germany and the postcolonial relationship between the Soviet Union and the GDR. Although the GDR is not named in the novella and biographical references to Honigmann's past are uncharacteristically absent, one could argue that the surface story about Sohara is actually a blind for the experiences of GDR citizens following unification. Without leaving their country, they have been, according to some critics, 'colonized' by the former West Germany. The straightforward narrative of Sohara's plight—the kidnapping of her children by her husband, an imposter and a wandering Jewish figure—is itself a cover for an intricate web of relations between Jews and Arabs, Jews and Germans, Algerians and French, Sephardic and Ashkenazic Jews, and Germans and non-Germans. A closer look reveals the interweaving of colonial and postcolonial experiences, exile and Diaspora, and the national memories of France, Germany, and Algeria that come to the fore in Strasbourg, itself a location of multifaceted histories, languages, and borders. The novel questions the consequences of colonialism on the identities of both subjects and colonizers and highlights the necessity of understanding how the Shoah exists within a structure of colonial oppression and genocide.

In *Soharas Reise* the Algerian Jewish Sohara and the German Jewish survivor whom Sohara befriends have not only their Jewishness in common but also the experience of exile and of locating themselves within a space (Strasbourg) whose apparent neutrality is itself an illusion. Honigmann writes of a chosen exile but harks back to the exodus and to the present-day position of the GDR vis-à-vis the west. She explores the tensions between East and West, choosing a borderland nexus of Germany and France, a place where the stability of national and ethnic identities are called into question. Her reliance on stock Jewish characters and practice is tempered by her willingness to differentiate between Sephardic and Ashkenazic cultures.

The complexities of Sohara's identity as an Algerian Jew living on the border of Germany are underscored by her relationship to her German Jewish neighbor, Mrs. Kahn, a Holocaust survivor who calls the Germans 'cannibals,' has not spoken German for more than fifty years, and even renounces the seductions of bargains from the discount grocery store just over the border. Mrs. Kahn, the emblematic Ashkenazic Jew, is forever making gefilte fish, which the narrator describes as 'the second most sacred object of the Ashkenazi after the concentration camps.' By positioning herself as a Sephardic Jewish woman who stands outside the dominant western Jewish culture (marked by gefilte fish), the narrator distances herself not only from Germany but also from a Jewish identity for whom the Holocaust is the first *Heiligtum* (sacred relic) and gefilte fish the second. For Sohara as a Sephardic Jew, the Ashkenazim are the 'elite among sufferers, the world champions of martyrdom,' whereas she perceives that for the Ashkenazim, Sephardic Jews are 'novices, placed in the lowest ranks, semi-Arabs (*halbe-Araber*).'

The Holocaust serves as a marker of hegemonic domination of the Ashkenazim over the Sephardim, another way in which the Sephardim are cast as hybrid and subaltern (semi-Arab); the Holocaust is in the domain of the shared memory of the Ashkenazim, a memory of space and geography that underscores Sohara's exclusion as an Algerian Jew. The presence of the Holocaust pervades the novel, yet as an elliptical trace of memory that serves to demarcate Sephardic from Ashkenazic Jew; its 'dispersal' throughout the narrative is seen by the way in which it is elided in language: 'Mrs. Kahn always says "these camps" and "the cannibals," she has found a new language for "it," because, as she says, one cannot describe "it." Many who have gone through "it" show up at schools and talk about "it," they write books and publish them and have transformed "it" into a story that one can tell and that they feel compelled to tell again and again.' The prevalence, and yet at the same time the elision and slippage of the Holocaust is suggested further as Sohara muses on how 'the Ashkenazim' constantly tell stories about the Holocaust, how the subject is present in the media: 'everything I have heard or seen has been transformed in my head into a single huge story or, even more, into a terrifying landscape. A landscape of horror with Polish and German place names,

Auschwitz, Warsaw, Treblinka, Nuremberg, Berlin, Dachau; by the way, these are the only Polish or German place names I know at all, not counting Kehl.' Sohara is brought into the narrative of the Holocaust—an exclusively Ashkenazic narrative—through the landscapes of destruction with which she is familiar, a litany of points on a map that echoes the points on her own nomadic map of personal and historical memory (Oran, Amiens, Marseilles, Lille, Metz).

The Germany that lies just over the border—'over there'—stands as the unmarked, the exotic, the 'dark continent' that bears the imprint—reversed—of a buried colonial past and a not so buried Nazi past, a place inhabited by—as Mrs. Kahn repeatedly says—'the cannibals.' When Sohara's husband kidnaps their children and Sohara thinks he might have taken them over the border, she pleads with Mrs. Kahn to call 'Germany' to get them back. Mrs. Kahn replies, 'I can't just call "Germany!" We need to know whom to call, a phone number, a person.' Mrs. Kahn looks for Germany on the atlas but only sees it as it exists in relation to other places in Europe, such as Antwerp, described as the most Orthodox site in Europe, thus suggesting the spaces of Europe as defined by their Jewishness. Yet the question remains whether Algeria, in the novel, is a fully realized place, or if it exists solely as a space within the imagination of the narrator, a space also marked by elision, by a blurring of colonial (or historical) and personal childhood memory. The Algerian War for Independence is the reason Sohara's family leaves Algeria for France, yet this historical trauma is also elided as the narrator can recall the war with only a vague memory of distant gunshots.

The desire to escape the burden of Jewishness, imposed in part by non-Jewish Germans and the weight of history, is a theme in Esther Dischereit's writing as well. The exasperated sighs of one of the narrators in Dicherheit's *Joëmis Tisch* express this sense of burden. After she overhears a father tell his son that 'a Jew after all is human-too' (*Auch-Menschen*), the narrator wonders if she will ever escape being Jewish, a stigma that manifests itself in her anxiety attacks at border crossings and during encounters with Germans in uniform. The search for normalcy, according to Dischereit, is not the same as Martin Walser's plea in his 1998 Frankfurt speech that Germany be 'allowed' to be a 'normal' nation among other 'normal' nations. Rather this search stems from a desire for the pressure often placed upon victims to explain their shame to be transferred to the Germans. For Dischereit the normalization is not a matter of forgetting but of taking care of one's own business.

The texts by Honigmann and Dischereit question fixed notions of identity and express the desire to recover lost or thwarted moments of a female Jewish subject. The genealogical structure of texts such as *Joëmis Tisch* by Dischereit and *Eine Liebe aus Nichts* by Honigmann evokes the deep loss caused by the atrocities of the Shoah while at the same time attesting to the strength of genealogical ties that have survived the Shoah, even as they are constantly on the verge of breaking apart. By engendering a female Jewish identity that is neither fixed nor homogeneous but rather fragmented and heterogeneous, Dischereit and Honigmann present a differentiated picture of the oppression of women within Jewish culture and German society.

Esther Dischereit was born in the former Federal Republic in 1952 and lives in Berlin. Her Jewish mother survived Nazi Germany in hiding. Her father was a non-Jewish German. Her works include *Merryn* (1992), *Joëmis Tisch: eine Jüdische Geschichte* (1988; Joemi's table: a Jewish story), a recent volume of essays, *Übungen jüdisch zu sein* (1998; Exercises in being Jewish), and a volume of poetry, *Als mir mein Golem öffnete* (1996; When my golem opened himself to me). In addition to writing poetry, essays, novellas, and radio plays, she frequently contributes Op-Ed pieces and reviews of films and books to German newspapers and journals in which she confronts the dilemma of being Jewish in today's Germany.

In her essay on Nelly Sachs, Dischereit contemplates the impact of growing up in the postwar era, the daughter of a Jewish mother who survived in hiding. As one of her narrators exclaims in *Joëmis Tisch*, 'I am fed up with wearing a face of incarnate suffering.' Dischereit takes up the challenge to deconstruct the meaning of Jewishness in contemporary Germany while at the same time criticizing the German obsession with Jewish culture. She pokes fun at the fascination in the German media for things Jewish, but she laments the lack of insight into the meaning of the Shoah and the tremendous loss of life and heritage for Jews despite the plethora of writing and films on the subject. Often Dischereit chooses to take a stand and writes about a current event from her perspective not only as a Jew but as a German with ties to the feminist movement and union organizing. In her writing, Dischereit presents Jews not as outsiders to German society but as major participants within that society where Jewishness or Germanness are but two markers of identity.

Like Biller, Dischereit's work is suffused with satire. In her text, the self-absorbed, callous remarks of Germans intent on establishing their victim status are interrupted with critical asides by a Jewish narrative voice. In one scene, for example, a German figure, Martha Elisabeth, asks her Jewish friend, Ruth, to find the grave of her husband, a member of the Wehrmacht who had been killed in the Second World War in France. The narrator muses, 'Along the Drôme river. Why is that mentioned here? Ruth drives along the entire road, gets out; do you see an honorable soldier's grave? There is no grave; that's what she'll tell Mrs. Steder. She has done her best.' Ruth notes the impossibility of inviting her German friend to the mass graves where her father and brother were shot. The disparity between the ways of dying—'falling' heroically in the war versus being shot to death at the edge of a mass grave—accentuates the incongruity between the descendants, despite the repeated attempts at dialogue or the supposed return to 'normalcy.'

The decidedly gendered perspective in Dischereit's writing marks the gender and class differences among Jews both within and outside of the Jewish community. This narrative style can also be attributed to Dischereit's conscious placing of herself within the tradition of German feminist literature. In *Joëmis Tisch* the bodies of the female protagonists are sites of remembrance, topographies that are littered with traces of the Shoah, reminders of the rift that Behrens identifies. Dischereit gathers these traces to be decoded but without forcing them to coalesce into a unified or coherent structure. The incoherence and narrative indeterminacy of the fragments in *Joëmis Tisch* suggest the indeterminacy of the voids—linguistic, aesthetic, moral—left behind in the wake of the Shoah.

Instead of dwelling on her position as Other within German society, the female Jewish protagonist in Dischereit's *Joëmis Tisch* questions the 'normalcy' of the dominant culture in which she lives. The novel intersperses images of the narrator's dead Jewish mother, Hannah, with conversations with Germans about the German past and present society. The narrative, which consists of a series of more than fifty scenes, moves back and forth between the past and present, between individual and historical experience, and between third- and first-person narration. The daughter seeks to reclaim her Jewish identity '[a]fter twenty years of being an un-Jewish Jew' (*Un-Jude*) and imagines her mother's history against the backdrop of her own sense of alienation in postwar Germany. In Dischereit's novel, the process of 'coming out' as a Jew in Germany takes place through the reconstruction of the narrator's mother's life and in confrontations with non-Jewish Germans.

By shaping her novel around the narrator's taking on of a lost or repressed Jewish identity in Germany after the Shoah, Dischereit insists on the impossibility of remembering in isolation. The ritual of conjuring the past in order to live in the present is not simply a practice undertaken in the company of the Jewish community but also in the company of Germans. The 'German' Germans are the 'resident other' (Plank 274) with whom Jewish Germans must reckon. By objecting to the prejudices and misconceptions that reduce living Jews in contemporary Germany to iconic figures, the female Jewish narrator dismantles the structures that enable Germans to complain that the Shoah has placed the heavy burden of guilt upon their shoulders.

Dischereit's text exposes the unwillingness of many Germans to name the perpetrators or to take responsibility for the remembrance of the Shoah. By inserting quotation marks around statements by Germans and then interrupting them with the narrator's sarcastic monologues about the blindness of many Germans to their false piety, Dischereit exposes the lack of communication between Germans and Jews. In one conversation, for example, a Sudeten German complains about the hardship he experienced as a refugee in 1945. While he remembers having to leave the family dog behind on a 'beautiful May day' as they left the Sudeten, the narrator interjects the description of the deportation of her Jewish relatives. The juxtaposition of each experience exposes at once the historical abyss between most Germans and Jews and the inner conflicts experienced by the narrator as she attempts to come to terms with her Germanness despite her Jewish heritage.

As in the texts by Behrens and Honigmann, the memory of the Shoah in Dischereit's work is but one constitutive element. As these writers conjure up images of the past and attempt to write genealogies marked by interruptions and loss, they also suggest the possibility of Jewish identity that is based not in absence but in presence, in a Jewishness lived, practiced, and experienced in present-day Germany. If the figures in these texts are consumed by the imperative to remember, they are also insistent upon the right to be not only Jews but Germans, writers, women, politically engaged people, and historians.

Maxim Biller, the youngest of the authors presented here, was born in Prague in 1960 and immigrated with his family to Hamburg in 1970. He studied German literature and journalism in Munich and writes regularly for *Die Zeit*, *Tempo*, and other journals devoted to literary and social commentary. He has published two collections of essays and several collections of short stories: *Die Tempojahre* (1991), *Wenn ich einmal reich und tot bin* (1991), and *Land der Vater und Verräter* (1994). His short stories and essays are biting satires of the present-day relationships between Jews and Germans. Biller exposes the distinction between victim and perpetrator status as complex and ambiguous while showing how this distinction is etched into the very fabric of German culture.

In 'Harlem Holocaust' a young German writer named Ephraim Rosenhain contemplates the failure of his life and directs the blame toward a New York son of German Jewish immigrants whose writing about the Shoah has earned him fame in Germany. The story parodies the German literary market that celebrates Jewish writers whose writing in English has gone unnoticed but whose translations into German are a great success. Ironically, the German-speaking Jew's books are translated from the language of his country of immigration (American English) into German. His return to Germany represents, intentionally or not, the voice of those Jews whose status as survivor seems to give them free rein to become the 'authentic' spokespeople for the impact of the Shoah on the lives of the Jews and on the lives of the Germans. By foregrounding the role of language and literary style, Biller thus suggests that any correspondence between the 'original' text by the Jew and the 'translation' by the German is itself always a chimera. Further, 'Harlem Holocaust' addresses the issue of the popularity of Jewish writers in Germany by suggesting that the Jewish writer is successful only because of work that is fundamentally uninteresting to an American readership, which strikes a nerve with German readers. Ironically, in Biller's novel the German writer can only be published after his suicide by the Jewish writer, who decides to publish the manuscript because 'it is a document of a self-destrucive talent and, at the same time, of the great German disease.'

The tension created by the compulsive speech patterns of the Jewish writer and the self-pitying litany of the German translator form the backdrop to the multilayered story within a story. The Jewish writer from New York goes by the Polish-sounding name Warszawski. From the perspective of the German figure (whose name, Ephraim Rosenhain, connotes Jewishness but whose family roots are entrenched in National Socialism and anti-Semitism), Warszawski is an outsider who wields a 'moral cudgel' (*Moralkeule*). As in the works of Henryk Broder and Georg Tabori, Biller breaks taboos in order to tear away the mask of false piety and rote commemorative practice still prevalent in the German public sphere. In many of Biller's works, the events of the 1980s (such as the protest by members of the Frankfurt Jewish community that blocked the premiere of Fassbinder's play, or the polemical and heated discussions within the Jewish Community about the conservative politics of Heinz Galinski, the former director of the Jewish Community in West Berlin) are filtered through the subjective experiences of mostly male Jewish and German protagonists. In 'Harlem Holocaust,' for example, the first-person narrator is not Jewish but becomes obsessed with his struggle to enter the world of the Jews, even as he is unable to overcome his resentment at being excluded. The German figure feels victimized by the Jewish one, and his description of the Jew leaves no stereotype untouched, whether it be the rounded cheeks, the big nose, or the lively hand gestures. Rosenhain, the German, hates the Jew, Warszawski, least of all because he has stolen his pregnant girlfriend, who responds by aborting his child and abandoning him. His fantasies about the sexual encounters between Warszawski and Ina Teutonia Polarker—as she is called by Warszawski—are, at least on the surface, blatant renditions of anti-Semitic notions of the male Jew as the predator of innocent, helpless German women. In a striking scene in 'Harlem Holocaust,' it is the Jewish male who protects his body from contamination by the German female. Before having sexual intercourse with Ina in a stopped elevator, he pulls a blue condom dotted with stars of David over his erect penis and proceeds to orally stimulate Ina until she succumbs in a powerful orgasm in which she cries out in garbled Yiddish. Significantly, Biller often chooses confined spaces, such as the closet or the elevator described above, to suggest the closeted erotic tensions between Germans and Jews. Biller's explicit description of Rosenhain's fantasy is a startling reminder of how sex has often been removed from the telling of the story of the Shoah and from its remembrance.

Biller's texts have had a mixed reception from both Jewish and non-Jewish readers, in part due to their exploration of sexual issues. As the publisher's blurb for his second collection of short stories announces, Biller is both condemned and celebrated as an 'inconsiderate breaker of taboos' because his texts deal with 'our country [Germany] . . . its present and its past, the crimes of the perpetrators, the deeds of the victims and above all with the children and grandchildren of those who have survived all that.' The use of 'our country' in the blurb situates Biller as an outsider in the society in which he lives, even as he is presented as a German writer.

In 'Harlem Holocaust,' Biller also mirrors a phenomenon in present-day Germany by portraying the German's indignation and despair at being confronted with a Jew who has the freedom to say and do whatever he pleases. In 1998, in his acceptance speech of the German publishers peace prize, Martin Walser made waves by accusing certain German and Jewish factions of 'instrumentalizing' the Shoah and using it as a 'tool of intimidation that can be deployed at any time.' Walser objected to the moral imperative that makes it difficult for him as a German to return to 'normalcy' and for the German nation as a whole to be seen as the democratic, open nation that it had become, not the hotbed of neo-Nazi terror that one might deduce from the media. Biller's story, written before Walser's speech, attributes similar sentiments to his German figure—he is the victim who is beholden to the Jewish writer whom he translates.

Translation is a major trope in the story—the German writer translates the Jewish writer's English into German, the language of the Jew's origin. The German can only mimic the Jew, who writes in a 'foreign' tongue; he cannot become the Jew. The Jewish figure has no illusions about his difference within German culture, even as he cashes in on his ability to hit the Germans where it hurts—below the belt as it were, by placing Rosenhain's masculinity in question. The mimetic quality of their relationship makes identification impossible and illuminates the absurdity of the German's self-pity. He blames the Jew for his lack of self-fulfillment: the very presence of the Jew reminds him of his Germanness and thus his place in the legacy of the Shoah.

While the satire exposes the everyday anti-Semitism in today's Germany, it also emphasizes the fruitlessness of relegating all Jews to the status of victim and all Germans to the status of perpetrator. Furthermore, Biller follows in the tradition of Tabori, whose satires encourage Germans to stop hiding behind official acts of commemoration and to confront the remnants of fascism in their everyday lives. Biller counters an artificial symbiosis in which Jews assume a moral authority that consequently casts Germans as bearers of guilt. By presenting differentiated images of Jewish figures modeled after real figures in contemporary Germany, Biller breaks down the dichotomy that petrifies the Jew as victim and the German as perpetrator without erasing the context in which this dichotomy has arisen.

In 'Harlem Holocaust' the absence of moral and historical coherence is seen in the figure of Warszawski, the writer from New York who attempts to locate himself in the position of the Other in American culture, the Black, only to return to his Jewish roots. The elision of the difference between Black and Jewish history provides a brief refuge for the Jewish character from the demands of forging an identity as a European Jew. The young Warszawski's appropriation of Black culture in the form of jazz proves to be dishonest, just as the appropriation of Jewish culture by non-Jewish Germans in the form of Klezmer music smacks of displacement and voyeurism.

The mazelike tributaries of the text emulate, to some extent, Warszawski's commentary on his writing style as *surfiction*. This fiction is a mixture of allusions to actual historical events, people, places, official and personal documents, and is characterized by a seismographic style that records the contradictions of a new Germany and the passing of a German Jewish culture. It is a record of the first-generation's memories (a generation that is itself dying out) and the implications of relying solely on fictive renditions to represent the Shoah. The composite image of the Jewish writer, Warszawski, whose narrative style draws from Jewish American writers such as Philip Roth and Saul Bellow, is a mosaic of characters to be found in texts by the Jewish German writer Edgar Hilsenrath, the Hungarian-born George Tabori, and the American-born Irene Dische. Writing about the Shoah has necessitated an imagining of the past; much of this writing is not about the Shoah but rather about its vicissitudes and aftermath as well as about the industry that has developed around the Shoah, cynically known as 'Shoah-business.' Whereas the false piety of the Germans is placed in question, Biller suggests nonetheless the need for developing a modus vivendi for living as a Jew in contemporary Germany.

As Sander Gilman has discussed at length in his article 'Male Sexuality and Contemporary Jewish Literature in German: The Damaged Body as the Image of the Damaged Soul,' the stigma of circumcision as both a physical and metaphorical marker of male Jewish identity plays a major role in the work of Biller and of another contemporary male Jewish writer, Rafael Seligmann (not included in this volume). In *Rubensteins Versteigerung* (Rubenstein's auction), for example, the constant anxiety of Rubenstein, the main protagonist, over his sexual performance and virginity at the age of twenty-one is linked to his condemnation of his German Jewish parents for returning to the 'Naziland' from Israel. As he attempts to sleep with a number of Jewish and German women, he links his failure to achieve an erection to his parents' decision, a decision that subjects him to perpetual alienation and the predicament of being a German Jew without a homeland. As Gilman has shown, the male Jewish body functions in these texts as both a sign of difference and as a stigma of illness. The male protagonists are often ill in the work of Biller and Seligmann, an indication of the no-win situation of being Jewish in Germany and of being an outsider obsessed with the task of being Jewish and observing the Germans observing the Jews.

In Biller's text, Jewishness is marked on the body of the characters. The Jewish body becomes the sexual fantasy of the German, and his vivid image of his former girlfriend's first sexual encounter with the Jewish writer—in a halted elevator no less—stands in for his own desire to be Jewish, to take the liberties that the Jewish male takes. Dichereit's *Joëmis Tisch*, in contrast, shifts the attention to the Jewish female body; by focussing her critique on the female Jewish body, Dischereit suggests the correlation between fascism and patriarchal forms of sexism and misogyny and the objectification of women within Jewish tradition.

While the writings of Biller and Seligmann have been associated with the Jewish American tradition of Philip Roth and Saul Bellow, as Gertraud Koch and other critics have pointed out, Dischereit and Honigmann create their own models based as much on German literary tradition as on Jewish women's writing.

Our intention with this volume is to present a range of Jewish voices and identities in Germany and to counter the notion that Jewish writers can be categorized. Indeed, 'Jewish writing' has become a genre in Germany due to the German literary market's readiness to appropriate Jewish authors as representatives of Jewish culture. There still remains a facile assumption of a monolithic Jewish community and tradition; equally facile and problematic is the notion that the work of Jewish writers will perform the task of mourning, that it will reenact traumatic experiences for the reading 'pleasure' and personal 'absolution' of non-Jewish German readers. Jewish writing in Germany evokes the absence that is, ironically, present in the repetition-compulsion of non-Jewish Germans to commemorate the Shoah. The authors included in this volume present a strong critique of these fetishized commemorative practices that embrace nostalgic images of Jewish culture and that have resulted in a confused mixture of remembering a rich culture in a void (Libeskind) through voyeurism and nostalgia. At times Jewish culture becomes reduced to Yiddish theater and Klezmer music, Jewish cemeteries, kosher delis, and guided tours of past and present Jewish sites. Even the heterogeneity of Eastern European Jewish culture becomes subsumed at times into entertainment for the *Volk*.

Yet despite the prevalence of a cultural need to create unity out of destruction, the narrative styles of these texts reflect the fragmented remnants of the past. A common theme in these works is the search for family ties that might survive despite fragmentation and destruction. This search is reminiscent of Walter Benjamin's notion in *Einbahnstraße (One-Way Street)*, the notion of exposing the layers of history that are part of the story of the present. Thus these writers enact genealogical (in the Foucaultian sense), archaeological, and pathological studies in their remembrance of the Shoah. The narrators in Behrens's 'Arthur Mayer oder Das Schweigen' and Dischereit's *Joëmis Tisch* engage in a search for evidence of the crimes of the past *and* the present. Thus Dischereit and Behrens, in particular, seem to perpetuate the image that Germans have learned nothing and that Jews are carrying the brunt of the mourning process by showing traces of anti-Semitism abounding in everyday language and in flippant comments.

For the most part, the main characters in the stories in this volume are marked by their status as outsiders, a status that at times joins them to other minorities in Germany or, in the case of 'Harlem Holocaust,' to minorities in the United States. In *Soharas Reise*, Sohara bears the marks of Jewshishness and Arabness—she is a 'foreigner' in two senses as her religious practice and identity are as exotic to the German Jewish survivor as they are to her white, non-Jewish French neighbors.

Furthermore, in all the works, the Jewish characters are characterized by their feelings of shame. The one exception is Biller's 'Harlem Holocaust,' a text representative of a new trend in contemporary Jewish literature (seen as well in the work of Rafael Seligmann) to draw on anti-Semitic stereotypes in order to provoke readers and to expose the prevalence of anti-Semitism in Germany. Shame is a common emotion among the female Jewish characters in these texts, a shame rarely expressed by their German counterparts. Whereas the Jewish figure in Biller's 'Harlem Holocaust' manages to outgrow any feelings of shame or guilt for feeling sexual pleasure, the female characters find their lives dictated by shame, often passed on to them by a mother figure. In *Joëmis Tisch*, Hannah's daughter experiences shame in the proverbial locker room when other schoolchildren remind her that she has a Jewish mother and cannot be Protestant. The narrator in Behrens's short story overcomes her shame by directly confronting the Nazi past of her neighbors.

Although Jewish identity and relations to non-Jewish Germans are major themes in most of the works represented here, the experience of being female and Jewish distinguishes the work of the women writers. Whereas texts by Biller often address the anxiety over the stigma of circumcision, the double stigma of femaleness and Jewishness is an implicit theme in the works of the Jewish women writers. In addition to the dilemma of identity, a shared characteristic in these texts is the development of a genealogical memory that recalls the destruction of the Shoah as a process that could only have taken place in confrontation with non-Jewish Germans. Given that the authors' German heritage complicates the division between Jewish and German identity, the interactions with Germans brings more confusion than clarity. Instead of concentrating on the past, the writers in this volume address the events of the 1980s and 1990s as symptoms of a recurring problem among non-Jewish Germans who are incapable of dealing with the presence of living Jews, even as they go to great lengths to commemorate past Jewish victimization. For many Jews, living in contemporary Germany means juggling the remembrance of the past while building a future in which Jewish communities become a vital part of German society without being marginalized.

In the texts by Biller, Behrens, Dischereit, and Honigmann, the metaphorical packed suitcase remains. The tense encounters with Germans and the sense of alienation that pervade these texts are not responses only to the destruction wrought by the Nazis against Jews but also to present-day anti-Semitism and the constant reminder that Germans and Jews are bound by history now more than ever. The writing of German Jews in the 1990s suggests that this dilemma will continue to occupy Jewish writers and their readers in Germany for many years to come.

Leslie Morris,
University of Minnesota

Karen Remmler,
Mount Holyoke College

Works Cited

Behrens, Katja. *Die dreizehnte Fee*. Frankfurt/Main: Fischer, 1994.

——.'The Rift and Not the Symbiosis.' *Unlikely History: The Changing German-Jewish Symbiosis*. Ed. Leslie Morris and Jack Zipes. New York: St. Martin's, 2002.

——. *Salomo und die anderen: Jüdische Geschichten*. Frankfurt/Main: Fischer, 1995.

——. *Die Vagantin*. Frankfurt/Main: Fischer, 1997.

——. *Die Weiße Frau*. Frankfurt/Main: Fischer, 1994.

Biller, Maxim. *Land der Väter und Verräter*. Köln: Kiepenheuer & Witsch, 1994.

——. *Die Tempojahre*. München: DTV, 1991.

——. *Die Tochter*. Köln: Kiepenheuer & Witsch, 2000.

——. *Wenn ich einmal reich und tot bin*. Köln: Kiepenheuer & Witsch, 1991.

Broder, Henryk M. and Michel Lang, ed. *Fremd in eigenem Land: Juden in der Bundesrepublik*. Frankfurt/Main: Fischer, 1979.

Dischereit, Esther. *Als mir mein Golem öffnete*. Passau: Stutz, 1996.

——. 'Ein sehr junges Mädchen trifft Nelly Sachs.' *Übungen jüdisch zu sein*. Frankfurt/Main: Suhrkamp, 1998.

——. *Joëmis Tisch: eine jüdische Geschichte*. Frankfurt/Main: Suhrkamp, 1988.

——. *Merryn*. Frankfurt/Main: Suhrkamp, 1992.

Fleischmann, Lea. *Dies ist nicht mein Land: Eine Jüdin verläßt die Bundesrepublik*. Hamburg: Hofman & Campe, 1980.

Gilman, Sander. 'Male Sexuality and Contemporary Jewish Literature in German: The Damaged Body as the Image of the Damaged Soul.' *Re-emerging Jewish Culture in German Life and Literature Since 1989*. Ed. Sander Gilman and Karen Remmler. New York: NYU Press, 1994.

Hartman, Geoffrey, ed. *Bitburg in Moral and Political Perspective*. Bloomington: Indiana UP, 1986.

Honigmann, Barbara. *Am Sonntag spielt der Rabbi Fußball*. Heidelberg: Verlag das Wunderhorn, 1998.

——. 'Selbstportät als Jüdin.' *Damals, Dann und Danach*. München: Hanser, 1999. 11–18.

——. *Eine Liebe aus Nichts*. Berlin: Rowohlt, 1991.

——. *Roman von einem Kinde*. Frankfurt/Main: Luchterhand, 1986.

——. *Soharas Reise*. Berlin: Rowohlt, 1996.

——. 'Von den Legenden der Kindheit, dem Weggehen und der Wiederkehr.' *Nach der Shoa Geboren*. Ed. Jessica Jacoby, Claudia Schoppmann, and Wendy Zena-Henry. Berlin: Elefanten Press, 1994. 35–40.

Koch, Gertrud. 'Corporate Identities: Zur Prosa von Dische, Biller, und Seligmann.' *Babylon* 7 (1990): 139–42.

Lappin, Elena. *Jewish Voices, German Words: Growing up Jewish in Postwar German & Austria*. Trans. Krishna Winston. New Haven CT: Catbird, 1994.

Ochse, Katharina. ''What could be more fruitful, more healing, more purifying?' Representations of Jews in the German Media after 1989.' *Reemerging Jewish Culture in German Life and Literature Since 1989*. Ed. Sander Gilman and Karen Remmler. New York: NYU Press, 1994. 113–129.

Plank, Klaus. 'The Survivor's Return: Reflections on Memory and Place. *Judaism* 38.3 (Summer 1989): 263–277.

Seligmann, Rafael. 'What Keeps the Jews in Germany Quiet?' *Reemerging Jewish Culture in German Life and Literature Since 1989*. Ed. Sander Gilman and Karen Remmler. New York: NYU Press, 1994. 173–183.

——. *Rubinsteins Versteigerung*. Frankfurt/Main: Eichborn, 1989.

Stern, Susan, ed. *Speaking Out: Jewish Voices from United Germany*. Chicago: Edition Q, 1995.

Walser, Martin. 'Die Banalität des Guten.' *FAZ* 12 Oct. 1998: 15.

Wolffsohn, Michael. *Eternal Guilt?: Forty years of German-Jewish-Israeli Relations*. Trans. Douglas Bokovoy. New York: Columbia UP, 1993.

Zipes, Jack. 'The Contemporary German Fascination for Things Jewish: Toward a Minor Jewish Culture.' *Reemerging Jewish Culture in German Life and Literature Since 1989*. Ed. Sander Gilman and Karen Remmler. New York: NYU Press, 1994. 15–45.

Notes

1. Although the term 'Holocaust' is the more common term for the genocide of six million European Jews by the Nazis and their collaborators during World War II, we use the less familiar term 'Shoah.' Whereas the Greek word 'holocaust' refers to a sacrifice consumed by fire, the Hebrew term 'shoah' connotes total destruction without the religious reference to scrifice.
2. For a more in-depth discussion of postmemory see Andrea Liss, *Trespassing in the Shadows*. Minneapolis: U. of Minnesota P, 1998. Marianne Hirsch, *Family Frames: Photography, Narrative and Postmemory*. Cambridge: Harvard UP, 1997.
3. Katja Behrens, "The Rift and Not the Symbiosis," p. 9.
4. Jews living in Germany represent a diverse, multiethnic and multinational population, which is reflected in the changing makeup of the Jewish religious communities. Since the fall of the Berlin Wall, a grow-

ing number of Jews from the former Soviet Union have immigrated to Germany under a special agreement that grants them automatic refugee status.

5. In the United States, two collections of Jewish writing in translation appeared in this period. See Lappin; Stern.

Katja Behrens

Arthur Mayer, or The Silence

1

Transported, said Mr. A, as in Anders or Anhalt. Transported with not so much as a word. Mr. A and I have known each other for a long time, many years, almost two decades. He has always had this kind of tongue, sharp as a knife, and a certain gentleness, which won me over, even though he has always been anything but gentle when the discussion turned to 'that' time. We get outright hostile toward each other; we stare at each other, and his eyes appear to me like thistles. I don't know whether he was a soldier, whether they took him out of school to put a rifle in his hand; we don't talk about those kinds of things; we never talk about it. A dead silence hangs over that time in which he grew up and must have worn a uniform just as everybody else, sang around the campfire and learned from the adults who their friends and who their enemies were. Almost half a century has gone by since then. Mr. A has been a good father; soon he'll be a grandfather. At the moment he engages in endless talk about our loquacious brothers and sisters from the East. He requests, no, he demands silence.

The stone is located on a main artery, and Mr. A discovered it by accident when the road was closed for a while and he had to go on foot to get to his house. Usually nobody walks around there—a narrow roadway, no sidewalk, speeding cars. I knew nothing about the stone in this place off the beaten path, nor did I know anything about Arthur Mayer.

He was very well liked, said Mrs. B, a good doctor . . . treated me when I was a child.

Transported, said Mr. A. Transported without a sound.

2

The road passes through a valley between dark, thickly forested hills. It continues uphill.
It takes me a while to find the stone. The inscribed side faces the roadway.

> IN MEMORY OF DR. ARTHUR MAYER.
> BORN 20 JANUARY 1888, DIED AT AUSCHWITZ
> WE REMEMBER HIM IN PLACE OF ALL THOSE WHO LOST THEIR LIVES FOR POLITICAL,
> RACIAL, OR RELIGIOUS REASONS.
> THE CITIZENS OF TOWN S

3

S, as in Schönberg or Schwarzdorf: population 10,494, two churches, two banks, one savings bank, one old-age home (beautifully located at the edge of the forest, right next to the cemetery), three pharmacies, one athletic and cultural center, four real estate companies, one old and one new city hall, one square (named for its French sister town, with a fountain and benches where trucks pass at high speeds on their way south and motorcyclists rev their engines), fourteen restaurants (among them one Italian and one Portuguese), three gas stations, one ice cream parlor (in the summertime people sit around on nearby curbs, stoops, or motorcycles eating ice cream; in the wintertime it turns into a place where fur coats are sold), five bakeries, three boutiques, one old-fashioned clothing store (for more than eighty years), one ophthalmologist, three gynecologists, five family doctors, and three hairdressers.

4

Dr. Mayer, says Mrs. B, as in Brunner or Brauner, was still treating me when I was a child. She says this like someone who likes remembering the old days, days long ago, when she was young and Schönberg was still a small town, with a population of not more than a few thousand. He was a good doctor, that Dr. Mayer; I knew him well, she says, unaware that a few months later she would not remember him at all.
I always admired her. She is in her late seventies; her movements

are young and so is her laughter. She and her husband look like happy people who enjoy their bodies and life. Mr. B is in his mid eighties and has a head of white hair like an artist. Sometimes he kisses my hand, and they are always friendly to me. In the summertime she bakes cherry pies and invites me to go cherry picking.
He was very well liked, she says, with a Hessian accent, and I think there are still people who knew him. I could try to bring him back to life with words. I am sure Mrs. B will tell me about him.

5

When exactly did he disappear? asked Mrs. B. I really don't know exactly when he left. When did he go away? I think he had already left before the takeover.
Before what takeover?
Well, before the takeover.
What do you mean?
Yes. '33.

6

What got you started on Arthur Mayer anyway?
Now she uses the formal address again. For a while we were on familiar terms. I start telling her, but she no longer listens, rummages around in a drawer, says something about her great-grandfather, searches for his photograph and his will; that's what she wanted to show me. Tenaciously, I turn the conversation back to Arthur Mayer; tenaciously, she talks about her great-grandfather, who had been an adjutant of the grand duke.

7

—but the aunt, she would certainly remember.
She is still well put together. Mr. B nods. Perfect memory. His voice is soft, and it is difficult to determine from his accent where he is from. The aunt is eighty-seven years old. Her short-term memory isn't particularly good.
. . . but she knows everything about things from the past.
The aunt settled in Schönberg in 1918. I'm counting. So she lived in the same town as Arthur Mayer for sixteen years.

Mrs. B says she'll ask the aunt when I can visit her.
Mrs. B calls me promptly the next day.
The aunt said she knows nothing. She remembers nothing. She knows absolutely nothing. My aunt has a poor memory for such things. She said you should get in touch with Mr. Conrad; he too is investigating.

8

It's not only Mrs. B, the woman with so much gusto for living, who points me toward Mr. C, as in Conrad and Clemens. Mr. D, as in Daniel or David, also says:
You can't get around Mr. Conrad. He has a monopoly around here.
I know. On the occasion of the fiftieth anniversary of the pogrom, an exhibit was held at the Schönberg athletic and cultural center (the same place where the annual ballroom dancing competition is held, as well as the exhibit of purebred chickens, the meeting of postage stamp collectors, the firemen's ball): *Jews in Schönberg.*
When I entered the hall, I was met by a tall, good-looking elderly gentleman, who extended his hand.
I'm particularly glad to greet *you.*
Since we didn't know each other, I presumed what he meant was that a Jewish woman was an adornment for his exhibit. Still chatting, he led me around. I was somewhat confused. The photos, the letters from survivors to Mr. C, all gave the impression that sometime, *somehow,* a natural catastrophe had befallen the Jews.
I give Mr. C a call.
You won't believe it, he says. I was just holding a photograph of Arthur Mayer.
Mr. C is working on a book about the Jews of Schönberg. He has been commissioned by the town and has been very generously funded, says Mr. C.
Mr. C was a teacher. Now he is retired, has been to America five times visiting survivors, and soon he will make his third trip to Israel. He visited Auschwitz twice, as well as Dachau and Treblinka, and just this very morning somebody dropped a number of documents, previously unknown to him, in his mailbox.
The county police report of 1936 . . . people just know that I am the competent authority.

9

Arthur Mayer's family had been living in S since 1698, that is, for 235 years, about ten generations before the Nazis.
He was very well liked, says Mr. C. When he treated poor people, he told them 'no charge,' the others will make up the cost.
On 10 October 1933, his wife, Margarethe, declared her change of residence and moved to Metz. Arthur Mayer followed her six months later. He was forty-six years old when he left his hometown, his house, his medical practice, his family to live with his in-laws, who had a shoe store in Metz.

10

Jews had been living in S since 1698. Most of them were in the cattle and fodder business.
They weren't permitted to practice a trade, to acquire land. Only in 1848 were they granted civil rights.
Fifteen Jewish families lived in S in 1867. The Jewish community purchased the farmland and residence, where they built a synagogue with a mikvah, a school, and living quarters for a teacher, from a farmer who had emigrated to America.
In 1936 the synagogue was sold to Willy Schneider. I ask a woman I know on the town council why there is no memorial plaque on the former synagogue. She tells me that when the current owner, Mrs. E, as in Ernst or Engel, was asked for permission to put up a memorial plaque, the old woman started to cry.
For God's sake, they'll smash my windows.
That's why we decided to do without a memorial plaque.

11

I get a call from a Mrs. F, as in Faust or Fischer. You don't know me, she says, but I am in the same situation you are.
I know immediately what she is talking about. She means what my mother, decades after the danger had passed, still called it, as if nothing were over, as if time had stood still, since it was better not to say the word *Jew* out loud, just as one avoids talking of death or walking through a cemetery at night. Mrs. F says she wrote something about that time. Was I willing to read it.
Mrs. F says she wrote the story of how she survived the Nazis. She would like to get it published.

It would be interesting were it not written with the chronic caution of a person who has lived in hiding, all traces blurred, personal feelings suppressed, an underground existence whose space is inside; on the outside is a life for all to see, seemingly completely normal, like everybody else but with a life-threatening secret—the fear that it may be *discovered*, which links the victims to the perpetrators.

I ask Mrs. F whether she is prepared to abandon her cover.

No, she says, with determination. Until then she had spoken in a hesitant, uncertain tone. I have children, and one never knows how times might change.

12

A sunny winter's day. The vaulting sky above S, as in Schönberg, is pale blue. Yesterday, I called Mr. G, G as in Gärtner or Grimm.

He was a good doctor, said Mr. G, when I asked about Arthur Mayer. He was very well liked, but I can't tell you anything.

Was he perhaps a patient of Dr. Mayer's.

Absolutely, said Mr. G.

I encouraged him.

He pushed himself. Then come tomorrow afternoon about three.

I arrive a few minutes early. Since he lives so close by, I was unable to estimate the time.

I ring the bell. Nothing stirs in the house. I feel bad, afraid to disturb Mr. G's afternoon nap. Finally, a head peeks out from behind the door, and a little man in a sweat suit appears, tilted body, a squint in one eye, watery blue.

Are you a writer?

I say yes, and he holds up his arms defensively.

I can't tell you anything more than what I told you on the phone. It's useless; you are wasting your time . . .

He is apparently determined not to let me in. We face each other in the yard, halfway between the gate and the door to the house. I see his hand trembling. His entire tilted body speaks of fear. Nevertheless, I ask whether he might anyhow . . .

Nothing doing, he says. He meant to call me this morning. He recites a telephone number and asks if it is mine.

I say yes, surprised that he should know my number by heart. He probably had been overcome by fear during the night, had been lying awake in bed, thought about that time, and got so scared that he wanted to cancel immediately but didn't dare leave a message on the answering machine.

I don't remember anything, he says, it's been sixty years.

But you were his patient.

He says, yes, and forgets for a moment that he doesn't remember anything. Even in '32. I was out cutting wood . . . infection . . . Doctor Mayer treated, he was a good . . .

As he speaks, he pushes me toward the door.

I can't tell you anything. It must have occurred to him suddenly that he didn't remember anything.

Don't even know when he left . . .

I say emigrated. Already in 1934.

1934? he says, relieved. At that time I was already in the labor service. I really can't tell you anything. And with that, he has opened the gate and forcefully offers me his hand. No hard feelings. Can't help.

No wonder, says Mr. H, as in Hartmann, Hoffmann, or Hübner. Fritz G was a member of the SA.

13

The Nazis received 692 votes in the Reichstag election of March 1933 in Schönberg, almost 50 percent of the votes. There were then about thirty Jews living in Schönberg.

On 28 March 1933, 'the national boycott against the Jews' began.

On 29 March 1933, 'our people's chancellor and Führer, Adolf Hitler,' was declared an honorary citizen of S. Railroad Station Street was changed to Adolf-Hitler Straße. The mayor announced the decrees during the membership meeting at the local inn. Parade through the town, visit by Adolf Hitler.

I try to imagine how Arthur Mayer must have felt about all this, the buildings decorated with flags, the crowds lining the streets, the extended arms; here, where I go shopping every day, look into the windows of the boutiques to see whether they have something nice, where I buy Band-Aids, envelopes, and new batteries, where he grew up among people who knew him for as long as he could remember. A few years before, he was a member of the town council and now . . . *and when the Jews' blood spurts from the knife's edge, then all goes twice as well.*

At first he probably didn't believe what he was hearing, the way people were suddenly talking, Krüger, Anheißer, and Kammler and Fritz Gärtner, whose father sat with him on the town council, representing the Social Democratic Party. Fritz Gärtner, says Mr. H, as in Hartmann or Hübner, probably got a pack of cigarettes for joining the SA . . . many joined for a pack of cigarettes. And then they marched through the streets shouting, passing Arthur Mayer's family home and Arthur Mayer's medical practice, which presumably almost no one visited anymore. *Germany Awake, Judah die*, not just some fellows in uniform; no, it was Fritz and Hans and Ludwig, with whom he and his brother had played and roughhoused. They went to school together, copied from each other on tests, and received a paddling together. Later he drank beer with them at the harvest festival and even later danced with their sisters, and then they went to war together. At times they may have forgotten who he was, a Jew, one who didn't belong, a bad Jew, but when the fellows from Schönberg met those from Neunkirchen, then he was a Schönberger, and during the war, during endless days and nights on a ship, he probably longed as much for Schönberg as did the fathers of Fritz and Hans and Ludwig, who were stuck in the mud somewhere far from home.

After he had returned home, he helped their children into the world, listened to their hearts, bandaged their wounds, tapped their backs.

They didn't forget this.

He was a good doctor.

He was very well liked.

In the beginning, Arthur Mayer may still have felt safe. They can't hurt me; after all, I was an officer. And then, fewer patients in the office, fewer greetings in the street, fewer chats, many evading glances, a strange emptiness, and maybe now and then a slap on the shoulder, don't take it personally, or a shrug of the shoulders, well, there is nothing one can do.

Slowly understanding, not all at once, and with the understanding came fear, first kept in check, not wanting to believe it, but then calls at night, somebody asks him to come deliver a baby; then there is nothing.

14

Shortly before Christmas, a pale blue sky and empty streets. It's a Saturday afternoon.

19 Hauptstraße. City hall, the fountain, the inn, and this old brick house, two stories with gables. So this was the house of Arthur Mayer's parents. These are the stone steps he walked up when he came home from school, from the university, from the war, from the town council meetings. Members of his party, a farmer, a furniture varnisher, and a mason, they too probably turned to him with stomachaches or when the saw cut someone's leg.

On the ground floor, where Arthur Mayer's parents sold cattle feed, there is now a stationery store with display windows to the left and right of the door. Postcards *Honey-Sweet Greetings from Schönberg*, then . . . all varieties of wrapping paper and rolls of ribbons in all colors. In the other window is a little Christmas tree decorated with ribbons and artificial candles as well as cards *Only Uphill in the New Year* and *Christmas? Winter? Cold Weather? No Thanks!* A cigarette vending machine, an ad for Camels.

15

24 December, in the morning. Mr. D, as in Daniel or David, my fellow Jew in Schönberg, at the newspaper vendor.

Mr. D kneels at the magazine stand.

An old woman rams against him, as Mr. D assures me, with amazing force, her knee into his back.

Make way; this is no reading room.

Exchange of words.

The way you look, says the old woman, you're no German. Why don't you go back to your country. You have no business being here.

I am as Aryan as you are, replied Mr. D. If you are a typical German, then I'm glad I'm not like you.

Aren't you German? I ask Mr. D.

Well, yes, he says, I just forgot for a moment.

16

It's Sunday morning. The church bells are ringing. Something glistens in the mail slot. Perhaps a hand-delivered letter. It's a flyer.

Germany is in the Hands of Foreigners!
Do we need more proof? Aren't all Germans aware of the unrestrained alien influence and destruction of our culture. Isn't the unchecked stream of asylum seekers oppressively obvious?
'The Federal Republic must remain a land of immigrants or the Germans will become a shrinking people due to the decline of the population.' Thus says H. Geißler, member of the CDU *leadership in a recent interview with* Bild. *In plain German, Geißler wants to 'honor' our people with Negroes, Asians from the Middle to the Far East. Is this man insane or a criminal?*
'White women are to mate only with members of dark races, and white men should be allowed to mate only with dark women. This way the white race will disappear, since miscegenation between dark and white people means the end of white people, and our most dangerous enemy becomes a memory.' Thus the argument of Rabbi Rabinovitch.
Our people have always been derided and slandered by mean-spirited, corrupting elements. With the fall of the criminal communist system in central Germany, those people are now visible, those who have deceived our people and have proven to be the upholders of the oppressive system. One need only point in this connection to Hilde Benjamin, among others, and the Judaized red 'writers' association of the GDR,*' whose members tried for decades, with selfless dedication, to explain to the German people the 'blessings' of socialism.*
How many of the 'chosen' supported this criminal regime remains to be determined. Turn the page to find a small selection of the better known among them. They all enjoy freedom unscathed . . . —Therefore, there is only one solution for us Germans:
MAKE GERMANY FREE FOR GERMANS!

17

When I drive now from Schönberg to Walldorf, passing the Walldorf Valley, between dark forested hills, I keep an eye out for the stone whose upper part becomes visible for a moment between the tree trunks. In the time it takes to bat an eye, the weathered stone appears in my field of vision, and in my head, I see pictures of Arthur Mayer's life.

18

When the Germans marched into France, Arthur Mayer and his wife, Margarethe, and his mother-in-law fled to Lyon. Mr. C, as in

Conrad or Clemens, Schönberg's expert on Jews, explains to me over the telephone that a classmate of his wife's was there when Arthur Mayer, his wife, and his mother-in-law were 'picked up' in Lyon.

Only now I wonder how it was possible that a soldier from Schönberg 'was there' when the family was being 'picked up.' Did the soldier just happen to walk down Rue Git le Coeur and happen to see two SS men come upon the Mayer family? The enemies of the state, Dr. A. Mayer and Margarethe Mayer, born Benetik, had been deprived of their German citizenship on 5 December 1940. It was 1943 when the Mayers were 'picked up,' and maybe among those who 'picked them up' was the schoolmate of Mr. C's wife, who is a native compared to Mr. C, who is a latecomer. I wonder what it must have been like in the French city of Lyon when the boy from Schönberg happened to meet the doctor from Schönberg, Arthur Mayer, who probably not too long before had examined his throat . . . and now say ahhhh? So many questions: Did the classmate of Mr. C's wife let it be known that he knew *this Jew*? Was he ashamed? Did he sleep well that night?

Dr. Arthur Mayer was declared dead on 29 December 1949 at the district court of Z.

19

Mr. C, complains Mr. H, who is a history teacher and says he is willing to tell me what he knows, Mr. C has a monopoly on Jews around here. He has been permitted to examine the records that have to do with Jews. He knows which houses were transferred from their Jewish owners to whom and at what price. Mr. C was an elementary school teacher; he was among the founders of the Christian party in Schönberg, served on the town council for twenty years, was county representative, one of the powerful, says Mr. H, the history teacher.

20

I am sorry, says Mr. C; in the meantime I've received several phone calls . . . You have apparently . . . under the circumstances, I cannot tell you anything. I must warn you, I must say. You are putting yourself at risk. You are talking with people without knowing anything about their pasts . . . I proceeded in each case with great caution . . . intimate things . . . confidence was established, and now one thing worries me, dear woman, that some of the things you have been told are being linked with me, that the trust is being broken here. When it is a matter beyond mere facts, about what is known anyway, when it goes beyond, and you are told things, then I am involved as well. So, my dear woman, I spent six months telephoning back and forth, you know, because this would have become the story. I was advised, Mr. Conrad, let it be . . . let's keep a lid on it. You understand: we'll keep a lid on it; we won't touch this. That is the reason, I was told by a Dr. So-and-so (I won't mention his name now), why my mother didn't say anything. I accepted that. His cousin in Chicago spoke with living grandchildren and almost got them to say yes, what do we care; after all, he took a different name. Then I spoke with him again, and then it was: no, we'll keep a lid on it. My dear woman, I live here; in this regard, I am more than cautious, and when I heard that you had spoken to this one and that one, even to Fritz Gärtner, he too asked: What's the use of all this? You already know everything. But this isn't the point. Why I am so cautious, at any rate, my dear woman, is that my book will be published soon, and it contains a chapter on Rudolf Mayer. What? What did I say? Rudolf, he was the great uncle; that's the man on the exhibition poster, the man who owned the inn near city hall. I am also in close contact with his granddaughter; she was here and spoke with schoolchildren and rebuilt, so to speak, a certain trust, and she is working on removing distrust as well with another branch of the Mayer family, who hasn't answered my inquiries yet, but we'll get it, you know, and if things come to light now, that would be detrimental to the cause. I hear everything that goes on; people tell me everything because they know he won't talk, and now this comes to light. Nowhere, I can assure you, nowhere is there a greater trust than in Schönberg. Just today, I received from Carolyne, she is also a Mayer, a warm letter and, by the way, an invitation to come to Chicago; these are all things that are possible here in Schönberg, and I take partial credit for this, and when you are called to account today, when somebody denounces you, well then, my dear woman, I am sorry. I would have liked to help you, but I've thought it through carefully, also sought advice, and I'll hold to my position. No, I don't see you as competition; it's not about me personally or my honor; you may be seeing this the wrong way. That's not what it's all about. My concern is with the source, so to speak, from which these things come, and in this regard, I feel somehow, no, I don't feel, I *am* simply the injured party.

21

'Only compatriots will be considered by the town in the assignment of jobs and deliveries, only those who have nothing to do with Jews; don't buy at Jewish stores, and have no connection with them. Permission to settle in town and acquire real estate will not be granted to Jews; that is, no transaction with them will be valid.' (1935)

22

I meet Mr. I, an elderly gentleman who doesn't look like an elderly gentleman at all but looks twenty years younger. Mr. I, as in Ilse or Idel, lives near me. We see each other almost every day, and sometimes we stop for a little chat.

The line at the checkout counter of the supermarket is long. Mr. I lines up behind me. I have a basket full of groceries; he holds a box of breadcrumbs and a few bananas in his hand.

How are you, he asks, and whether the new year has started out well for me.

Yes, I say, and ask about him.

He stayed home, he says.

I ask whether there were a lot of fireworks.

This year, he says, there weren't as many as usual, and he talks about young people and old people who envy the young ones because they shoot off the fireworks.

Well, he adds, they are dying out anyway, and I think about what preoccupies me most these days, how it must have been for Arthur Mayer and those dear to him, and since I have a premonition of what is about to come, I force myself to ask.

Was he a longtime resident of Schönberg? I begin cautiously.

Yes.

And did you know Doctor Mayer?

Certainly.

The look in his eyes changes. Just a moment ago, he was still flirting with me, had moved close to me, transcending with blinking eyes the usual distance between human beings; all this with the bananas and bread crumbs in his hand and without any further intentions, out of a lifelong habit, and now it was all gone. He took a step backward. Distrust in his eyes.

What kind of a person was he, this Doctor Mayer, I ask, and he says, he was a good doctor; all this wasn't as it is today; not everybody had insurance, but Doctor Mayer didn't ask for it; he said the main thing is that you'll get well again first—very different from Doctor Jungmann, the one who came later.

Oh, he was a doctor too? I ask.

Yes, he says, but not a good one, and I bring the conversation back to Arthur Mayer; I would like to know very much what kind of a person he was.

Well, a regular fellow, he says.

And when did he leave, I ask. This is also a test of his memory, of how much he still knows.

Mr. I, as in Ilse or Idel, thinks for a moment, and then he says—'34, and I think, what an excellent memory, and I ask him about Arthur Mayer's wife.

She was rarely seen, doesn't know anything about her.

The word *Jew* occurs not even once. Where he died remains unsaid, as do words like National Socialism and Fascist.

23

From the chronicle of the Protestant Church of S, 1919–1922:

> *New disturbance was brought into the political life of Schönberg by Dr. Arthur Mayer, a Jewish libertarian physician originally from here, who returned in 1919, was leader of a democratic group, but later turned socialist, and August Anders, who switched to the bourgeois camp in 1922 once he was pushed out of his position in the party. Very talented, energetic, without scruples, Mayer constitutes a danger to the religious-moral fiber of the community. Everywhere I sense his antagonism toward the church. He is aided by the not very firm, gullible mentality of the people of Schönberg. Thus he was able, in late 1922, to gain a socialist majority on the town council, where he set the agenda. The old town councilors, who had calmed down as far as practical work was*

concerned, were, except for . . . , replaced by radical elements. So as not to be financially strapped, the church community introduced its own taxes. With God's help, we also hope to be able to withstand other challenges.

24

Opposite the store at 19 Hauptstraße, where newspapers, cigarettes, colored ribbons, and wrapping paper are sold today, is a beautifully restored timber-framed house.

The squat little house with ochre-colored lattice frames, white-washed walls, stood opposite the massive, two-story, red brick house of Uncle Mayer's brother Solomon, a splendid mansion with wide, stone-framed windows along the broad front. Uncle Mayer's house too had a second floor, but the house was so low that the red roof tiles almost touched the ground. The front room on the second floor of my uncle's house, actually only a garret, was set up as a guest room.

This is where Henry Buxbaum of Friedberg lived during his summer vacations. He too was a physician, like his cousin Arthur, but was not allowed to practice from 1933 on and just managed to immigrate to the United States, where, forty years later, he wrote for his descendants, in English, the story of what he had gone through and where he had come from.

I had just left S and had reached Hauptstraße at the other end of town when I realized that I would be confronted with an unpleasant situation. About half a mile away from me, a group of storm troopers was marching along the road, and I had to pass them on my bicycle. When the Nazis came to power, they instituted a special Sunday service, though not a new mass or church event. From then on, every Sunday, early in the morning, the members of the Nazi civilian guard, the SA, were called together for military exercises on the outskirts of town. Some people, probably only the non-Nazis, were not too happy to be dragged out of bed early Sunday morning to march about in all kinds of weather and lose the only day of rest in the entire week. But they had no choice in this, as in many other matters. The Führer and his followers were intent on preparing for war, and hardly had they come to power, when they began their preparations with German thoroughness. Preparations for war could be openly observed everywhere by everybody, and these para-

military exercises were a part of it all. They were an integral part of a network of special intensive training programs that at one time or another encompassed every segment of society, every profession, and thus superimposed a military structure on all of Germany. But now I was trapped. It was impossible to pass the Nazi formation in front of me without a confrontation. The road extended for three miles in a straight line without a cross road in any direction. I could have turned back, possibly, without arousing their suspicion. But I didn't want to do that. Something pushed me on and didn't permit me to turn back. I was well aware of the danger that I invited if I passed the Nazi formation without lifting my arm in the Führer greeting. In Griesheim, my hometown, it wouldn't have mattered. Everybody knew that I was a Jew, and nobody expected me to raise my arm. The Nazis wouldn't have tolerated a Jew besmirching the sanctity of their symbol by raising his arm. But the troop in front of me didn't know who I was, and nothing compelled me to tell them. But never would I raise my arm. I braced myself to pass them, no matter what might happen. At that moment, when I made this decision, when I looked it straight in the eye, a strange peace came over me, absolute serenity. Whatever I did from then on was in the nature of a reflex that had been set in motion by an unknown source in me and over which I had no control. I didn't know how this encounter would end, but I knew I could not raise my arm. Something inside of me would not permit me to do it. Slowly, I pedaled on. A group of Hitler Youth, marching in front of them, passed me, raised their arms, and shouted 'Heil Hitler.' I pretended that I wouldn't dare take my hands off the handlebars and answered with 'good morning,' holding on to the handlebars more tightly than before. They looked at me with surprise but continued their march. Another troop of boy scouts passed, and the same ritual was repeated. By now, my strange behavior aroused their attention. When I was getting closer to the SA formation, I saw their leader, a youngish fellow with stripes on his sleeves and shoulders, strutting at the head of the column, and who, all excited, now drew his men's attention toward me. He was a stage character in a play I had foreseen, where we would soon meet to play our various roles, and I was by no means excited: my decision had already been made. I was now parallel with the troop. The young fellow with the stripes jumped in front of me, threw his arm up as high as possible, and shouted a thunderous, provocative 'Heil Hitler' in my face. I turned around and said quietly: 'good morning,' while continuing to pedal on. He seemed frozen. And so seemed the others around him. It was unheard of that somebody didn't return the Hitler greeting! Two or three seconds passed, while I rode on, until he found his voice again and shouted after me, even louder than before, another 'Heil Hitler.' At the same time, two or three fellows tried to grab my bicycle and stop me. I turned around, looked at them, and asked: 'What's the matter? I already said good morning!' At that moment, even more baffled than before, they let go of my bicycle. I freed myself and rode on, gradually approaching the end of the column. But by then, the leader had regained his composure and loudly ordered his men: 'Catch him and hold him!' But meanwhile, precious seconds had passed since we'd first looked each other in the eye, and I had already passed the last man in the column. Two or three young men left the column and chased after me, but not for very long. They were confused, not knowing what to do, and soon I heard one of them call to the others: 'Oh damn, let him go; let's go back!' Slowly, I bicycled on without looking back. Did they really stop? I continued on my way for another two or three hundred meters, in a slow measured tempo, still tense the whole time, trying to determine from the noise behind me whether they were still following me. I still didn't dare turn my head.

(Hans-Helmut Hoos, 'Die Lebenserinnerungen des Friedberger Juden Heinrich (Henry) Buxbaum' [The memoirs of Heinrich (Henry) Buxbaum, a Jew from Friedberg] [Darmstadt, 1988]).

25

It's Sunday again, and again a flyer appears in my mailbox and only in my mailbox.

Heading: We Demand Truth and Justice.

Adenauer set the number of murdered Jews at three hundred thousand; yet soon there was talk about eight, or even ten, million. Today six million has become an incontrovertible number. 'Confession of Nazi crimes' has now become a sort of state doctrine, even a religious rite.

In schoolbooks, the minds of German children are being impressed with such claims by means of bestially embellished details of the supposed cruelties committed by their parents and grandparents. Television, radio, and almost all newspapers and magazines not only accuse us of millionfold murders but also present these murders as 'historical fact.' In 'documentary films,' whose titles create the impression that everything is documented, the perverse fantasies of those who falsify find their wildest expression, creating deep sympathy for the Jews and boundless contempt for the Germans. For prominent politicians, journalists, artists, or priests, it has become a dutiful exercise to espouse in public statements the unexamined slander against the German dictatorship, against 'the dark years in German history,' and against simply everything that is German.

This smear campaign and race hatred against all that is German has demoralized our nation. The result is a people with a compliant slave mentality who languidly accepts its own annihilation through alien penetration. The majority of Germans have fallen prey to the formula, concocted with the logic of hindsight by Rabbi Joachim Prinz, later taken over by the German political leadership: 'Although there is no such thing as collective guilt, the entire German people must be held responsible for the repercussions of the "Holocaust."' The repercussions of the 'Holocaust smear campaign' are fatal to our people: Payments to foreign nations for 'restitution' and 'solidarity' raise the burden of debt, which this government imposes on our children and their children. The opening of our homeland to settlement by foreign races and people, justified with 'all the terrible things that were done in the German name,' at first gradually, and now ever more quickly, destroys our nation. The illegal renunciation of ancient German lands in the East, justified by the alleged crimes of the German Reich against our neighbors, abandons millions of Germans to arbitrary foreign rule and expels them unceremoniously from the German people. Even worse than this is the ostracism imposed for the whole world to see by the Bonn politicians on the German people. The government leadership tramples the dignity of all Germans with the 'Holocaust.'

26

On the way to the supermarket, I run into Mr. C, whom I didn't recognize right away even though I saw him. When I recognize him and stop to greet him, I notice that he had been hoping that I would pass him by.

We say hello. I give him my hand, ask: How are you?

All right, says he, and you?

All right, I say, and how is your book coming?

He ignores my question and looks past me.
. . . was just at the *Schönberger Nachrichten*, have here a list of Jews who were killed . . . fiftieth anniversary of the Wannsee Conference. Mr. C, as in Conrad or Clemens, becomes agitated. This is new. Nothing was known about this until now.
I ask again about his book.
Yes, that will now come later, in May or so.
He lets his eyes wander. I look him in the face. A good-looking man, dark, not much gray hair even though he must be in his late sixties. I search his face for traces of that which Mrs. J, as in Jäger or Jung, told me yesterday. C, she said, was in the war. Soldier. Poland. Warsaw. Jews. Open question. Guilt feelings. The silence is awkward.
I guess I disappointed you.
Yes.
I have to be careful, very careful.
That seems to be necessary.
Yes, it is necessary.
Can you tell me why?
I don't have the time right now.
Mr. C points at his wife, who apparently had been shopping, and explains that he has to give her a hand.
Couldn't I at least see the photograph of Arthur Mayer? I know you have one.
I am inundated with a flood of words . . . only a group photo, Mayer was hardly recognizable . . . eyes were darkened so that one could hardly see anything at all . . . daughter-in-law has the photo, and she is pregnant; now I really must go . . .
Mr. C starts to walk away. On the other side of the street a woman is waiting. She must have passed us as I was asking about the photograph, didn't stop to talk with her husband, is standing there with her bags, a homely woman with gray curls. She is the one from a well-established family; he only settled here after the war. It had been her classmate who had witnessed Arthur Mayer and his family being 'picked up' during a raid in Lyon.

27

Mr. K, as in Keller or Kaiser, bellows into the telephone. Arthur Mayer was very well liked, treated the unemployed for free, and sent gift packages to poor people on Christmas.

On Christmas?
On Christmas, thunders Mr. K, a retired teacher who didn't grow up in Schönberg, moved here only after the war and became the local historian, maybe in order to make himself at home in the town where he was a stranger.
Mr. K tells me to contact Mr. C.
I tell him that I have already done that.
To his curt tone of voice is added an understanding undertone. Conrad also tried to get rid of Lauer when he showed interest in the Jews; he prevented Lauer from gaining access to the archives—and when Lauer took photographs of the Jewish cemetery, Conrad confronted him: What business do you have around here?
I am not particularly amused by the idea of an altercation over the absent Jews of Schönberg.

28

Ah, that Conrad, the Jew king, says Mr. L, when I call him. Why don't you ask him what he did during the war? He was in the army, in Warsaw . . . what did he do there?

29

What, says Mr. K. Arthur Mayer was in Auschwitz? I thought he had been finished off by the SS in France.

30

Mr. L, as in Lauer or Loos, is tall and thin. He wears a vest and slippers, leads me into his living quarters in the basement. Half dark. A desk. A bucket chair. A chair for me. We are both at a loss. I see Mr. L the way he described himself on the telephone; I see him in the year 1948 on a streetcar, a line that still exists today—a car shakes the walls of my living room every half-hour—on that streetcar in the company of veterans returned from the war, who are taking a ride into town. Adolf Hitler Square, they say, knowing full well that the square no longer has that name.
It took me a long time to really comprehend that the Nazis had lost, Mr. L, as in Lauer or Loos, had told me on the telephone. The economy was once again doing well, he said, and his father was earning a living again, *and among the young people, this wandering off*

into nature and then into the war; we are riding toward the East, the Ukraine, which today is important again, this granary.

31

Mr. K published a *Heimatbuch* about a town in the hinterland. It was commissioned by the town savings bank. Mr. K has a chapter about the Jews who had once lived there. The book was meant to appear on the occasion of the town's quincentennial celebration. The director of the savings bank asked him to drop the chapter about the Jews. He was afraid he would lose his best customers. All old activists, the director of the savings bank called them in so many words. Mr. K refused. As a result, the mayor of the town called him personally, pleaded with him. They will all close their accounts with the bank.

Well, let's just see about that, said Mr. K and turned to the local newspaper.

In advance, the newspaper ran Mr. K's chapter about the Jews of this town in the hinterland.

No one had anything to say after that, snorted Mr. K with self-satisfaction. It just goes to show what cowards they all are.

32

Mr. L, as in Lauer or Loos, the thin regional historian who is also a retired teacher and who had moved into town only after the war, this Mr. L pulls out a file card and reads out loud that in 1870 Arthur Mayer's father, Solomon, donated one mark for the war memorial. This goes to show, says Mr. L, that they saw themselves as integrated, and their thinking and feeling were typically German.

33

My mother knew from the beginning the meaning of the Nazi seizure of power. I visited her in Friedberg early in April 1933. She was sitting in a chair waiting for me to come up to her and kiss her because she couldn't see me. She was totally blind in the last three years before she died. And just as Jeremiah clearly foresaw the fate of Jerusalem, she leaned against me, and in a few words, she said everything that needed to be said: 'Heine, they have pulled us up by the roots.' [(Hoos, Memoirs) Heinrich Buxbaum's mother came from that same town in the hinterland where, a half-century later, no space was to be found for the Jews in Mr. K's town history.]

34

'Some communities are even worse. Wiesenbach, for example, is packed with Nazi followers and Jew haters. Somebody once wrote an article about the Jews. They called him day and night. You wouldn't believe what's going on.'
Mr. K, former teacher and local historian.

35

With a sure grip, Mr. L keeps pulling out new file cards. It's getting dark in the room. Mr. L gets up and flips on the light.
At the beginning of the First World War, Arthur Mayer was twenty-six years old. A ship's doctor, somewhere far away, maybe in America.
My confidential source, says Mr. L, who was a neighbor of the Mayers, still clearly remembers when he came to Schönberg to volunteer for the war.
It wasn't easy to get here; in those days it was a great distance.

36

The memorial plaque for Arthur Mayer had been put up in the summer of 1964. The stone itself had been a natural find and cost 3 marks. The expense for the inscription amounted to 420 marks.

37

In 1922 Arthur Mayer had a plaque made to honor those who lost their lives in the First World War and had it placed on a house owned by his relatives. The survivor commemorated his dead neighbors.
Forty-five men from Schönberg died in that war, which was not yet called the First, nor was it the only one of its kind.
Where was the plaque put up?
The corner of Bergstrasse and Schlossweg.
Which corner? Where the housewares store is now?
Mr. L equivocates. I ask again. Mr. L is evasive. I am well aware, of course, that questions of this sort are forbidden; former houses of

Jews and who lives in them today is a topic that is not discussed, a silent agreement; there wasn't anyone who wouldn't obey this rule. Corner of Bergstrasse and Schlossweg, a few steps from the Gärtner family's yard, where the gardener Fritz—don't take it amiss, I can't tell you anything—accepted candy, or was it apples, from Uncle Arthur and didn't yet care that he was a Jew and didn't yet know that one day he would join the SA to spite his father, a Social Democrat who, together with Arthur Mayer, served on the town council and who would rather commemorate the war dead in the open street than in the semidarkness of the church, where the women of Schönberg, presumably at the behest of the priest, had erected a wooden plaque.

38

Mr. L pulls out another file card and reads aloud what the butcher Willi Goldschmidt, a survivor born and reared in Schönberg, said when he visited the town on the occasion of the opening of the exhibition *Jews in Schönberg*.

I'm a Jew, but I slaughtered whatever came my way, and I also ate pork.

Willi Goldschmidt, says Mr. L, he was a sly dog.

Mr. L sits haggard in his swivel chair at the desk, and I sit on a chair in the corner by the door, my notebook on my knees.

He bolted, says Mr. L, when I ask him what was so sly about him. A clever fellow.

Mr. L says this with the grudging recognition one accords a criminal whose crime one disapproves of but whose skill one cannot but admire. He took advantage of all sorts of hiding places to evade the Gestapo. He was picked up in France but got away again . . . must have been a real fox.

Mr. L gets up and pulls out another card from a different file box.

In 1931 Willi Goldschmidt was the county champion of the Schönberg wrestling team.

39

That Arthur, says Willi Goldschmidt, he was in the camp with me.

In Auschwitz?

In Auschwitz.

I found Willi Goldschmidt's number in the telephone book.

His wife and mother-in-law, they were gassed right away; he continued to work as a doctor . . . and then all of a sudden he wasn't there anymore. Whether he was gassed or died just like that . . . he wasn't there anymore.

I hold my breath. Nobody had told me of the existence of somebody who knew Arthur Mayer at Auschwitz. I ask Willi Goldschmidt for a meeting and try to explain why I want to write this story. A woman's voice interrupts.

. . . that's ridiculous . . .

I beg your pardon? I ask.

That was my wife.

What did she say?

My wife says, why all the fuss.

What kind of fuss?

Well, you know; my wife, she knows nothing about all this.

Apparently Willi Goldschmidt is trying to indicate to me that his wife is not Jewish, and suddenly he is in a hurry to be rid of me.

Listen, why don't you get in touch with Conrad, the teacher; he knows everything.

I don't give up; I try to get Willi Goldschmidt to agree to a meeting.

A click. The line is dead. I hold the receiver against my ear; I listen; suddenly I feel discouraged.

I go into the kitchen and wash the dishes. I can't stop thinking about it; I have to ask; I want to understand; I drop the dish scraper, dry my hands, and rush to the telephone.

This time the wife answers.

I tell her I don't understand why her husband cut off our conversation.

I did that, she says firmly and without hesitating, like someone who is absolutely certain about something and does not have the slightest doubt about being right. All this leads to nothing.

But he was a friend of . . .

That was fifty years ago. It's all forgotten and over.

But . . .

Willi Goldschmidt's wife had hung up.

40

Whenever I have some business at town hall, I am reminded of Arthur Mayer's uncle Rudolf, who was a horse and beef butcher and already an old man when he sat here waiting to be picked up. The woman, whom Mr. L conspiratorially calls *my informant*, said she couldn't forget how the old man sat there at the town hall . . . Mr. L says, *didn't want to believe it and completely broke down*, and now I don't know who, his informant or Rudolf Mayer, who died in Theresienstadt in 1943, like Franziska Weber, who may have been his sister, born Mayer, and a few years older than he. I wonder whether Rudolf and Franziska and Moritz and Juliane saw each other there; they were all old people born and reared in Schönberg who died in Theresienstadt, who probably didn't have the strength to speak to each other and to reminisce about their hometown, which, supposedly, was suddenly not theirs anymore.

41

Again I am standing in line at the supermarket, and again Mr. I, as in Ilse or Igel, the elderly gentleman who doesn't look like an elderly gentleman, is in line behind me. This time he holds four kiwis in his hand. I ask how he is doing, just to say something and not be standing around mute.

Fine, he answers.

We are silent.

I push my cart a few steps forward, turn around to Mr. I, and ask directly whether there was any rivalry between Doctor Mayer and Doctor Jungmann, who had arrived in town later.

Mr. I doesn't give a direct answer. He says, Mayer was a good doctor, Jungmann wasn't.

I continue to probe. Yes, he confirms hesitantly, Jungmann was a bit envious. I ask whether Jungmann was a Nazi.

God no, he says.

I tell him I heard he was. He says, and if he was, and shrugs his shoulders, who wasn't?

I am no longer the same person I was at the beginning of my investigation. Now I take the bull by the horns with questions I wouldn't have dared ask a few weeks before. I have become much bolder. I ask directly and am just as surprised as he:

And you, were you a Nazi too?

He stands there quietly with his four kiwis and nods his head. Yes, I too was one of them.

I always thought you had been a Social Democrat.
That, I never was. They did everything wrong. Nobody who wasn't alive in those days can truly understand this, how poor we were, poorer than the third world today.
All three men in my family lost their jobs at once, he says.
You cannot imagine what it was like.
I say that I can and that I am sure it was very bad. The cashier rings up the prices on the register. I bag yogurt, cheese, cottage cheese, and Mr. I says, nothing happened to those Jews; it's all untrue; they all got away, and in the neighboring town, a Jew had said to his brother, if he weren't a Jew, he too would be a Nazi.
Didn't he feel sorry for Doctor Mayer, I ask, putting my change away without looking at it.
But he was able to get away, he says quietly and with conviction. Nobody around here came to any harm; that, you can believe.

42 Register

Jewish persons residing in the service district of the Police Station A, as in Altdorf or Abenden, and belonging to the Jewish community B, as in Bensbach or Buchen.
Cutoff date: 1 March 1936

TOWN S

No.	Last name	First name	Occupation or status	Date of birth	Place of birth	Jewish, political orientation
1	Kohn	Martha	no occupation	2/10/07	C	neutral
2	Mayer	Rudolf	butcher	5/4/68	S	‘
3	Mayer	Ludwig	butcher	5/17/02	S	‘
4	Mayer born Maas	Lina,	housewife	3/9/98	G	‘
5	Mayer	Milton	merchant	12/15/88	S	‘
6	Mayer	Hedwig, born Grüne-baum	housewife	5/14/93	B	‘
7	Mayer	Max	merchant	2/21/86	S	‘
8	Rosenfeld	Hermann	merchant	7/7/73	A	‘
9	Rosenfeld	Emilie, born Mayer	housewife	4/14/88	S	‘

10	Rosenfeld	Herbert	pupil	6/22/25	S	‘
11	Rosenfeld	Erich	pupil	2/22/22	S	‘
12	Gold-schmidt	Cäcilie, born Roth	widow	12/5/91	S	‘

43

In my dreams I tell my grandmother, who is lying in bed, about my meeting with Mr. I. Suddenly, I fling my arms around her neck and burst into bitter tears. I tell her that Mr. I said nothing happened to the Jews.

44

Mr. C had a plaque made for the exhibition *Jews in Schönberg*. ‘All Jewish fellow citizens who were victims of the Nazi terror are listed here.’

*Bamberger, Moritz * 11/8/1869 S.*
died 10/14/1942 Theresienstadt
*Ewald, Selma, born Goldberg * 3/17/1879 S.*
missing in Poland
*Goldberg, Auguste * 10/4/1873 S.*
died 8/20/1943 Theresienstadt
*Goldberg, Edmund * 9/27/1877 S.*
missing in Izbica/Poland
*Mayer, Nathan * 3/7/1895 S.*
missing in Auschwitz
*Steinthal, Betty born Feistler * 1/1/1860 S.*
died 1/29/1943 Theresienstadt
*Weiler, Franziska born Mayer * 5/29/1876 S.*
died 8/6/1943 Theresienstadt
*Bachenheimer, Ruth * 3/1/1905 S.*
missing in Poland
*Ettinghausen, Bethge born Feitler * 7/11/1861 S.*
declared dead in Sobibor
*Rosenfeld, Emilie born Mayer * 4/14/1888 S.*
declared dead in Poland
*Mayer, Max * 2/21/1886 S.*
died 3/17/1941 in Cholm
*Mayer, Rudolf * 5/4/1868 S.*
died 1/2/1943 in Theresienstadt

*Mayer, Arthur medical doctor * 1/20/1888 S.*
missing in Auschwitz
*Mayer, Margarethe born Benetik * 6/5/1902 F.*
missing in Auschwitz

45

Until a few years ago, there was a small green common at the upper end of the Ober-Beerbach Straße, which was very popular among the town residents and, until 1939, also among the Jewish fellow citizens. The children delighted in splashing around in the creek and building little dams. Evergreens, which surrounded the common, set the area off from the road. Benches that invited the visitors to rest could, however, get unpleasant in the middle of summer. Whole swarms of mosquitoes, bred yearly in the damp field, demanded their blood tribute from the wanderer. Appropriately, the untiring visitors were dubbed mosquito killers. Exactly when the common was laid out and for what reason can no longer be determined. The first record of it that anyone can put a finger on is the minutes of the beautification commission meeting of 28 March 1925. This record shows that Dr. Robert Mayer offered to have the common expanded and renovated at his own expense. What he had in mind was a living memorial, embedded in nature, for his parents, Solomon and Gertrud Mayer. When it was made clear that no change of name favoring one family would take place, the board agreed unanimously. The work was contracted and proceeded with due speed. According to the minutes of 13 June 1926, the commission expressed its heartfelt gratitude to the generous benefactor.

It is probably safe to assume that R. Mayer's great interest in precisely this area had to do with the fact that it was the destination of the Jews' Sabbath walks. According to the prescribed rules and the habits that developed from them, Jews were not allowed to undertake far-flung excursions on the Sabbath, and their walks were restricted to about one thousand steps from their place of residence. And this is exactly the case here.

After the Second World War, our veteran mayor, A B, was the driving force behind a memorial for the Jews as well as for others who had been persecuted for political, racial, and religious reasons. He selected Dr. Arthur Mayer, the popular physician and brother of the aforementioned Robert Mayer, as sole representative, and talked the young socialists into taking the necessary steps. In the summer of 1964, they erected the now existing stone and created a modest separate area in what was then a densely overgrown little evergreen garden. [From an essay by Mr. L, as in Lauer or Loos, local historian and retired teacher.]

46

In 1941 Arthur Mayer's assets became the property of the German Reich.

47

Why don't you hit the bad Jew in the mouth.
This sentence sticks in my mind as well as the fact that Mr. L read it with meaningful intonation from one of his file cards. It wasn't some villager who was supposed to have said this to Arthur Mayer but his own mother. There you have it . . . and now I don't remember what this sentence was supposed to show; it was to prove something, but I don't remember what.

48

The *House of Fashion M.* I usually stop in front of the display windows for a moment to look at the clothes, beautiful fabrics, beautiful colors, a little grandmotherly, a little old fashioned; you may as well forget it—all this was always separate in my head, the conventional clothing store of M and the wife of Mr. C, who knows all the Jews; she is a born M, you know, the House of Fashion M. I am standing in front of it and looking around; this time I have no eye for the garments. I see only one thing: Mrs. C's parents' house is situated between Arthur Mayer's parents' house, which later became his medical practice, and the Town Hall Pub.
The Town Hall Pub had been a horse and beef butcher shop that belonged to Rudolf Mayer for as long as Jews were allowed to own something. When he was taken to Theresienstadt, the butcher shop was already in the hands of N, as in nobody.
An old timbered house, bull's-eye windowpanes, beer by Schmucker, bowling alley. A Yugoslav name on the door.
I open; I am immediately in the semidark pub. Closeness. Stench of beer. Two men at a table, a woman behind the counter. More men in the corner. All heads turn toward me. The woman is blond and wears a white apron. She is no longer young.

I hesitate at the door.

Hello, says the woman. Hello, I reply, smile, and close the door again behind me.

Outside the sun shines brightly. As I walk past, I look up at the magnificent facade. So this was Else Mayer's parent's house. This is where she was born in November 1905. Her father, Rudolf, was a butcher and cantor of the Jewish community. Her brother, who was three years older, also became a butcher. And a member of the 'Harmony' singing society. Else played the piano. Her family probably didn't like it when she married a goy. Girls who married Christians were generally considered as good as dead by their families. It was customary to say the prayer for the dead over them, to spit them out, reject them, just as the body rejects a foreign organ. But it was 1931 and the prospective son-in-law was willing to be married in accordance with Jewish ritual. His name was Willy, and he played the violin. Maybe it was the music that brought Else and Willy together. I can see Mr. L in front of me, holding one of his file cards up to the light . . .

. . . played together at weddings.

She, hands on the keyboard; he, the violin under his chin. An exchange of glances, a nod, and the first note resounds, the first sounds, melting, rising, carrying them away from everyday life, the village, the hick town, which is by far not as picturesque as it will be one day when a writer arrives who only wants to tell the story of Arthur Mayer, who, enraged and made curious by the threats of Mr. C, will stubbornly continue to ask questions when Käthe O, as in Opper or Ortlepp, who was just about to rebraid her nine-year-old daughter Gerlinde's ponytail, the daughter of House of Fashion M, sways to the music and who, on a sunny afternoon in spring 1992, answers the telephone with a cheerful voice, only to slam down the receiver after saying, oh, it's you; what do you want from me now; I'm just getting dressed. And when the last tone has faded, and she lifts her hands from the keyboard, and he lets the violin sink, their eyes will meet, and perhaps her father is there, and perhaps Else gives him a quick glance to make sure that he doesn't notice anything and then goes on flirting with Willy, and perhaps Arthur, her cousin, also participates in the festivities; he's her cousin and will deliver the child that will be conceived that very night.

In 1936, when only a handful of Jews are left in the town, and Else Schneider's brother receives permission to emigrate with his wife, the Jewish community, probably the father, Rudolf, sells the synagogue to Willy Schneider.

The day came, or was it the night, when hairdresser P, who at that time was acting mayor, the mayor having been drafted into the army, came to see Else Schneider to tell her that she would be 'picked up' the next morning.

Leaving everything behind. Money. Papers. Jewelry. The violin. The goodbye from her father.

The old man had to endure many goodbyes before he said goodbye himself in order to be 'picked up' at the town hall.

One of Mr. L's file cards notes that Else and Willy Schneider escaped to Austria where they went into hiding.

What the neighbors remember about that morning is the bucket with the chicken feed, which was still standing in front of the former synagogue.

49

I have taken the bull by the horns. Everywhere I have been proclaiming how my investigation of the Schönberg physician Arthur Mayer is going. I was awarded a literary prize and took the opportunity: Schönberg politicians at the award ceremony. Television, floodlights. One day after the award ceremony, I receive the key to the town archives. I already know that there is nothing left to find; the Mayer file has disappeared together with everything else *from that time* that might have been of interest. But I take the key anyway, sign in, and turn toward the picture archives.

Mr. Q, as in Quilling or Quambusch, has pulled the records for me. Up until now I have known Mr. Q only by sight. He works for the town government; I live next to the town hall; so it's natural that we should see each other. A young man, early thirties I guess. A surprise: also an ally. Soft voice, hands rattling the key chain. Hurriedly, he comes and goes. But don't let anybody know it was I . . .

The town secretary accompanies me on my way through the hallways of the town hall. Mr. Q comes to meet us. We exchange a conspirators' glance.

Official room. Open doors. Dry air.

The young woman who works in the room where the file shelves are located pays no attention to me. I pull out the first file and start leafing through it. What excitement to be looking through a telescope at the town where one lives. I recognize the streets, the corners, the house at a two-, three-minute distance from this office, only much drabber than today. Cobblestones. Weatherworn shutters. Crumbling walls. No concrete blocks yet, no neon advertisements, parked cars, traffic signs. Through these streets, so familiar to me, marching boys, marching men. Flags. Swastikas. Each photograph has a typewritten caption. Harvest festival. October 1935. Between the inn and the drug store a swastika like a full moon over the crowd of people. For the first time I understand what *gleichgeschaltet* means.

Mr. Q passes as though by coincidence, looks over my shoulder, turns a few pages without saying a word.

Breathtaking, I say.

He points at Adolf Hitler standing in an open car, from the front, from behind.

In the hall is a copier. I rush out with the file to seize the opportunity now. Mr. Q sets up the machine for me, disappears.

I hurry back and forth between office and hallway. The open files pile up on the table.

Willi Goldschmidt, 1931 member of the sporting club's youth team. They're lined up like organ pipes, posing, hands behind their backs, left leg turned outward. Third from the left, a robust fellow in a black training suit. Nothing points to the fact he would soon be a hunted man. Willi Goldschmidt in 1988 at the opening of Mr. C's exhibition *Jews in Schönberg*. An elderly gentleman, white hair combed back, white sweater, black suit. He stands erect, turned toward an unseen speaker. Nothing points to the fact that he was once a hunted man.

Mr. Q reappears, hisses at me in the hall, don't leave the files lying around so openly . . .

I try to cover them up, but I am far too excited to do this, and I know today I have the upper hand; today nobody can touch me.

Mr. Q sets the copier so I can magnify.

Girls in a long line. Braids. White blouses. Ties. I walk my dog along this same path through the woods. BDM, I say, just imagine that.

Mr. Q makes a psst sound and says something so softly that I am unable to understand.

What do you mean?

I still don't understand.

Mr. Q leans toward me. In here the walls have ears.

I fall silent and make a photocopy of the town council in 1935, all in uniform, in front of a swastika flag three or four times as big as they are.

Singers at the song festival in 1934, that was the year Arthur Mayer left, arms raised very high, it seems to me, higher than necessary.

An elderly town employee, whose name I have been unable to remember to this day because we can't stand each other, comes into the room, looks at me over his shoulder; oh, that old stuff, he says, what do we want with that stuff; it's old hat, over and done with.

A class photo. A girl in the first row holds a sign inscribed in gothic script: *Schönberg* 1892. The little boy in the last row, third from the right, white collar, puffy cheeks, that is Arthur Mayer. And then I find what I hadn't been looking for: the photo that Mr. C said wasn't available, in Frankfurt with the pregnant daughter-in-law.

Under a stage sky, in front of what looks like a red velvet curtain, Arthur Mayer, this time in the front row, at the center. Hands on his knees. Suit. Tie. Vest. Eyes and mustache painted over. I remember Mr. C's effusive speech, only a group photo; Mayer is barely recognizable; *I had to retouch the eyes black so one could see anything at all.* Little pen-drawn *x*'s over Arthur Mayer's eyes.

50

A call from Helga R who would like to help but had nothing to report herself because she is my age and came to Schönberg only a few years ago.

. . . but Susi Sturm, she is quite nice and will, I am sure, be able to tell you something, really an incredibly sweet old lady who likes to talk about the old days and tells stories so well.

Helga R is willing to talk to Susi S, as in Sturm or Stein.

You'll see; she's really very nice.

51

Hilde T, always somewhat breathless, marriage, children, work, political work. Hilde was there when the first flyers appeared.

In the window the potted roses she had left in front of my door are blooming.

52

A call from Helga R. She spoke with Susi Sturm, she says. And, of course, she is willing.
I'll give you her number.
I call immediately. Susi Sturm has an energetic voice and really does seem very nice, but at the moment, unfortunately, she has painters in the house. I should call again in a few days.

53

Hilde shows me a copy of the charges she is bringing against the authors of the flyers. I don't feel so completely alone any more.
Why don't you call Liesel Uhlmann; they call her the mother of the SPD [Social Democratic Party] around here. She told me how she was harassed by BDM girls in the schoolyard.
Hilde and Liesel U, as in Uhlmann or Unger, are in the midst of preparations for some big party. I believe they were cutting cucumbers, onions, or tomatoes for the young party members. When the fingers are moving, the mind comes to rest, memories come back, a willing ear is there. It is impossible today to imagine what it was like in '33, how she was chased around the schoolyard. The father was a Social Democrat; that was enough. Liesel, the old woman and longtime resident, and Hilde, the young woman who recently settled in town, who breathlessly feels for her.
The worst was Anna V, as in Volz or Veit, unbelievable how she harassed her.
Her father was the head of the local farmers, says Hilde, and when he left for the war, her husband became head of the local farmers.
I search among my photocopies. There is a photograph of Anna V, no longer in the schoolyard, at the time of Germany's greatest victories, on her parents' farm, high on a horse, in perfect position, white blouse, dark tie, short hair, the horse perfectly reined in. President of Farm Women, the caption of the photo says. *Farm Women have a solid position in the life of the community.* At an annual exhibition where one can buy hand-knit potholders and hangers with knit covers.

54

I give Liesel U, as in Uhlmann or Unger, a call. Her voice sounds young. She is friendly.
We were children in those days, she says. The one who has written a lot about this is Mr. C.
But, I say.
Liesel Uhlmann, listening amiably, obliging, willing to meet with me.
Not tomorrow, something else is going on then; we are both still very active even though we are quite old.
She laughs a coy little laugh, and my heart opens. Arthur Mayer, she says, he was my childhood doctor.

55

I give Susi Sturm a call. The painters are gone; yes that's true, but I can't tell you anything.
Her tone is so firm that I give up any further attempts to persuade her.
I know nothing.
In one of the files from the picture archives, in the back of the many BDM group photos, is a piece of paper with the names of the girls in the picture. Susi Sturm too is part of it. But that isn't possible, or is it?

56

Only Mr. Conrad knows who bought the Jewish houses, says Hilde. Only he is authorized to view the files in the land registry. He poses as the father of the Jews.

57

'The whole world knows that the Jews are the ruthless eternal EXPLOITERS of working nations. What did our GOOD MARTIN LUTHER say hundreds of years ago—the Jew is the pus-filled UTERUS of endless criminality.'
From my mailbox, 9 April 1992

58

When Hilde was a member of the town council, she introduced a bill for the community to erect a memorial for the murdered Jews.

It was Mr. C, as in Conrad or Clemens, who squashed her bill. After all, we have the Arthur Mayer resting place. The others needn't concern themselves at all.

59

A call from Liesel Uhlmann, the motherly one.
I can't tell you anything more than what Mr. Conrad has already told you. I am sorry; I wish I could be of more help to you.

60

Hilde says that everything has been deposited with Conrad. Do you know that even today people put records from the Nazi era in his mailbox? And he boasts about all the things they tell him, because they know that he wouldn't repeat their stories, and then he says, I'll take what I know with me to the grave. They have left everything to him. Those who feel guilty hand it all over to him in confidence, ask him to safeguard it like his own secret. He was a soldier in Warsaw; he lost a leg in Warsaw . . .

61

The literary prize brings this:

> *Those lying, dirty, false Jews. And you from the TV cultural department and all those who participated in the program are ridiculous fools. And that Behrens woman got free lodging for a year and most likely enough pay so she can prepare more lies and untruths for print. Carry on you fools! Adolf Jewlove.*

And then this:

> *First I would like to congratulate you on your success. Then I regret that I wasn't able to help you more with your investigation. Now I would like to draw your attention to a woman who is a witness and knew Mr. Mayer very well. Mrs. Weber is more than willing to talk about him, what kind of person he was, what impression he made, his dedication to sports and politics. She is ninety years old, but when she talks about the old days, she tends after a while to idealize the past. She can be reached through her son; just ask for Oma . . .*
> *With best greetings—Heinz Lauer*

62

Mrs. W, as in Weber or Walter, leads me into a quiet dusky room. Outside the sun is shining. In the garden, behind the curtains, the yellow of the narcissus is glowing. Dark wallpaper, heavy dining table with a fringed tablecloth, empty chairs, and an old-fashioned display cabinet.

Mrs. Weber is short, thin, and well-preserved, leans only lightly on a cane. She offers me something to drink and pours with a firm hand.

Of course, she says. The Mayers were our neighbors.

It's quiet in the house. She does not live in the room where she receives me.

That is only for visitors.

It used to be nicer in the old days, says the old woman. More peaceful. The mooing of the cows. Baying sheep. Roosters crowing. Every once in a while the wheels of a horse-drawn cart. Later, but only very rarely, the revving of a motor. Doctor Mayer was the first in town to own a car.

He treated the old woman free of charge, helped her children into the world—he was also a very good gynecologist, she says—and when her father was leaving this world, he stopped by three or four times a day to look in on him.

His mother and her mother died almost at the same time in 1924; Mrs. Weber was then in her early twenties.

Her name was Gertrud, but she was called Treidche. She had a Christian name but kept the Jewish laws.

Fleishig, milchig, says the old woman next to me like someone who knows. And on Fridays, they didn't turn off the lights. Sometimes they would call and ask one of us to turn off the lights.

I hear that she grumbled a lot about Treidche and that her sons would go through fire and water for her, and I hear about Solomon, the father, who was a quiet man.

She was the one with energy. But he went about his business, first cattle, later cattle feed. The old woman also remembers where they lived before they built the house on Hauptstraße. After all, it's not that far from the old house to the new one, only a few steps down the street. Solomon's parents lived next door, 13 Walldorfer Strasse.

And who lives there now? I ask.

Somebody by the name of Volz, replies Mrs. Weber hesitantly.

A brick structure. In the garden there's a drooping flag. A little gust of wind reveals a Berlin bear. On the roof is a satellite dish. In the place where the big cattle shed once stood, a giant thermometer with an advertisement for Underberg; in the front, where the little shed was, a twelve-thousand-liter oil tank for steam heat.

Mrs. W also knows what became of the brothers. Robert went into hiding in Holland and has a son who's a lawyer. Milton went from Schönberg to Frankfurt, must have gone through very hard times.

I wonder which of the brothers doesn't accede to Mr. C's wishes . . . but we'll straighten that out too, believe me.

Mrs. W has put her cane against the chair, placed her hands on the armrest; her gaze wanders into empty space, into that distant past when her son was born and Doctor Mayer said: Give him to me!

To this day she has not forgotten how the doctor stood there, looking at the boy, and said: Give him to me!

Margarethe was not a doctor's wife . . .

The old woman's voice still echoes something of the estrangement between the people of Schönberg and the woman from Alsace.

They were not well matched. He, he was a genuine native of Schönberg, and she . . .

I remember Mr. I, as in Ilse or Idel, and his disinterested response to my question about Arthur Mayer's wife.

She was never seen. Her mother visited frequently.

For a moment, the fog lifts. I can see the Alsatian woman, who is much younger than her husband and apparently an only child, reared in the city of Metz between women's and men's shoes, possibly doted on by the customers, and now stuck in this Hessian village, where her husband knows everybody, plays politics, backs sport organizations, plays theater, and sends Christmas packages to the poor. She probably felt alone, this Margarethe from Metz; her mother's visits were her only solace. Many lonely evenings. What did she do when she was finished with her housekeeping chores? Did she read? Did she wait? Do needlework? Possibly not a happy marriage, and yet Arthur Mayer was persuaded not to do what he thought would be the thing to do: to immigrate to America or Switzerland. Margarethe didn't want to leave her parents, and so he let her go, sent her ahead immediately after the elections. Six months later he followed.

The medical practice had shrunk; nobody came anymore. They were all afraid. Then the sudden news: Doctor Mayer was gone. They were standing in front of his house with shotguns in their hands, but he was already gone.

Now the tables were turned. Now it was he who lived in a strange land, and his wife was at home. What did he do with his time all day when he no longer had patients to take care of, no more brief chats in the street, nobody who would call him 'Attur,' no more altercations with the parish priest, no more club meetings. Nothing. Maybe he was glad now that he didn't have children about whom he would have to worry in the years to come when Mrs. W, as in Weber or Walter, would have to smuggle this or that remaining Jew who had a toothache through the backdoor into her husband's office.

They brought bed sheets as payment since they no longer had any money.

I watch the old woman's face, her gray eyes, in which there is nothing for me to read, a hard gaze, without a smile, without kindness, which I return while I am taking notes on my knees about how she was called to the town hall, and there was Rudel sitting with his pillow in his lap.

It was the old town hall, a Renaissance building that has now been beautifully renovated, renowned in the area for its beauty. All Rudolf Mayer had to do was cross the street. Mrs. Weber indicated how the old man was sitting there, hugging his pillow as if he were seeking solace like a child from a doll.

I was close to tears; I'll never forget the scene.

Mrs. Weber knows that Rudolf Mayer died in Theresienstadt and Arthur Mayer in Auschwitz.

Of homesickness, she says.

Excuse me! I ask, unsure whether I had heard right.

He died of homesickness.

Who?

Doctor Mayer.

My stomach turns into a knot. I stare at her, say, I can't believe it.

Heard that from a Jew, she says, as if that were proof enough that it was true. He said that Doctor Mayer died of homesickness.

In Auschwitz?
Yes, in Auschwitz.

63

The mayor's front office. A telephone ringing constantly, people coming and going.
Everybody wants something. Flower bouquets wrapped in cellophane paper for some anniversary, bottles of wine in gift boxes. Marianne X, the town secretary, about fifty, not from among the long-established residents but grew up in Schönberg after the war when she settled here as a refugee. Marianne wants to help. Flings herself into the questions about Arthur Mayer. Full of enthusiasm, raring for action. Let's see about that; I'll help you. There are so many old people whom we can ask.

64

Marianne called Mr. Ä. Mr. Ä said she should contact Mr. Conrad or Mr. Ü. Marianne called Mr. Ü. His son answered the phone and told her to contact Mr. Conrad. It was true his father was a good friend of Mr. Conrad, so he probably wouldn't want to say anything. Marianne called Mrs. Ö. She told her to contact Mr. Conrad.
Marianne says, now I know how you must have felt.

65

Marianne spoke with Mr. C.
Mr. C said there was no material; he had given me everything.
Mr. C said there was no Mayer file; it never existed.
Mr. C said there's nothing that's been held back; people just don't know anything.

66

Marianne now knows why people don't want to say anything.
Jews too were only human beings, and some of them were bad, and people don't want to say this.

67

Hans Y, about fifty, a university professor and newcomer who enjoys living in Schönberg, where he is the co-publisher of the local newspaper. Helpful without many words. Confidence inspiring aloofness. Support. Hans sends an inquiry to the memorial at Auschwitz. Documents are found.

For the first time Arthur Mayer becomes for me a person of flesh and blood. Not one of all the people I had spoken to had described his looks, his gestures, the sound of his voice. It is strange to be reading now that he was a short man. Only now do I see him before me, wandering through the streets of S, short, broad shoulders, compact. And only the personnel form of the concentration camp at Auschwitz reveals that he was a multilinguist, that Sh. Jew, Arthur Mayer.

What's that supposed to mean, Sh. Jew? asks my friend Werner. Shit Jew?

NI – 10186 109.

Lfd. Nr.	Häftl. Nr.	Name	Zugang	Abgang	Bemerkungen
13358	150791	Schickler, Artur Isr.	14.10.43	28.10.43	Entlassen
13359	106792	Silberstein, Alfred Isr.	.	21.10.43	Entlassen
13360	115462	Nowak, Jan	.	25.10.43	Entlassen
13361	106661	Gutreich, Hans Isr.	.	27.10.43	Entlassen
13362	157243	Streicher, Karl Isr.	.	21.10.43	Entlassen
13363	116272	Scham, Alois Isr.	.	18.10.43	Entlassen
13364	150671	Hoed, Simon Isr.	.	.	Entlassen
13365	157107	Voorzanger, Herbert Isr.	.	9.11.43	Entlassen
13366	139733	van Coevorden, Abraham Isr.	.	21.10.43	Entlassen
13367	115951	Chaleo, Salomon Isr.	.	14.10.43	nach Auschwitz
13368	123984	Kaspar, Josef	.	.	. .
13369	105147	Simon, Heinz Isr.	.	.	. .
13370	132047	Hamerla, Wladyslaw	.	.	. .
13371	116917	Farbiarski, Arthur Isr.	.	.	. .
13372	127104	Winter, Walter Isr.	.	.	. .
13373	156984	Bacicurinsky, Ar... I.	.	.	. .
13374	156987	Bálint, Géza Isr.	.	.	. .
13375	156993	Boriat, Maurice Isr.	.	.	. .
13376	157009	Dana, Ichona Isr.	.	.	. .
13377	157063	Guetzowitch-Airkine, Benjamine Isr.	.	.	.
13378	157081	Holdner, Finkas Isr.	.	.	. .
13379	157101	Klotz, Gaston Isr.	.	.	. .
13380	157107	Kleinmann, Lazare Isr.	.	.	. .
13381	157118	Kupperwasser, Eliasz Isr.	.	.	. .
13382	157145	Luft, Isacher Isr.		.	. .
13383	157148	Mayer, Arthur Isr.	.	.	. .
13384	157155	Mendelsohn, Avram Isr.	.	.	. .
13385	157217	Spatzierer, Kuna Isr.	.	.	. .
13386	157237	Staniy, Robert Isr.	.	.	. .
13387	157250	Totis, Bela Isr.	.	.	. .
13388	157268	Wormser, Jacques Isr.	.	.	. .
13389	157272	Wohlmuth, Moritz Isr.	.	.	. .
13390	157273	Weiss, Gabor Isr.	.	.	. .

Konzentrationslager AUSCHWITZ Art der Haft: Sch. Jude Gef. Nr.: 157148

Name und Vorname: M a y e r Arthur

geb. 20.1.1888 zu: Seeheim Hosnen

Wohnort: Lyon, rue d'Colombier 33

Beruf: Arzt Rel.: kos.

Staatsangehörigkeit: staatenlos Stand: verh.

Name der Eltern: Rasse:

Wohnort:

Name der Ehefrau: Margarite-geb- Benedykt Rasse:

Wohnort:

Kinder: keine Alleiniger Ernährer der Familie oder der Eltern:

Vorbildung:

Militärdienstzeit: von — bis

Kriegsdienstzeit: von — bis

Grösse: 1,62 Nase: langgebogen Haare: dkl. braun Gestalt: oval

Mund: normal Bart: keinen Gesicht: oval Ohren: normal

Sprache: deutsch, franz. engl. griech. Augen: dkl. braun Zähne: 1 Schemh, 2 Gold

Ansteckende Krankheit oder Gebrechen:

Besondere Kennzeichen: keine

Rentenempfänger:

Verhaftet am: wo:

1. Mal eingeliefert: 10.10.43 2. Mal eingeliefert:

Einweisende Dienststelle: RSHA IV B 4 a 3233/41 g (1085)

Grund:

Parteizugehörigkeit: von — bis

Welche Funktionen:

Mitglied v. Unterorganisationen:

Kriminelle Vorstrafen: angeblich keine

Politische Vorstrafen: angeblich keine

Ich bin darauf hingewiesen worden, dass meine Bestrafung wegen intellektueller Urkundenfälschung erfolgt, wenn sich die obigen Angaben als falsch erweisen sollten.

v. g. u. Der Lagerkommandant

KL/42/4.43 500.000

70

'The arbitrary Jewish fixing of six million JEWISH DEAD shrinks in view of the official publication from international archives (see Poland). The JEW and his ceaseless marketing of his dead, a very profitable Jewish business without work.'
From my mailbox, 1 May 1992

71

The marketplace is brightly lit. Alpine orchids and geraniums. As on almost every Saturday, I run into the editor of the cultural pages of the local newspaper, Mr. Z, as in Ziegler or Zeiler, who lives in Schönberg. Usually we just say hello, a nod of the head, a good day, and we go on with our shopping.
Mr. Z is a cheese lover. He buys the good, expensive, fat kind. Slender, about my age, a goatee. We meet again at the vegetable stand. He is in line in front of me. When he has bought everything he needs, he turns to speak to me. I have just selected the most beautiful red peppers and am about to move over to the zucchini, when he says, I heard you're having difficulties?
My colleague and I too have received anti-Semitic flyers and that kind of stuff on occasion.
Exaggerating, he says, that's a journalistic sin.
Exaggerating?
We always hear that the forest is dying, and when we go to see it, it's all still there.
That's not what this is about.
Or when there's a flood in some godforsaken village in South Africa, don't scream right away that all of Africa is flooded.
It's a matter of silence, I say.
That's normal, he says. Journalists experience this all the time; nobody wants to talk.
Meanwhile, I have handed the peppers over to be weighed and decide to do without the zucchini, was just able to grab a melon. We are in the midst of a real altercation, facing each other, from an unusually large distance. I have put my shopping bag down and, across the distance, tell him my experience with Fritz G.
That's normal, he explains. Somebody doesn't want to talk, we must respect it.

But, I say, if nobody talks about it, then it becomes frozen.
Why? Some people like to talk, and others prefer not to think about things. One must respect that.
He too has put down his shopping basket. Every once in a while somebody passes between us. Every once in a while I catch a curious look.
Apparently, people are still afraid if one cannot talk about it even now.
They don't want to listen to other people's opinions.
They must hear what other people have to say.
It's not a matter of people's opinions. It's a matter of completely erasing a part of history.
You are exaggerating.
Somehow I paid for the vegetables without noticing; I presumably put the change away.
After all, it wasn't a particularly good time.
That's why . . . and maybe people would feel better if they finally talked about it.
You are saying that truth makes one free, he says. The Stasi made the same claim.
I am furious and tell him that I think this comparison is unbelievable, unheard of, outrageous, that I would never have expected this from him, ettzettera peepee. I am too enraged to think clearly; otherwise, it would have struck me immediately that *truth makes free* was never a motto of the Stasi and that Mr. Z, perhaps somewhat confused, was thinking of the motto over a certain gate.
Mr. Z realizes that he has gone too far.
Mr. Z becomes conciliatory.
I didn't mean to annoy you.
That's really outrageous.
Sorry, he says. I let myself get carried away. A joke between friends.
I don't think it's funny.
With you, I'll never joke again.
His wife, who had been standing behind him for some time, pulls his sleeve.
I am done; we can go.
Mr. Z repeats that he will never again joke with me. His wife gives up and walks alone toward the parking lot. He pays no attention to her.

You have no sense of humor.
Unfortunately, I feel the need to point out to Mr. Z that I do indeed have a sense of humor.
Some people think they have a sense of humor but don't really have one, Mr. Z remarks.

72

'JEWS as exploiters of laboring nations! These are the harbingers of death for the German people—kill them!'
From my mailbox, 6 May 1992.

73

The local newspaper carried a big article by Hans Y about Arthur Mayer's time in Auschwitz. The documents were printed, interpreted, explained. The editorial department asked Mr. C for a photo. Mr. C took a photo to the editorial department. A half-hour later he returned and demanded to have the photo back. He couldn't do that to his wife. That's how the photo I had discovered in the town picture archives was printed on the front page of the local newspaper, which was financed by the merchants of Schönberg: Arthur Mayer, painted over by the guardian of history, free of charge, in every mailbox in Schönberg.

Katja Behrens

Solomon and the Others

Shlomo!

Yakov!

Yitzak!

I am sitting, looking out over the water, listening to the ancient names. Only yesterday I was still at home. Here they say *shama*, which means simply *there*, but they don't mean simply *there*. They mean a place that is so terrible it is better not to name it; to call it by its name would be to evoke the memory of it. If one doesn't talk about it, then it isn't real, perhaps not real after all, or at least not quite real. Silence is like a bandage over that which happened *shama*, *there* in the land where I was born and where I grew up. There my friend was the fatherless Wolfgang; he was a cheeky brat and blond as straw, and we climbed trees together to smoke our first cigarette—if I am not mistaken, it was a Juno, and my nose was not yet fully grown, and we didn't know anything about what had happened and that more than the usual things separated us. A war had ended; that much we knew. We also heard it being said that the *Russians* had wrought terrible havoc; the rest was silence. Silence reigned as if it had been snow that had fallen rather than bombs, entire hosts of snowflakes ordered to bury everything and to swallow every sound. And now, more than four decades later, here on the beach, these names from an unimaginably remote time.

Solomon, Jacob, and Isaac are playing soccer.

Solomon shouts to Isaac to pass the ball to him.

Solomon wears a headband. His hair is long, curly, and wild. His sneakers are worn and have holes. He plays with absolute concentration, with glowing red cheeks. I watch him and feel a childish pride coming over me—I have only been here for a few hours, and I know that later I will become annoyed with *the land*, as they call it quite arrogantly, *ha-aretz*, as if there were no other. But I haven't reached that point yet; I still feel the exhilaration of a castaway who feels firm ground underfoot again, who has escaped the hostile element, who just shortly before was very small, timid, and helpless and now is the greatest, triumphant, boasting, cocksure . . . I would now like to have one of those Nazis here to whom I would say: Just take a look; you weren't able to wipe us out after all.

Jacob makes a foul.

Jacob and Isaac fall down, tumble over each other, and before you know it, Isaac is back on his feet, spitting out the sand, starting to run, while Jacob rubs his ankle, swallowing the pain like a man.

Isaac's body is sinewy, dark-skinned, and when he shouts to Jacob, his voice comes from deep inside his throat: he is probably from the Levant, chews sunflower seeds when he goes to the movies, breaks them open one by one with his teeth without stopping, all the while staring at the screen, and spits the shells on the floor.

Solomon shoots a goal.

The two squatting onlookers, who are somewhat older, exchange an appreciative remark. Solomon fixes his headband and bends down to tie his shoes. His skin is so light, his eyes so blue; maybe he has a German grandmother who calls him Shloimele and was perhaps herself once married to a Solomon. Maybe her oldest son's name is Sally, and maybe he's a good American who has almost forgotten what it means to be a stranger in the big melting pot, who hardly knows anymore what it means not to be at home anywhere, to be straining for the sounds in between, to be testing the air to determine whether it is time to move on, at times almost deeming himself safe and already too deeply rooted to be able to make a quick getaway; then they are not just robbed but also murdered, the survivors driven out, there, where I come from; they were last seen at the Romanisches Café, where some had a premonition of what was in store for them and others did not, in the twentieth century as once in Egypt, strangers, who interpret dreams; they had forgotten that they were what they were, betrayed by the pride, the sadness, and the animal fear in their eyes, today as once in Egypt, before they got out and made their way through the desert under Moses' leadership, who is now the goalie and wears a Coca-Cola T-shirt. There is something stocky, broad about him, and he stands with a forlorn look, firmly stationed with both feet in the sand, battle ready and bright eyed; his parents might have come from Poland.

Two young German couples have appeared, very blond, very young, perhaps still in school. They are sitting down in the sand to watch the game, four backsides against the wood hut where the lounge chairs are stored. I wonder whether it makes them uncomfortable when somebody asks them where they are from or whether they are able to answer freely. Their faces are open, still unmarked. I would like to know why they came here. Maybe the descendants are bothered more than the participants, Grandma and Grandpa, who paid for their skateboards, their mountain bikes, and video recorders. Only yesterday, a grandfatherly man was standing in front of my house. I have known him for years by sight; his face displays the scarlet redness of someone who drinks or has a heart ailment, and, rain or shine, he wears sunglasses, and perhaps he actually believes he can hide behind them, and perhaps he really doesn't know that everybody in town *knows*, even I. He wears sunglasses, but he tells his podiatrist quite openly his dreams about the Führer . . . He stood there bending over his little grandchild, full of love. The child wobbled on the new roller skates, tipped forward and backward, and Grandpa held her gently by the hand, as if she were something precious that couldn't be handled carefully enough, and I wonder what will happen when this child grows up and hears rumors or reads trial reports and can't believe that her grandpa could have done *something like that.*

Solomon dribbles the ball to the Germans and says something. The two boys get up immediately, as if they had been waiting to be allowed in the game. One of them is as straw blond as Wolfgang, the fatherless friend of my childhood. Isaac and the others join them. Handshakes. Solomon, his cheeks flaming with red spots, fixes his headband. Jacob turns toward the girls, waves to them in a Middle Eastern manner, with the fingertips turned downward: *come play, come.* The girls shake their heads, remain seated. *Come.* Grins appear on the faces of the two squatting onlookers. The older one, already a man, curly-haired and dark-skinned, probably from Morocco, shouts something to Jacob that I don't understand and yet understand—it's a matter of getting them to change their minds.

Jacob turns around briefly; then he turns again toward the girls, extends his hand toward them as if wanting to help them get up, the very embodiment of chivalry and innocence. *Don't be afraid . . . come.* However, if his sister would get it into her head to play soccer, he would have to regard it as an insult to his honor, and he would, if necessary, by force, lead her back to decency and modesty, but then Lea or Rebecca or whatever her name may be would never think of playing soccer, not even in her wildest dreams. The girls have a disagreement. One wants to and the other doesn't, but she wants to only if the other plays too, and it takes some time before she's persuaded.

Two teams are being formed. Herbert, Solomon, Jacob, and one of the girls against Isaac, Fritz, Moses, and the other girl. All of them put themselves into the game with heart and soul, full of energy. Solomon shouts: *Erbee! Erbee!*

A couple comes strolling hand in hand down the beach, both in uniform, he with a machine gun slung over his shoulder, she eating ice cream. Their caps stuck under their epaulettes. Heavy boots. Children's faces. He takes on a knowing air; she, a disinterested one. Every once in a while her tongue runs once around the scoop of ice cream, pulls back quickly into its cave, only to come out again soon to lick the melting scoop. Herbert's girlfriend is a good player; I don't know her name, but I can see that she has not quite overcome her shame, shying away from colliding with the other body. When she has the ball, she hesitates a bit. She needs to halt a split second in front of the strange foot, the strange leg, before penetrating the other body. Slowly, she finds her way into the game, runs like a boy, rams the opponents. Her cheeks begin to glow. The other, the girl who had permitted herself to be pushed aside again, follows the human tangle around the ball only listlessly, then turns away and walks toward the side of the wood hut. Solomon positions the ball for a penalty shot; he takes his time, turns it into a big production; the wind carries me a few fragments of what is being said.

. . . first you talk me into it, and then . . .

But the girl who had been pushed aside is already sitting in her old place, a lonely back against the side of the wood hut. The girl with the glowing cheeks hesitates, doesn't know what to do, her arms hang down, apparently torn between wanting to play, she was just getting into it, and the call for solidarity, which told her to stop, not to leave her friend alone, to keep her company. She stands there and wavers until Solomon has scored his goal, then suddenly turns and runs, flinging herself into the tumult, mingling with the rest.

Shlomo!

Yakov!

Fritz!

Susanne! Here! Over here!

The two onlookers are still sitting next to the goal, which is marked with a jacket and a shirt. Their eyes follow Susanne, who has large breasts and wears only a thin T-shirt. She seems to have forgotten about it, so absorbed is she by the game; her cheeks are almost as red as Solomon's. The onlookers and Moses, the goalie, who has nothing to do for the moment, exchange remarks; the kinky-haired guy nods without letting the bosom out of his sight while he is talking. Moses laughs salaciously, so it seems to me, but at the same time shows his admiration by putting his thumb and second finger together and flipping his wrist: he appreciates an athletic accomplishment; all three of them, though put off, appreciate it.

The kinky-haired guy must have felt my gaze. He looks in my direction and calls to me: *hi messacheket tov*—again I have to get used to the fact that the language separates men and women even in their activities; of course, she plays well, *hi messacheket*, but *hu messachek;* later it will again become second nature to me; now all three of them are looking at me, as if I were the mother; they nod and purse their lips, *be-emet* and *be-chayai.*

The soldier couple disappears along the beach, two uniformed figures strolling hand in hand by the edge of the sea.

In the distance are the centuries-old towers of Yaffa. The water glistens. The sun has come out from behind the clouds. On the horizon is a ship, small and picturesque in the blue mist.

Moses stands slightly bent over, his hands on his thighs. A clash near the goal.

The lulling cluck-cluck sound of the tennis balls . . . *matkot* . . . everywhere along the beach people play *matkot.* The cluck-cluck sound and the pauses in between when they run after the ball that jumps around somewhere in the sand or swims in the water, only in this country the cluck-cluck sound of Ping-Pong paddles and tennis balls was already heard long before the high-rise hotels, now in a state of decay, were being built.

Shlomo!

Yitzak!

Susanne has the ball; Isaac tries to take it over. Susanne won't be pushed aside; she passes the ball to Solomon. At that moment Isaac grabs her with both arms and wrestles her to the ground; he rolls with her in the sand without letting go of her, he holds her close, not only with his arms, his legs too hold her in a firm grip. For a moment they are two bodies rolling in the sand—the others rush over; nobody pays attention to the ball rolling away; Susanne gets up, shakes the sand from her hair; that was a *foul* and the signal to stop.

Barbara Honigmann

EXCERPT FROM Sohara's Journey

'He must have mentioned some place,' Mrs. Kahn kept asking me over and over again. 'He must have said something about where he wanted to take you and the children. A city, a country, a region, at least he must have indicated a direction. After all, it is customary to say we'll take a trip to the south, to the Mediterranean, to the mountains, or to some town.' —'No, nothing,' I said. 'I really can't remember anything.' Mrs. Kahn had been pushing me, but it was no use; I just didn't know any more. All I vaguely remembered was something like 'Kehl'—'Maybe he said Kehl,' but Mrs. Kahn thought that made no sense at all since we were already in Kehl. 'Maybe he said Köln?' —'Kehl, Köln—he abducted my children; they are gone; I don't know where.' I should calm down, Mrs. Kahn said; we would think about it some more; we would do everything possible; first we had to think, to find some way. She took out an atlas and showed me where Köln was located, up there in Germany, up the Rhine; I asked her if it was kosher there; he would, after all, take the children only to a kosher place; to which she replied only, 'Oh my God, no!' But then I saw on the map that Antwerp wasn't far away, the most orthodox place in all of Europe. 'But that's no vacation place for children,' said Mrs. Kahn. I asked Mrs. Kahn to do something, to make a telephone call to Germany; the last message had after all come from Germany, from Kehl. 'How am I supposed to place a call to Germany?' said Mrs. Kahn. 'I don't even know where. I can't just call "Germany"! We need to know whom to call, a phone number, a person. I haven't spoken German or spoken with a German in fifty years. Sometimes I listen to the radio, and, wait a moment, sometimes they announce telephone numbers for "further information" or in the case of a prize question, "Password: Lucky Strike."' Mrs. Kahn turned on the radio, a German station; for about an hour we sat in front of it and listened to the music, the commercials, like soldiers listening to reports from the front to find out who was being threatened and where. Suddenly Mrs. Kahn started to yell, quick, quick, quiet psst; first it was hard to hear anything, especially since she kept yelling 'quiet psst, quiet psst,' but then everything was being repeated, and she was able to write down the number 07221-920. We were so excited, as if the battle of getting the children back was already half won, as if I at least had a thread in my hand that I only needed to follow to the end, and then everything would be all right again, and it would only have been a bad dream that my husband stole my children from me, that he's a lunatic or a criminal. This nightmare of suddenly being all alone and of wanting nothing but to jump off a high-rise building or from the bridge into the Rhine.

Mrs. Kahn mumbled something, and then she called out very loudly, 'For fifty years! For fifty years!' She started phoning around in that language of which I don't understand a word, in German. It all turned out to be very complicated; they kept giving different numbers and again others, and then they continued to connect with others and made the caller wait and connect again and again, and at some point there was actually a voice that said, no, basically not, actually never, but in the end they accepted our announcement anyway: 'Simon Serfaty is urgently requested to return home.'

By fifty years, Mrs. Kahn meant to say that she hadn't spoken German for fifty years. Burnt all bridges. She didn't want to see or hear or know anything about Germany, she said. She never drove to Kehl to shop at Aldi's as everybody else did. At first I had suggested that we go shopping together. —No, she didn't want that. Or I could at least get something for her since everything was much less expensive. —No, she didn't want that either. Nothing. Never again. The valerian drops she gave me, her cure-all that nobody here knew about, she got for herself from Switzerland. She had organized an entire chain of shoppers and suppliers, which hadn't broken since 1945, and saw to it that her supply was always well stocked. 'I always hear now of the good Germans,' she said. 'I, for my part, haven't met them. I no longer need anything from them, no cheap stuff from Aldi's either. Cannibals!'

Mrs. Kahn always called the Germans cannibals. For a long time

I hadn't known Mrs. Kahn's story. Sometimes, when I got the mail for her from the mailbox, I put the magazine *Le Deporté* on her table with the rest of the mail and advertisements. And in the summertime, when she was wearing a short-sleeved blouse, I could see the tattooed number on her arm, and I could imagine what had happened. But I didn't ask questions, and she didn't say anything. Once we saw a film on television, which we had chosen foolishly for it was about the Nazi period and Jewish children who had first been hidden but were then discovered and deported. When the movie was over, during the commercials, I still remember it very well, a blonde was running and skipping along the beach, tossing her blond hair from side to side while she was warbling; Mrs. Kahn began to cry and cried more and more, until she dissolved completely in tears. That's when she told me how at the last minute, before she was picked up, she had tossed her son, a tiny baby, over the balcony to her neighbor; that was in Belgium. Her husband had already fled to Italy. There he was first hidden by monks in a seminary and was later taken, as had been his wish, to the partisans by Don Pauli; what a courageous man he was. But due to his blond hair and blue eyes, her husband stood out too much in Italy; the cannibals caught him and killed him. After the war, Don Pauli managed to find Mrs. Kahn and told her the whole story. 'I'll spare you the details, Mrs. Serfaty,' Mrs. Kahn said to me. 'Just be glad that it wasn't that bad in Algeria.' The baby that she had tossed over the balcony is her son, Raphael, who has now been living in Israel for a long time and visits her once or twice a year, of course, much too rarely, and unfortunately is also not married.

Actually, she didn't want to talk about this anymore, never again, said Mrs. Kahn. 'But sometimes I have to talk about it anyway, and then I can't stop. It seems to me then that it is impossible to talk about anything else ever again because it is, after all, the most important thing in the world. But one would be called crazy, and look at me, I am quite reasonable, a quite reasonable neighbor.'

I felt embarrassed when Mrs. Kahn was crying and telling me about these things. I was unable to console her; what could I possibly say. I've heard about such things from other Ashkenazim on occasion; some actually talk about it all the time, even during a chance meeting in the marketplace, and, of course, one reads about it in children's school books and learns about it on television too, and there are frequent movies about it, and everything I have heard or seen has been transformed in my head into a single huge story or, even more, into a terrifying landscape. A landscape of horror with Polish and German place names, Auschwitz, Warsaw, Treblinka, Nuremberg, Berlin, Dachau; by the way, these are the only Polish or German place names I know at all, not counting Kehl. It doesn't keep me from shopping at Aldi's; it just remains a store. After all, I didn't encounter the cannibals in the midst of a harmless everyday life as Mrs. Kahn had.

In Africa things were not all that bad for you; the Ashkenazim told us when we arrived here, but they knew little about what was really going on in Africa. The Ashkenazim, at any rate, are the elite among sufferers, the world champions of martyrdom. We, by comparison, were novices, placed in the lowest ranks, semi-Arabs, and we first had to learn everything, absolutely everything, from them.

However, between Mrs. Kahn and me, this was never of any importance, the fact that she was Ashkenazic and I from North Africa. She is not proud, and neither am I. We are two women who are pretty much alone, and who for that reason befriended each other a little. She mistrusted Simon from the beginning.

Immediately, on the day after we had moved into the apartment building, he had invited her over so we could become acquainted. I placed a few dates, figs, and pistachios on the table, which she didn't touch, and then Simon started to interrogate her about herself and the people in the building, and then he didn't stop talking about himself, about his travels all over the world, the things he saw, how he approached wealthy people to collect money for Russian or Syrian Jews and for the yeshivas in Israel.

'So you are a rabbi?' Mrs. Kahn had asked. On our door there was a big sign saying 'Rabbi Serfaty.' 'Yes, of course,' Simon was already losing his temper. Then she wanted to know what kind of rabbi. — 'Well, what kind of rabbi, a rabbi!' —She meant where he had become a rabbi, with whom. 'I studied a long time, and then I just became a rabbi,' Simon had answered.

'But where, with whom?'

'In Singapore.'

'In Singapore?'

'I am the rabbi of Singapore.'

Mrs. Kahn burst out laughing; even though she was usually reserved and controlled, she laughed in his face, and Simon threw her out, put her in front of the door and said that he didn't want to see her again. I asked him if he didn't have any respect for the old lady, but he insisted that she should respect him; he was a rabbi.

After that Mrs. Kahn came over only when he wasn't home, and that was more and more often. For weeks, months, he didn't come home. I had long lost all respect for him.

One evening, a long time ago in Amiens, Simon had appeared at our door. I was always working at that time, the day and night shift and, of course, on Christian holidays, Christmas, Easter, New Year's Eve. The other nurses were glad when I filled in for them, and to me it made no difference. For my part, I took off on Rosh Hashanah and Yom Kippur and for Pesach. Most of the nurses came from all kinds of other countries, but we never really talked about where we came from. None of the women said anything about her country, her town, her language; I never spoke about Oran, never about Algeria and how I came to France. And yet we were friends and banded together because we recognized in each other the newcomer, human beings without deep roots here but all with the difficult task of just holding on to the surface of this strange place.

In those days, I believed that I would remain with my mother forever and would never get married. In Oran we always had a few women who had been left out, who couldn't be married off, and who would then be invited everywhere, who only ate at strangers' tables and would always remain a guest.

Actually, I had hardly known any men in my life. My father was long dead; I had no brothers, only an uncle back in Oran, who studied the weekly Torah with my sister and me every Shabbat afternoon. My cousins were either too old or too young for me.

Later in Amiens, I did go to school with boys and always had a crush on one or the other, like all the other girls. That remained, of course, a secret; God forbid, whom could one have told about it. Only on occasion, at the birthday party of a girlfriend perhaps, a boy would look at me for more than a minute or brush against my hand or shoulder while passing me something, and then I would wonder for weeks whether this had been love. If my mother had known that there were also boys at those birthday parties, she would never have permitted me to go, not so much because they were boys but because they were mostly non-Jewish boys. There were simply too few Jewish boys in Amiens, and the few that were there I had known for far too long to be interested in or to fall in love with them. Almost all of them later married non-Jewish women or immigrated to Israel.

My sister had it easy, for she was naturally pretty and outgoing with her dark eyes and dark curls. She was always being courted, like Rachel, and I felt ugly with my ash blond hair, and slighted, like Leah. I was often jealous of her, but later God rewarded me, like Leah, with six children, and my sister has only two, like Rachel.

Elijah, who is now her husband, was the brother of her best friend in school. She had an easy time finding him, and everything was simple for her and remained simple; she was always lucky. Immediately after graduating high school, Elijah and my sister got engaged and married quickly and moved to Paris. My mother didn't tell Elijah, as Laban told Jacob, it is not our custom to marry off the younger before the older one, and so my sister moved away, and I stayed. In Paris they set up and expanded a kosher catering business in the 19th Arrondissement. This was an ingenious idea since just at that time people were again starting to have kosher parties for brisses, bar mitzvahs, and weddings. Today they can hardly keep up with all the demand. Both of their grown sons are, of course, working in the kosher catering business.

My mother often asked the rabbi of Amiens, who was also from Algeria, to find a husband for me, if possible, one from Algeria or, even better, from Oran. Two or three times I was introduced to a young man. We sat somewhere at somebody's table on Shabbat or on a holiday; the young man sat on one side with the men and I on the other with the women. We'd look at each other from time to time; after the meal we might exchange a few words, and then he would say that he would write or call, but I never heard anything again from most of them.

Only once did I meet one of these young men again. His name was Yehuda, and after his first visit, I waited every day for him to call. Then he sent a card, an old picture postcard of the town where he was living, which said 'greetings and see you soon.' I read this card over and over, as if it were a love letter, until Yehuda actually came again to Amiens for Shabbat. In the afternoon we took a walk through the town and the park, and we sat on a bench, quite close together. Yehuda spoke, and I mostly listened; I was unable to speak since I was so excited. Along the way we, of course, met one or the other friend of my mother, and I could well imagine that the news of what they had seen would spread like wild fire; Sohara with Yehuda, they will soon become engaged, hopefully.

Somebody once told me he had read that being in love was like being insane. In fact, after this afternoon, I was for weeks in a state of madness, and all I could do was picture Yehuda sitting on the bench with me, and everything else, my mother, my sister, and the rest of life, I perceived only as from far away, through a fog.

But Yehuda never wrote afterward, never telephoned, and after many weeks, my madness of grand passion collapsed into itself, and everyday things and matters moved again to the places they had occupied before the great storm. I knew that all was over long before I was told that Yehuda was engaged to a girl from Paris. Then I again sat every night alone at home with my mother, listened to her complaints about her lost life, about her broken family, which was now dispersed over the four corners of the earth, torn apart in all kinds of cities, Paris, Tel Aviv, Montreal, and about the daughter who couldn't find a husband. We quarreled a lot, and I cried a lot and thought that it was unfair of my mother to blame me for everything.

Even then, when he first suddenly appeared at our door, Simon had white hair and a white beard. He introduced himself and said that he was collecting money for the Jews in Russia and for the Jews in Syria and for the yeshivas in Israel, where men learned Torah all day. They are the elite of our people, and we, who work, must support them, for they need, of course, money, a lot of money, which after all doesn't fall from heaven. The elite of those who are not Jewish are at the universities, where they earn a lot of money and receive prizes; among us, it is customary that those who don't themselves study feed the elite; from each, one-tenth for the mind.

In those days I admired these men, and I admired Simon for taking such a life upon himself, being on the road for weeks, approaching strangers, begging, explaining in order to get the money together. Schnorrers, they are called, Mrs. Kahn once told me.

I asked Simon to come in and made peppermint tea for him; my mother had bought fresh leaves at L'Oriental, imported directly from Morocco. The store had opened just a few months before, and we at last could get the spices and herbs we needed for our recipes.

When Simon smelled the tea, he said, ah, genuine *Nâr Nâr*! I knew then that he too came from an Arabic country. Yes, from Morocco, he said, like *Nâr Nâr*.

Actually, I didn't know why the Jews of that country had left, for there was no war as in Algeria, nor was the country occupied by the Germans as Tunesia had been. Of course, Simon, like all Moroccans, began immediately to talk about Mohammed V, of blessed memory, how he had protected the Jews and all he had done for them, a courageous, benevolent king!

No, it was because of Israel that we had to leave, said Simon, because of the wars with the Arab countries. He made the blessing before he drank the tea, just as he later never took a bite without first making the appropriate blessing. We spoke a bit in Arabic; later, my mother joined us, and we spoke all evening about Oran and Marrakesh, the city in which he was born and reared, and we drank freshly brewed *Nâr Nâr* and ate sweet sesame cookies.

I trusted him, his different expressions, his heavy body, and his stories, which he told all day long, about our great rabbis, of Baba Sale of Morocco and of Rachbar of Algeria and of Rambam and in general about the Messiah and the time when the Messiah will have come, the savior of Israel and of all nations. Mankind will be relieved of all woes of this world, of hunger, disease, and senseless hatred, and all nations will recognize our God as the only one; oh, if only the time had already come. My mother and I sighed as all Jews do when this subject comes up, and Simon said he was sure the time of the Messiah couldn't be all that far away; we wouldn't have to wait an eternity for him, for it is said that before the coming of the Messiah, the evil will gather and pile up to a mountain of depravity and rancor. All one had to do was look around. We would also have to be able to recognize the Messiah; he wouldn't just make his entrance, as we might imagine it, with great pomp, inspiring awe. It is said that he appeared once before, or perhaps even several times, in some godforsaken place in the person of a schlemiel about whom everyone laughed themselves to death: What, he is supposed to be the one, the greatest good-for-nothing among us, who knows nothing, who has no skills, who has nothing, and who always laughs when we cry and cries when we laugh? The dumb guy, that ugly thing, he is supposed to be the one? they said and simply couldn't recognize him, and so he turned back again, the Messiah, for he had really been it, the ugly one, the schlemiel, the dumbest of them all.

When I didn't get pregnant right away after we were married, and I was afraid I might be infertile, Simon took me to Troyes. There the greatest scholar of our people, Rashi, was born and had died, and it was there that a miracle had happened. However, there is no sign in the town pointing to it, neither to Rashi nor to the miracle, even though almost every house bears a plaque for some unknown general. Of course, the insiders know the place of the Rashi miracle. All one has to do is turn a few corners in the old city and look around with a roving eye, and immediately somebody will come along or call from the window, it's farther up, back there, to the right.

When my sister and I were reading the Torah weekly with our uncle in Oran, we also read Rashi's writings, sentence for sentence, first the Torah and then Rashi's commentary about it. It took seven years to complete, since during the first year we read the first of the seven paragraphs of the weekly Torah respectively and in the following years the second, the third, and so on until we had once gone through the entire Torah. I always imagined Rashi as one of us; that is, somebody from Oran, one of the famous rabbis whom we revered and in whose names we made mutual promises and blessed each other. Now it turned out he was from Europe after all, from such a cold country, almost on the German border. He studied in Germany, Simon told me. He led me through the old town where the streets are so narrow that it is almost impossible to walk next to each other and dark because the sun's rays rarely fall vertically here. We stopped in front of the remains of a wall. What is this? I asked; there is nothing to see here. But Simon guided my hand over the wall, and I noticed that it was uneven; it caved inward, and Simon said that it had been here, that this was the place of the miracle, there where the wall was folding inward. It had been in this street, nine hundred years ago, that Rashi's mother was walking along in an advanced stage of pregnancy. At that moment, a goy approached her from the opposite direction with a horse and wagon and called out to her: Hey, make way; get out of the way! However, she wasn't able to get out of the way because the street was much too narrow. The goy screamed, well then don't, and spurred his horse and was just about to simply gallop over Rashi's mother with his horse and wagon, when she turned toward the wall, imploring God to help her, not for herself but only for her child, and at that moment the wall of the house moved inward so that she was able to push in and was spared from any harm. It was through this miracle that Rashi was able to be born. Simon showed me the place, and I felt the cavity with my hands. Soon afterward I became pregnant with our first daughter, whom we called Zipporah, like the wife of Moses. Our second daughter we called Elisheva, like the wife of Aaron. I dreamed about having many more children with Simon, boys, to whom he would teach Talmud, and girls, to whom he would teach the Torah with Rashi's commentary, the way my uncle had taught us back in Oran. I would busy myself in the kitchen with housework and fix peppermint tea; the door would be open; I would be able to look in and hear their voices reading and translating, and Simon would explain the text to them patiently, proud of their eagerness to learn, and in the end he would call, 'Sohara, bring the children something sweet; they have been studying so diligently,' and I would, of course, always have a store of marzipan and candied almonds in a tin can.

Simon also thought that our names were a good match, Simon and Sohara. He spoke much that first evening about the meaning of the two names and how they complemented each other: Simon derived from *sh'ma*, that is, 'to hear,' and Sohara is 'to see,' of 'light,' 'splendor,' that is, 'the splendor of heaven'; as it is written in the Book of Daniel: 'The teacher will shine like the splendor of heaven and all those who have guided the people toward justice.' Simon spoke about his years of studying the Zohar, the most mysterious and most difficult of all books; he was so excited about it that he was unable to sleep for nights on end. Now that he had met me, Sohara, the same was likely to happen again. I blushed. Then he said that the Zohar had been written in our North Africa and that we Sephardim were in general not proud enough of our culture. We shouldn't permit the Ashkenazim to humiliate us, and we shouldn't always try to imitate them. That was ridiculous, he said. As if we had lost all our dignity. 'They call us superstitious and uneducated, but the truth is that they, with all their education, have lost their faith. And *Nâr Nâr* like this one, they don't know anything about it, and they can't make a real couscous, not to speak of dafina—they don't even know what it is.'

We laughed, and my mother laughed too. While talking with Simon, she drifted more and more into Arabic; she searched around in her Arabic treasure troves and took out the best pieces in the way of phrases and wise sayings. And yet, while doing this, she was observing him with quite a critical eye.

A few weeks later, he visited us again one evening; then he spent Shabbat with us, and soon more and more often, and finally regularly every Friday. My mother and I offered at that time, of course, the more extensive Shabbat menu, not the limited one, which we prepared for ourselves alone. Already on Monday we started making plans for the following Shabbat, what kind of salads, fish, soup, meat, dessert we would serve. On Monday we thought about it; on Tuesday and Wednesday we did the marketing for everything we needed; on Thursday we baked and marinated; and on Friday we did the cooking. My mother remembered recipes that she used to cook during the time of her engagement to my father; she used mysterious ingredients and little tricks to give the matter of the wedding a push. She also gave me many hints and much advice on how to handle a man and what not to say or do under any circumstances, as if such a man were a precious china plate that might accidentally be dropped and broken irreparably. I told my mother that if we love each other everything would go well. It's as simple as that.

I went on a long journey only once. From Algeria to France. I never returned from this journey. Actually, I didn't experience much of the Algerian war myself. I only heard a few shots from far away in the evenings and at night when all else was quiet; but from one week to the next, we were allowed to move only within ever narrower confines: don't go there, no longer there either. Every morning my mother would set new limits for my sister and me, to keep us from getting caught in a crossfire or some other awful event. Every day another girl, sometimes two, would be missing from school. They had already departed with their families, had left Algeria, and nobody was allowed to know anything about it beforehand. It was dangerous to flee; after all, the outcome of the war was not yet decided, and the OAS threatened anybody who, so to speak, gave up Algeria voluntarily. And yet, the school classes were emptying out, and the houses too became empty. Every day brought a new surprise—oh, they are gone, and they too. But, out of fear, it was better not to talk about it. Then one day, the war was over, and our life in Algeria was over too. We and I-don't-know-how-many thousands of others were placed in a transit camp at the edge of the sea and waited for passage on a ship, my mother, my sister, and I. We had two suitcases; we were not allowed to take more. Both suitcases were primarily filled with paper bags and tin cans in which my mother imported all kinds of spices that she rightfully assumed we wouldn't be able to find again so easily in Europe and that were absolutely indispensable for our meals. 'If nowhere else,' my mother said often, 'we can at least find the smell and taste of Oran in our kitchen.'

On the day before crossing the sea, mother took us to our father's grave for us to say goodbye to him and our grandparents and all the other ancestors who rest there in the graveyard. Next to the graveyard, directly next to it, is now, so we hear, a new housing development. The 'former' citizens of Oran had, for a long time, collected money that they would send over for the maintenance of the graveyard, which really, so we hear, is supposedly still in halfway decent condition and has not been razed as in other countries, thank God.

Then one day we were standing on the deck of a big ship that was moving off the coast, and everybody was crying, all the children, all the women, and most of the men. This farewell was different from other farewells. Not one for a short distance, for a vacation, a few days or weeks. This time it was a farewell from everything, from an entire country, and forever. Two thousand years we lived there! Sixty generations! Not just a laughable three or four like the French, who had gambled away everything. Everybody moaned, groaned, and lamented: We are now the last of so many generations. The very last. What a misfortune! What will become of us?

When nothing but the sea was visible anymore, an indifferent gray sea, everybody left the deck, and for three days all was very quiet on board, as if the passengers had fallen into a deep sleep. Not until the opposite coast of the Mediterranean, the French coast, came into sight did they reappear. The majority hoped to be able to stay right there on the coast, in Marseilles or Nice, at least at the edge of the sea on whose other coast lay the forsaken country, as if they then would not be so completely cut off; isn't it said: Oceans cannot separate us; oceans unite us. However, only a handful were able to settle in those towns, only those who already had a brother, a cousin, or a brother-in-law who would take them in and help them along. We, however, were sent to Amiens. This was the place to which we were assigned after spending days and days again in a camp, and in Amiens we were housed in a former chocolate factory, always ten women to one room. It was October, and the weather turned cold right away; the darkness and the long hours of dusk, this eternal indecision between light and dark when the day dies a painful death, not short and painless as back home; 'beheaded clean as with a guillotine,' as my uncle once said. Then winter came quickly, and we had no winter coats or warm clothes, no warm shoes or boots; we never needed those in Oran. And we no longer had the sea or anything to which we had been accustomed. Every square, every street, every tree, every house, and every human being was new.

The displaced Algerians huddled together, but they came from completely different corners of the country, and it is impossible to imagine the difference between these people, let alone between them and those from the Sahara.

There was nobody else from Oran in the Jewish community. My mother befriended women from other Algerian cities; they exchanged memories, lamented, and told each other about the things they had left behind, their residences, their businesses, the graves of their parents. 'Somebody must try to imagine this: after living there for two thousand years, we are driven out like dogs! After two thousand years!' They did not mourn their 'fatherland' but rather their homes, their gardens, the sea, the beach, the mild climate, and a different way of life, a lighter, more generous way, they had said.

Our mother cried for some time, beginning in the morning when she got up until evening when she went to bed and during the night as well. She cried for three years, and I have no other memory of her during this time than of seeing her sobbing, blowing her nose, wiping her tears, spreading herself out on the table, her head buried in her arms, weeping, for years.

Maybe others were more fortunate and had an easier time adjusting, got a better job faster, and became accustomed to the new situation more easily. Maybe they understood earlier that their time in Algeria was coming to an end and had prepared themselves over a longer period of time, at least mentally, for a new life in another country. If my father had still been alive, he would immediately have gotten a position as a public servant with the railroad, but my mother never worked outside the home; all she had to live on was a small pension. But this wasn't the worst. The worst was that she didn't know what to do with herself all day; there was nobody to visit, to talk to, to cook or bake for, or to prepare holidays for; the entire family was torn apart and dispersed to different places; some had even ended up in Canada.

In Oran—when our father was still alive—how many people sat at our table on Friday nights, the whole clan, uncles, aunts, and countless cousins. They all lived in close proximity to each other anyway and visited each other constantly. Locked doors were unheard of and so was being by oneself; what would be the point? The women, of course, lived in a more or less separate world where no news ever remained hidden or without comment, and, as during a permanent emergency session in parliament, there was always much to be talked about, to be discussed, and to be decided.

My sister and I tried to make a fresh start; we told our mother that we wanted to start a new life, here in Amiens—why had you always spoken about France with such reverence and love: a civilized country! Land of liberty! You were granted equal rights and even French passports. So please stop crying, stop it already!

We wanted to befriend other girls in Amiens, meet with them after school, go to the movies. But mother didn't permit it. She didn't permit us to do anything; we were not allowed to go to the movies or to the park, and visiting somebody's house was totally out of the question. She was afraid whenever she lost sight of us. During this time, we collected postcards of movie stars, as our girlfriends did, and sent them off to be autographed; we hadn't seen the movies, but we at least had a look at the photos in the display cases outside the movie houses, and our girlfriends would tell us all about them. However, when mother discovered the collection, she threw it away just as she threw away everything else that in her eyes was frivolous, superfluous, and senseless; none of the objects in our apartment were older than three years. She said she didn't want to become attached to anything anymore; she didn't want to collect new memorabilia that she would have to throw overboard anyway, that would sink irretrievably to the bottom.

It has only been a year since my mother died, and I cried for a long time even though I, myself, am past forty and have six children. Thank God she did not die in the hospital but at my sister's house where she had lived for the last few years, since she was no longer able to really care for herself. All her life, reading and writing had been a great effort for her, and she never learned to speak French without making mistakes. For this reason alone it was necessary that one of us be close by to take her, for instance, to the doctor. Though she was able to recognize the doctor's name plate, frequently there were several next to each other that looked alike, pediatrician, ophthalmologist, and cardiologist, she had to be dropped off at the right one, at least on her first visit.

Since coming to Europe, her heart had been beating less and less and increasingly softly, and in fact she wasn't really able to live; she spent the remainder of her life just waiting, acquiring, in a motionless state, the rings of age like a tree. She turned inward or stared out the window, as if she could thus recover the lost and mourned homeland inside herself or outside in front of the window. Her heart attacks were like fits of rage against her unjust fate and against the Arabs who had robbed, cheated, and expelled her even though she had been their friend. Remote, but friends, and, after all, the Arabs had come to *our* rabbis for advice and blessings, and they had called *our* physicians when they were not well. And we had lived there *before* them, meaning for two thousand years, before the Arabs invaded the country, coming from I don't know where.

Very slowly, my mother faded away. I was able to see this when I visited her at my sister's in the summer, year after year. For that's where we spent our summer vacations together. My sister's house is located on the outskirts of Paris, and she has a lot of room for the children, a medium-sized garden where they can romp wildly to their heart's content. The greatest attraction was the dog, Billy, with whom they wandered around and to whom they tried to teach tricks, which he, however, never learned. At the house, the walls are plastered with photos, Billy eating, Billy sniffing, and Billy in the garden.

Shortly before her death, I took my mother again to a doctor in this suburb when she complained about her heart all night long. The doctor asked her to get undressed and lie down on a stretcher for an EKG. I had to help her, for she was too weak, and we took off her clothes very slowly. Never in my life had I seen her naked, and I now turned my head. She asked me to please stay with her; her fear of death was greater than her sense of shame. Suddenly it seemed that we had exchanged roles, as if I were the mother and she my child, and this thought repulsed me even though I was quite willing to take care of her in her sickness the way I had taken care of many people in the hospital, but I didn't want everything to be turned upside down so suddenly.

My mother always had a great sense of shame and would lock herself in her room or cover herself in front of my sister and me. We always sniffed the eau de toilette that was wafting through our apartment like the wind from the Sahara desert. It was 'Je reviens' by Worth. Even now I can sometimes see the round bottle with the little angel sitting on top with crossed legs. I even ask sometimes for a sample. The saleswomen then ask me if it's for an elderly lady since there is no longer much demand for it and it had gone out of style a long time ago. Then I reply, yes, yes, for an elderly lady.

In the last weeks before her death, our mother toddled around with tiny steps in ever-narrowing circles, only a few blocks, only in front of the house, only in the garden, no longer out of the house at all, and then no longer outside the room, and finally no longer out of bed. My sister told me on the telephone, she is already partly on her way—do you understand. And one morning she found her dead, covered with her wool blanket, the television still running from the night before.

My sister's kosher catering business remained closed during the week of mourning. Elijah could have kept the business open by himself, but the two are such a well-coordinated team that one of them was probably unable to function without the other. We were sitting on the floor in our torn clothes; a few friends and people who had known my mother came by, former citizens of Oran or elsewhere in Algeria. Once again they exchanged memories of the old days, the town, the sea, the crossing. Conversations during the time of mourning are difficult, for the callers belong to the living, whereas the mourners belong, for this time, more to the dead or at least to the world in between; no longer is it possible to speak and feel as before when they too still belonged completely to the living; their world had suddenly become a strange place.

Some people now approach us in a different way, with a look of understanding, a sense of closeness, as if they had been admitted into the secret society of those who have lost their parents and have moved in the succession of the generations to the front line where they are no longer shielded.

Sometimes when I am walking in the street, and I happen to catch my mirror image in a display window, I see more and more my mother rather than myself, and I wonder whether I will soon become her, my face, my body, my behavior. For I already feel this transformation in my walk, in my movements, my gaze. I hear myself talking with the voice of my mother, and I see myself motioning with her hands. Oh no, oh dear, God forbid.

Barbara Honigmann

EXCERPTS FROM On Sunday the Rabbi Plays Soccer

The Dead Men of the Donon

We want to take a ride to the Donon to see if perhaps there isn't already some snow. When we arrive at the wooded parking lot, we have to decide whether we want to climb the Grand or the Petit Donon, and since we are not in the mood for either a television transmitter or a Gallic, or whatever kind of temple it is, we decide to take the path toward the Petit Donon. Snow—yes, the ground is covered with snow; the children are totally euphoric and start running around like three-year-olds, tossing snowballs (snow spheres, they translate back from the French) all about them. But we insist we must press on with climbing since daylight won't last forever, and it is already afternoon. We take a shortcut that is quite a strenuous climb, but this is not yet the summit. We arrive at a plateau that is strangely barren, with fallen and cut-down trees and chunks of boulders arranged in a round. We climb over them and stand on top of them to get a good view of the valley. Suddenly Ru, who enjoys shoveling the snow everywhere, calls out, look here, there is an inscription on the stone. He is right; it reads, *two Germans;* we scratch some more, *Sapper Batt.* 134 K. A boulder like any other, but now we take a closer look at the others and make a horrifying discovery. The entire mountain is strewn with such chunks of graves made of the red sandstone of the Vosges. They are lying flat on the ground or are half erect or leaning against a tree. I remember a color among my oil paints that is called *caput mortuum*, an iron red like these stones, and I always wondered about the origin of that name. *Two French soldiers, Inf. Reg.* 21; *eight German* KJR 119; *six French lancers* R21; *one French lancer* R. 21; and so it goes all the way to the summit of the mountain, and up there, hewn into the rock: *In Memoriam*, and so on, *of the victorious German soldiers; victorious* has been chipped off and is almost illegible. A few more meters, at the very top, towering over the summit, so to speak, for the rock is like a table for giants, hewn in once again: *à la mémoire éternelle*, and so on, *glorieusement le 21 août 1914*.

What a sight all around us. These dead men, turned into red stones, are crawling forever up the mountain, barely hidden by the trees and covered with snow. Then the children discover one more thing, the shed; they had been here before on a school excursion during some past summer; now they remember they had built this shed; yes, this one, this is exactly the one they had built back then, during one of those summers.

Greetings from New York

Dear Reader! I bet you are surprised. I am now in New York for the first time in my life. You can be even more surprised, for I feel so much at home here, you can't imagine, as I do hardly anywhere else in the world. I arrived, took a taxi to the hotel, walked for a bit around the hotel, Amsterdam Avenue and Eighty-first Street, that is, the Upper West Side, and immediately I felt as if I had always been here, as if I had lived here and in general belonged here. I am in a euphoric mood and don't even know exactly why. But the Viennese poet, who was also invited, feels the same way. The two of us can barely keep our feet on the ground; we're so filled with euphoria. I know, dear reader, that you will now say that I have to explain to you what I mean, for you have read and heard and seen on television that New York is a bankrupt, rotten, and violent town. That may be, but where I am, it's not like that at all. People are all friendly and polite to each other; nearby, Central Park blooms in the brightest colors—Indian summer—people are lying in the grass, basking in the sun; the lawns are dotted with sunbathers, and when you blink your eyes, you can see the skyscrapers surrounding the park; it all looks exactly the way we have seen it a thousand times in the movies, and that's just the beauty of it; you can actually find in reality the picture that you carry around in your head. And then, of course, you discover a thousand other things that you aren't even looking for. The Viennese poet and I just stumbled upon the round mosaic for John Lennon, *Imagine*, by Yoko Ono, and just then Yoko Ono passes by—she still lives nearby—and we smile at her bashfully and say Hi! and she returns our smile. Hi!

The Viennese poet and I are actually supposed to speak about Jews in Germany, even though neither one of us lives there, and at the moment there is no subject that interests us less. And in the evening we are supposed to give a reading at New York University of our writings, which are also at this moment very distant from us. More than anything we feel like strolling, walking, sauntering, roaming—oh yes, hiking shoes are very appropriate for New York—sometimes it turns into running and rushing, uptown, midtown, downtown, and how many people from different countries do I meet along the way! And then one day I am standing at the tip of Manhattan where the ferries dock. I take the ferry for the Statue of Liberty and Ellis Island. I don't get off at the Statue of Liberty. But on Ellis Island, that floodgate of mass migrations, there I remain a few hours, the entire afternoon. The great receiving hall has been emptied out, but in the side rooms and two projection rooms, the story of the immigrants is being told. There, now behind glass in showcases, are their passports, their photographs, the tickets of their passage, newspapers, diaries, and prayer books, their suitcases, baskets, and clothing, and all kinds of odds and ends, and it is as if something of the dreams and hopes of the one-time owners of these odds and ends were floating in the room, and I feel like crying a bit and don't know why. Now, the last ferry goes on its return run, and suddenly I am standing on deck myself, the wind in my face, the seagulls squawking; Ellis Island is behind me, and before me is the skyline of Manhattan.

I am telling you, dear reader, if you haven't seen it yet, it's worth a trip.

A Little Homage to MLK

My second trip to the United States took me to Atlanta, yes, to the Deep South, where the Olympic games took place and where thirty years ago the police had to, if not shoot, at least club their way into the university for the few black students who attended.

Today, the mayor of Atlanta is a black man, African American, as one says now, and almost the entire city administration is also African American, says Ann Kremer of the American Jewish Committee, who is also in the city administration and whose ancestors came from Alsace. I meet the famous black middle class on Sunday in the Ebenezer Baptist Church, the pulpit of Martin Luther King and his father before him. The service lasts for hours, but I wouldn't mind if it lasted even longer because one could listen forever to the gospel music and watch the people who, singing and clapping, can barely be contained in their seats; they are actually close to dancing. There are always a few visitors from far away, like me, since it is not an entirely normal church or an entirely normal 'service.' Everybody knows that, and that's why I don't feel like a voyeur; I am a tourist anyway. Visitors are sent on their way with a special blessing for themselves and their families and for peace in general.

Next door, at the Martin Luther King Center for Nonviolent Social Change, I visit a small museum and look at the Nobel Peace Prize, which is exhibited there. A whole school class is grouped around the showcase, and I listen to the black teacher's explanations. He says, 'By God, you know, if only Martin Luther King had lived to see a school class like ours, a mixed one, and all the black students, professors, politicians, business people, and mayors of the big cities! The majority of our minority has made it in the last thirty years; we live well, have gained influence, and only a small minority still lives in the ghettos of the big cities; you know what is going on there; you can see it on television all the time.' The children, meanwhile, are sitting on the floor with pencils and writing pads and are busily taking notes on what they had just learned about Martin Luther King's nonviolent struggle.

On the Banks of the Mississippi

And now I am in America for the third time, and yet each time it is different from a trip to a European country. I don't really know why I immediately feel so euphoric and filled with a sense of freedom when I cross the ocean and set foot on a different continent. The city in which I am now walking, Saint Louis, is situated on the banks of the Mississippi, and the name alone evokes myth and legend. Only one can't really speak of walking around since my hotel is fifteen kilometers from downtown and therefore also at some distance from the river. The man at the front desk looks at me when I ask how I can get to the Mississippi on foot. I had no idea about the fifteen kilometers, and, of course, now that I am fully rested and almost over my jet lag, I want to see the legendary river. Why don't you rent a car, said the man at the front desk, but I, not knowing my way around, wasn't brave enough for that; everywhere all I see are gigantic highways, and I am afraid I might drive all the way to the Pacific coast because I can't find an exit. So I take a taxi to the next Metro station, which exists here against all expectations and which resembles a streetcar more than a train, a high-speed one, and which also crosses the river. Actually, I had planned to walk back to the city from the other side, but since everybody is getting off at the last station before the river, I follow them instinctively. The people whom I tell about this in the evening wring their hands; what kind of adventure I had almost gotten myself into again; oh no, one doesn't set foot on the other side. Under no circumstances!

'The city'—I really must put it in quotation marks, for it consists only of sprawling concrete blocks strewn about in between large, wide, empty spaces, and me, a very lonely pedestrian, walking along the endless wide roadway. Life and people are somehow elsewhere, on the other side, for example inside the former train station, which, after all, had at one time connected the East with the American West. The train station has been transformed into a mall, a small town with streets and stores and restaurants, and indeed I find here the kind of travel bags that I have dreamed of all my life, half knapsack and half suitcase, and for only sixty dollars. Directly by the river, I visit, of course, the famous steel arch, designed by Eero Saarinen, the gateway to the West. It is higher than even the Eiffel Tower and at least as effective and actually more elegant and, in any case, impressive. However, the Mississippi itself is nothing but a brown brew and not even very wide, a disappointment. The same people who had been wringing their hands about me said, well, Tom Sawyer and Huckleberry Finn, where it's pretty and rural, that's also quite nearby, only a hundred miles away.

Barbara Honigmann

Double Burial from Novel by a Child

We were standing with Gerschom Scholem at the grave of his parents and brothers in the Jewish Cemetery of Berlin-Weissensee. It was cold; it was December. Gerschom Scholem and Fania, his wife, were wearing thin coats; they had just arrived from Jerusalem. Scholem should have known how cold it gets in Berlin in December, since he had, after all, lived here long enough, was born and grew up here. But this was probably too long ago. He left in 1923 convinced that he no longer had any business being in Germany.

We removed wilted leaves, twigs, branches, and tree limbs from the grave site and freed it of the relentless ivy that climbs from one grave to the next, from grave to tree, and from tree again to grave, carrying everything along and devouring it until the entire stony order becomes overgrown, so that not only the bodies of the dead but also the entire task of remembering returns to dust. 'One needs an ax if one wants to visit the grave of an ancestor, to cut a path through the overgrowth of time,' said Scholem.

The writing on the gravestone read:

ARTHUR SCHOLEM
born 1863 in Berlin died 1925 in Berlin
BETTY SCHOLEM, *born Hirsch*
born 1866 in Berlin died 1946 in Sydney
WERNER SCHOLEM
born 1895 in Berlin shot 1942 in Buchenwald
ERICH SCHOLEM
born 1893 in Berlin died 1965 in Sydney

Scholem spoke about his father, his mother, and his two brothers, about the one who had become a Communist and had been murdered in Buchenwald, and about Erich, who had immigrated to

Australia. He introduced them all to us, one after the other. And then we remained silent for a while, for as long perhaps as it takes to shake hands and to say 'Hello.' Scholem said a brief prayer. He said it very softly, whispering.

Near the entrance, on the way to the grave, was a construction site, even though what was being built was not discernible, and everything looked as it always did; a large section of the walkway was blocked by a rope, and a little flag was hanging from it with the words: 'Caution: Construction.' Fania Scholem removed the rope with the little flag, just so, the way one presses down the handle of a door through which one passes, and walked straight across the marked-off construction site. Gerschom Scholem called after her: 'Don't you see that the path is blocked?' But Fania answered: 'What do you mean; I won't let a piece of rope keep me from going my way! Can't you see that there is really nothing to see?' Scholem shook his head but nevertheless followed her onto the forbidden path across the invisible construction site, but not without replacing the rope behind him.

At the gate to the cemetery, a chauffeured black Mercedes was waiting for Gerschom Scholem and Fania, provided for them for the day by the head of the West German Mission to the GDR, Bölling or perhaps it was still Gaus, who had invited Scholem.

We drove to Schönhauser Allee. Scholem wanted to buy a pigskin briefcase like the one he always used to have in the old days in Berlin. This sort of thing was not available in Jerusalem, and he had loved this briefcase so much back then and later had always wished for one but had never gotten it.

Scholem and Fania, his wife, entered the shop through the wrong door and were sent back so they could enter once more through the right door, the one with the sign that said 'Entrance.' Then they failed to pick up a shopping basket at a specified place, for which they were scolded again. However, they didn't even notice it because they were talking to each other in loud voices, which probably also annoyed the saleswomen, who showed them a few of the briefcases only reluctantly. Fania was enraged about the discourtesy and constant reprimands, but Scholem asked her to restrain herself. In the end, they bought a briefcase and were happy because this had been such an old wish that now, after so long a time, had finally been fulfilled.

Fania Scholem spoke German. But where might she have learned it? Her native language was Hebrew, later she spoke Polish, Yiddish, Russian, and then, as foreign languages, English and French, but not German. So how did she know it now? 'She absorbed it somehow in the course of living with me,' said Scholem.

Later, Scholem sat in the rocking chair at our house. He had already read all our letters at Aunt Eva's in Jerusalem, and he told me not to go into the kitchen and make coffee since it would only take away precious time from our conversation. He asked questions and told stories, and we asked questions and told stories.

What stories he had to tell, a thousand episodes from German and Jewish and German-Jewish history, ancient, new, and ancient-new. He spoke of the Frankists, the Jewish Messianic sect in Poland whose adherents all later converted to Catholicism, about whom he had just been writing. And about Walter Benjamin's friend Noeggerath of Berlin, about whom he hoped to find out something while he was here. Then he railed against the Lubavitcher Rebbe, whose forgery of an allegedly historic letter he had proven; as a historian, he found something like that enormously troubling. Then he talked about the Jewish *Gesamtarchiv*, now located in the state archives of the GDR in Merseburg. He spoke about his first visit there, when he saw it with his own eyes, and about the library of the Berlin Jewish community, the once gigantic library at 68 Oranienburger Strasse. And we said, it's there again; only it's not as gigantic but rather tiny, but in the same street, in the same building. It had been there that he had taken out his first Jewish books, said Scholem, and we said, we had too. And this was where everything actually began, and we said, for us too.

Then Scholem told the story of the fate of this library. He had been sent to Berlin after the war by the State of Israel to find out what had become of this library and, if possible, to bring it back to Israel. The Nazis did not destroy Jewish books; on the contrary, the books had been collected and catalogued by ten Jewish scholars specially employed for this purpose (only two among them, married to German women, had survived). Later, the entire collection was stored in Prague because the Nazis presumed that this city would not be bombed, and when the war was over, that is, when the war would have been won, all the books that had been collected were to document the triumph over the Jews, like the treasures of the destroyed Temple of Jerusalem in Rome. The Czech government, which discovered the collection in Prague after the war, considered it its property and offered it for sale on the international market. This is how the books were dispersed, nobody knows where; now and then a book is found in some library or some antiquarian bookshop in some city somewhere in the world. Scholem found a few in the course of his travels in all kinds of cities and countries and bought them back; they are now with him in his home. It is said that five hundred very valuable handwritten Hebrew manuscripts had been among them, of which Scholem had discovered two in Warsaw. 'The books' fate was no better than that of the people,' said Scholem. He wrote a report about his investigations but never published it.

Later on, we were sitting in the Hotel Berolina. We had planned to take Scholem and Fania, his wife, to dinner there, and after he had told us how the Frankists, after converting to Catholicism, married into and thus Judaized the Polish aristocracy, we laughed about it; Scholem said to me and my husband Peter: 'It is said: Go to a land of knowledge of Torah (. . . and don't say, let the Torah come to you, for only in the company of others will it preserve you. Sayings of the Fathers 4:18). Jerusalem would be good, New York would be good, London would be good, anywhere would be good, but Germany is no longer good for Jews. There is nothing to learn here anymore, and therefore it makes no sense to stay; it is much too difficult. I don't know how we can arrange to get you there, but I'll think of a way.'

Both of them refused to eat meat. They did not keep strictly kosher at home, they said, but would prefer not to eat meat here in Berlin. However, the Interhotel had no fish, and so we could treat them only to egg salad, which was already partly dried out. Scholem and Fania spoke in loud voices and laughed loudly, and I felt the disapproving glances from all sides at this uninhibited old couple.

The chauffeur for the head of the mission was waiting in front of the hotel, and the two finally got into the limousine, and we lingered a little while in front of the open car door and said what a wonderful day it had been, and Scholem showed us once again the pigskin briefcase and said what a great success this had been for him, and then: 'Good bye. Well, I wonder whether we'll see each other again . . .'

The next day we rushed to the library on Oranienburger Strasse and took out all of Scholem's books. They were indeed on a shelf next to, as he had already complained to us, the 'German nationalist' Schoeps, with whom he felt no kinship.

Before long we received mail from Scholem. He sent us his book about the Frankists, which had just been published, and he asked us to present it to the Jewish community in his name after we had read it. And that's what we did.

A few weeks later I got a call from a friend who said she had heard something 'dumb' on the radio. I didn't understand what she meant to say, but then she said quickly that Scholem had died in Jerusalem and that his burial was tomorrow. That was 21 February 1982.

He was eight-four years old when he died. But for me, he had just been born; for many years, Scholem had merely been an inscription. The inscription of his name on the title page of his books and in the bylines of newspaper articles or a reference found when checking a footnote indicated by an asterisk. Or sometimes when he was quoted by this or that person, the sound of his name, this peculiar name.

This name had appeared in the flesh, as a true reality, with a loud voice, speaking a Berlin dialect, a beanpole with ears that stuck out, the entire mystique in our rocking chair. He had once again made the journey of his life, once again Berlin to Jerusalem and back, and he was wearing a coat that was too thin.

It is cold; it is December, three years later. I am sitting in the Petit Café on the Avenue du Général de Gaulle. So it is not New York or London but France; there I am sitting, thinking of Scholem in Berlin. The café is empty except for three Arabs at the next table, who are always there and with whom I am already well acquainted because we have spoken with each other several times, and they are friendly even though I explained to them that I was an *israélite*. They couldn't understand why I don't speak Hebrew (it is so similar to Arabic), and I had to explain that my mother tongue was German and that I was from Germany and was now living here because in Germany there are practically no *israélites* anymore. Whereupon they ask: Why not?

Soon after Scholem's death, I went one more time to the grave of his parents and his brothers at the Weissensee cemetery. I wanted to make some kind of gesture of remembrance, and I took the same path we had taken, unhooked the rope with the little flag that said 'Caution: Construction' and crossed the roped-off path, just as we had done. Then I was standing in front of the grave, and there I saw that his name appeared among all the names of his family. It read:

GERHARD G. SCHOLEM
born 1897 in Berlin died 1982 in Jerusalem

Most people have only one burial place. Gerschom Scholem has two. One in Jerusalem and one in Berlin. I guess he lived all his life in both cities. That's why he has two burial places. That's just the kind of life it was.

Esther Dischereit

Joemi's Table A JEWISH STORY

Can
the Unjust
make good
their injustice
through justice?
Yes, because
the injustice
of the
Unjust
is the
justice of
the Just.

Here I am sitting on this dumb swivel chair. After twenty years of being an un-Jewish Jew, I want to be a Jew again. I've thought about it for ten years. What is the man behind the desk saying about it? 'Tax evasion,' he says, with a smile. I would have to do penance for four years and pay my back taxes. I tell him: mother dead, father a goy—fourteen years old, off to the country, no mail, no nothing from the community—and I am coming back after twenty years, want to be a Jew again, and the Jew says to me: 'About eight hundred German marks, or should I have you assessed?'

Is it necessary to be a Jew, I've been asking myself long enough. The birthmark of Cain, forgotten under the waters of socialism, shines through my skin.

They caught up with me, the dead of history, and let me be a part of it. I didn't want to be a part, absolutely wanted to be a normal leftist—oppressed by the category of classes, class struggles, of oppressors and oppressed.

I thoroughly failed in the attempt. I am standing in the street, propagandizing class struggle, and somebody asks me about my nationality. Neither proud nor self-assured, and certainly not indifferent . . . should I say German? One would have to say German. Then, the BUT . . . what BUT? But Jew. There it is, thick and heavy, the word that is pinned to the lapel, hanging around my neck by strings. These strings are cutting my throat. My comrade at the drafting table, piled high with propaganda brochures, flyers, and a collection box, doesn't know anything about it. What does he care? No state can be built with these eternal losers of history.

I decide to forget this question about being German. In the evening there's the news. Something about Nuremberg flashes on the screen for some reason, and again I am as upset as I was this morning. Why do I get so upset about this kind of news? After all, there are plenty of horrible news stories—or not? Of course I know that . . . and get really upset. Dumb question, is this allowed? Dividing feelings of injustice equitably. Am I going nuts?

What a feeling—and although I don't like them—the rich, bad, fat Jews, and of course those who use other people's water to cheerfully plant little trees on top of the houses of foreign people, all as if it had to be that way and was justified by providence.[1] I too danced around the tree, faraway in a German city. We bought it—commemorating the planting in the foreign land with loud singing. A distant one that would always, always, always be a refuge? Maybe that's why we didn't go there. No, we didn't go, ever. To go there would be like a pilgrimage to Rome—or a hajj to Mecca. We didn't make a pilgrimage. It's possible that we might have seen the ruins of their destroyed houses. It's possible that we might have seen the children of the hajj. It's possible that we might have seen parents without their children. Or we might have seen none of this—and the Dead Sea, it buoys, buoys you so beautifully that nobody can sink. And yet, it is dead; perhaps it is impossible to live if one cannot sink.

The Jewish cemetery of Fes—do you know that there are no stones, after all those stones in Prague and Warsaw. No. In the middle of the mellah, the cemetery casts white light against the walls of the houses. Behind the walls are children's voices, women's talk, men's eyes. Each grave has been whitewashed with lime—on some graves the lime has not yet dried. I'm sitting here on this lime—enjoying its freshness.

Wherever dying is going on, there is also chatter, kaddish, Pesach, and circumcision. In my town, here in Frankfurt, people don't die.

Thus I was sitting in Fes and wept because in Frankfurt there is very little dying.

Flies are falling in the early morning hours onto the flat rooftops of the old city, chasing the sleepers from their places of rest. Blankets are being pulled back. Vibrations, the voices of the imams resound from the towers of the city. 'Allahu akbar—Allah akbar'—donkeys carry piled-up burdens through the narrow medieval streets. Customers have to jump quickly to the side, passing the tunnel alley of the blind beggars, smelling the stench of children's skin and freshly tanned leather that, still very new, is taken to market. Young girls fetch water in heavy pitchers, carry bread to be baked, and cook for their brothers, do their laundry, and pick up the pits the brothers spit on the floor tiles.

Calligraphic plaques in the bazaar give testimony to a center of learning and art. By late morning there is no more protective shade. The washer at the Hammam scrubs the skin raw. The pieces of skin smell brown, Moslem, Yiddish, and French.

Rabbi Didia is an old man. In his study, a Star of David crosses the hand of Fatima. He has been received by the King of Morocco. Nine candleholders are modestly silver-plated. 'Yehude?' 'Oui.' 'Yehude allemand?' His voice is soft, talking to himself. In a hidden corner of a wide street, where evening shoppers stroll, stand around, chat, is the hall he calls the synagogue. The old men embrace each other's heads and hands. There is almond milk in the mellah. Want to marry a Moslem? No problem. Military service? No problem. Now and again shared religious festivities . . .

A hand holds the microphone, wet with sweat. The device begins to stutter. Cool and white, the man remains seated in his dignity, while outside a young woman with a scarf knotted at the back of her neck scolds her young boy. Water from a plastic bottle seeps into the specially provided hole in the ground over which the boy stands, his feet wide apart.

The smell of local sesame cakes fills the air in the square of Córdoba. Turbans, long garments, a stonelike face in the daily life of an alley.

At the time of the Umayyads, he was tolerated until Isabella finally mistrusted even those converted. In a doorway, beautifully cultivated tropical plants. Hand-rubbed jewelry from nearby Toledo hangs on display. And what pillars! The child staggers at the foot of the pillar, holding a picture postcard; her blue sun hat has slid backward. Little fat legs stretch the white mesh stockings. Come here—the baby carriage rolls forward, unholy on the grounds of the mosque. The city battled too. But Maria had to win; lives ridiculously in the midst of stolen columns, the possession not of her soul but of the Carthaginians. She too will drive this rabbi off his pedestal—across North Africa all the way to Egypt. Camera—here take a picture of that, this beautiful old narrow alley. And here, the holy of holies, a beautifully circumcised heart with an opening for payment. Out of three hundred, this one alone has been preserved, the last remaining synagogue in the city.

Yes—it's a pity that so little life is visible in this picture. But they have beautiful cats in this town; did you see the little one? The travel guide states: The time of toleration has passed. Thus he drags his toleration with him through history. Rambam, Rambam, Maimonides. So many rest in peace, and those, of all people, who don't believe themselves resurrected, are supposed to live on?

Alhambra, the roadway whispers to me. Bleating, time keeps the Rif hidden—a goat, driven up a tree by hunger. The hemp blooms innocently. Carrying a pack and a jacket, a man wanders along the road, which is dotted with burning asphalt, in the midday heat. Drought, thistles, thistles, sand, and drought.

A boy is standing on a slope, looks around and stands and sits down and looks around. Bread, boy, bread. Middle fingers cover the mouth. Taken in deeply with the eyes. Hemp blooms gently between the hills.

Eight years, nine years old, perhaps seven—yes, seven years. I look past him, above him, through this mouth of his, beyond.

Rosa goes to school. In shoes and stockings. Her skirt is white with colorful hearts, matching her blouse perfectly, which is also white with colorful hearts. Small ladies' shoes on her feet—her hair parted on the side. Tied with butterfly barrettes. School bag—pink writing implement. A carton of Fanta.

The boy holds a little stick between his fingers—*un stylo;* Rosa has a decal on her notebook. Two slices of salami on the bread, real thick, she said. Butter sweats from the sandwich onto the wax paper. By noon, the salami forms a layer of grease.

The boy twirls the little stick between his fingers. The salami begins to roll up at the edges, curls, and hardens. Rosa opens her bag, searches for a piece of chewing gum—and, later, for the math notebook. The salami greases the plastic bag. Rosa tosses her shoes into the corner of her room.

A drumbeat on a sardine can, hands move up and down like a camel gliding on soft ground. The soles of his plastic shoes are attached to his bare feet by a string. The boy twirls the little stick between his fingers.

This road, this region, this drought—sand and thistles rake

about in the motor. Eyes follow me, gliding after me, until the road finally intersects with a crossroad. The waist-length jacket, the backpack—a man is sitting next to him. Perhaps the city, perhaps the trees against which they lean. Inside these stones, Allah is asleep.

The candleholder has been dusted and placed on top of the cabinet. The thin piece of silver forms a small rectangle ending in pointed corners. Two equally wide pieces of welded tin form the feet. The candles will be placed in three small holders that are spaced at an equal distance from each other. These holders are hooked into three circular openings of the candleholder—or unhooked, however one wishes to do this. If all three holders were to be unhooked, then a silver-framed candleholder would remain with three openings, three times emptiness, with no function. Maybe the manufacturer permitted housewifely professionalism to prevail. Just imagine, removable holders that can be filled with wax, how easy it would be to remove the leftover wax, simpler than other candleholders whose holders don't . . .

A candleholder with three arms in the same industrial design as, for example, our upholstered chairs with their thin, outward-turned legs. During the week these three holders usually contain bluish thin candles with wicks that are carefully singed at the tip. Unlit candles are bad luck.

And still, this flame is not allowed to consume even an iota of wax—at least not from Monday to Friday before sundown.

When the stranger enters our apartment, he sees the candleholder, a stylized brass swan that holds pretzel sticks in its belly, a wooden statue from Bali, whose filigree work wards off evil gods. An eagle's beak picks a person's eye. Embroidered, little round covers protect the gleaming polish of the table. The stranger takes a pretzel, politely admires the swan. Hannah smiles and offers him another glass of wine. The underside of the swan is engraved, from right to left, with the words *Made in Israel*.

At the time, it had surprised us when Hannah bought the candleholder. Her husband's monthly support for her and two of the children is barely enough. For lunch there is rice with cinnamon and sugar, or sometimes with tomatoes, for supper an apple and bread and butter. Nevertheless, she bought the candleholder, carefully selected after days of consideration.

On Friday, toward evening, Hannah takes the candleholder from the cabinet. She takes the middle holder from the opening and replaces it with a small container filled with flowers.

Thus it stands, two armed, in the center of a white tablecloth. When the rabbi comes, she will light the candles. Nobody will open the door. *Schabbes* begins.

What is it with this woman that she buys a three-armed candleholder when she needs a two-armed one?

Your eyes are so big, so dark. They would have betrayed you. Just because of these eyes. You are flesh, not a child. Your fidgeting, snorting, laughing stuck in your throat. Loaded into the railroad car. You didn't run fast enough. You peered through a slit in the car. The sun blinking in. You wanted to reach for it. It burnt you in return. And when the car stopped and the motor was still running, you looked at me. I know; I sensed your eyes.

We aren't in any railroad car. Standing here in a room with a bed and closet, and your eyes, they look at a dreydel.

Forty-five years ago, I had a sister. She was your age. Who can tell me that you are not my sister.

Or the years wouldn't have gone forward at all, rather they would have gone backward.

'A hat, a cane, an umbrella—forward, backward, sideways . . . three . . . a hat, a cane . . .' The child interrupts the game. Behind large windows that almost reach to the ground, people are moving about, spreading out sheets of paper on tables, walking among the covered tables, pointing a finger at one place or another. A man with a beard has a pencil stuck behind his ear. He reaches for it.

Steps sound on the pavement. The child turns around, almost touching the tail of a big dog. The child leans with her back against the windowpane, hands pressed against the glass. She yells. 'It's okay. My dog likes children,' says the man. The woman had taken the child by the hand. 'The dog's startled too,' says the man.

He wears a three-piece suit, polished shoes. Carefully combed hair, a cane. The woman and child continue on down the street.

'You know, I wouldn't know what to do without him. The dog hears everything. I can depend on this dog—a pointer.' The child's shoelace has come untied. 'You know,' says the man, 'he really is good with children. Only foreigners, that's strange.' He has a limp. 'Yes, that's strange, don't you think? He immediately goes on the attack.' Nine houses, eight houses. 'You know, their secretiveness. Somehow, he smells it—yes . . . and all the noise . . . you know what I mean.' Eight houses, seven houses, six houses.

He's been living in this area for twenty years, he says. Five houses, four houses. He's earned this afternoon walk at about four o'clock, he says. Gray eyeglasses follow the rhythm of the cane. Bad weather . . . well . . . then the entrance hall . . . The dog knew this. 'Same as with the Turks,' says the man. Five houses, four houses, three houses, two houses.

The woman holds the child's hand firmly. The cane moves along the pavement; the dog follows behind.

Hannah's daughter hears the bell announcing recess. The last class of the day was gym. Ever so slowly, she changes her clothes. She is ashamed, always dawdles, until all the other students are almost gone. So now only her shoes.

Kersten has come back. She takes a bite from her apple; the gym bag dangles from her right arm. She probably forgot something. She talks about something with the other two still left behind in the stuffy locker room. Between bites from the apple, Kersten asks: 'And your parents?' 'Catholic,' says one, the other: 'No, Protestant.' Kersten is standing in front of Hannah's daughter. 'And yours, what is your mother?' Hannah's daughter says nothing; she thinks. Hannah had forbidden her to talk about it.

Kersten repeats the question, louder.

The attention of the others is aroused; they come closer. Hannah's daughter wants to leave, get out of the clammy air in the locker room. The three now surround her—behind them is the door. 'I think Protestant.' Softly. 'You liar, you liar, she's a Jew, I know for sure.' Kersten stomps her foot yelling, 'She's a Jew,' at Hannah's daughter and in the ears of the other two.

The teacher has probably gone.

When the three have left, Hannah's daughter pulls the door shut behind her. With a heavy step, she goes home. She had been taught in religious instruction who Judas was.

She is afraid of the red spots on her mother's neck and the bottle of medicine that is within reach. We're living on the ground floor. Why, of all things, do we have to live on the ground floor. On the ground floor the windowpanes rattle so easily.

Bread and butter, tea—a slice of salami. Now a slice on the buttered bread that almost reaches to the front. With every bite, her fingers push it farther back to the edge of the crust. This way, the smell of salami lingers in the nose as if it were on the tongue until finally the person eating and smelling is rewarded with the meat at the end of the bread. Hannah still uses knife and fork when eating a sandwich, we don't. The doorbell rings. The tea sloshes in the cup.

Hannah's eyes rush toward the door. The bread in my mouth gets pasty. Her eyes flutter at the peephole. She turns back the security latch.

When she sits down again, and Günther comes in with a five-pound box of chocolates and an orchid, she has red spots in wide bands all over her neck.

Later, Hannah's daughter lives alone on the fifth floor. No peephole, no intercom. When the doorbell rings in Hannah's daughter's apartment . . . without announcement . . . the tea cools for the duration of five floors and splashes in the saucer. Viewed from the upper balustrade, a hand or hands, sometimes not even that, make their way up the stairs, come up the steps along the wall. Her neck is not red with spots. Her skin is darker than her mother's.

His son overhears my conversation. 'Papa, what is a Jew?' Now the father can say, be quiet, my boy, after all we are all human. A Jew after all is human-too, just like you and me. 'No,' says the child, 'I'm not. I'm German. I won't be burnt like the others.' So the father says nothing; I don't say anything either—I, the human-too, think about whether there are more humans-too out there. There are Turkish humans-too living on the other side of the street. Would it serve any purpose to create a community of humans-too, a class division into humans and humans-too? Difficult at best for Marx, and only in the early writings. According to Lenin, I am a marginal contradiction. Is it possible to just be a Jew again?

I'll become a Turk—at least that. At least we could then populate our other sides of the street very densely.

She is standing in front of Rose's door holding her mother's hand. The rattling of silverware is heard through the vestibule. Meta's hand is sweating in her mother's. At this early hour, the sun has risen and makes the chimneys gleam on the roofs across the way. Knightly armor perches on them like ravens. In one of these ravens crouches Meta's father, Felix Zacharias, and plays the piano. Surrounded by smoke, the notes flow over the railing and don't want to fly. Meta thinks of the candy in her pocket. She is wearing a lot of clothes today on this hot summer morning. A wool jacket under the coat, and under that, two blouses and three undershirts, topped by a very ample scarf. Meta's mother lifts the doorknocker one more time and lets it drop. A small side window next to the entrance door permits the mail to be passed through and the visitor to be inspected. They feel the shadow behind the wall.

Meta's mother knew nothing about this shadow in the old days. They listened to Joseph Schmidt—and dreamed of a husband; exhilarated after her Graues Kloster, she performed her Latin lesson wearing pointed boots.[2] And when things got too calm for her, she just laughed and laughed herself silly.

Felix Zacharias doesn't rhyme with Epicurus, as old as Zeus or Methuselah. And still she went there with her wonderful violin. After that, she didn't often knock on this heavy door.

The little window turns hesitantly on its hinge. The rattle of silverware swells in Meta's ear. Rose looks at the two visitors, sees Meta's much too heavy coat. And Meta's mother with the bag, worn out. Meta believes she clearly hears the sound of the piano. 'Well, I really don't know; how shall I tell you?' The sun gleams on the chimney. 'Since last week he was' '?' 'already here—and three at once, you understand—I don't know what to say.' Through the open door to the room, an egg is being cracked.

Meta's mother is sweating into her hand. The stairs turn slowly from the door. And the little one comes in a coat that is much too heavy. With heavy shoes and candy in her pocket, she follows.

Ruth Walter. Do you know Ruth Walter?

Nobody knows Ruth Walter. And yet, Ruth Walter is lying in the drawer with all the effects that were left behind. And writes to Meta, Heidi, Elke who came to Berlin from Niederlausitz. Talks about lard traded for a school bag and butter for eternity. Her daughter, as Elke, is kissing a woman with hair pinned up. The lard is our daily pay.

Meta, Heidi, Elke first went away with Ruth Walter. Meta, Heidi, Elke is locked up in the room. Ruth Walter is on the street now; she is looking for a store whose coupons she sometimes forgets at home. She looks the woman directly in the eyes. If only the man outside would stop moving. 'Excuse me,' says Ruth, and Hannah quickly leaves the store. Finally—after two or three blocks more—Hannah, Ruth buys Meta, Heidi, Elke this apple.

In her room, Meta urgently needs to go peepee. Somebody walks on the creaking floor behind the adjoining wall. When Ruth Walter finally turns the key to the room, Meta's head is all flushed and she presses her legs together. Tears roll from her eyes, and her stockings are getting wet. Very slowly Ruth Walter peels this apple, hands it to Meta, piece by piece, and finally eats the peels and the core.

Then she pulls Meta onto her lap, warms her against her skin, places her on the coarse sofa bed. In the apartment next door, the woman leads the dog to the wall. 'How's my dog . . . good dog . . . good, my dog . . .' The child's arms flail about. Soon the dog will go for a walk with his owner, isn't that right—morning, noon, and night. Meta smells the air in front of her door. What if she put herself on the leash . . .

Hannah Walter took her away—to the end of a world with Königsberg dumplings. She writes cards with fat blond girls on the picture side; she sends lard and sometimes sugar, dear Ruth, with many, many fond greetings.

Neukölln, 18 August 1943

Mrs. Gertrud Baer!

At the request of Mrs. H. R., for the next two weeks I am sending you the butter and margarine coupons that are still missing. Under separate cover, you will also receive a package containing the lard Mrs. H. R. has been promising. I presume that Mrs. H. R. has informed you about the details.

Please say hello
to little Heidi and tell
her to be good.

With best regards,
H. Walter

Mrs. Baer reads the letter and wonders about the coupons for the third week. Only death is free of cost. Four months earlier, H had sent best wishes for her birthday:

Berlin, 5 April 1943

To the birthday girl
May destiny bring you as your guide
Sunshine for future journies far and wide.
And our child, this I wish with all my might,
May she bring nothing but joy and delight.
Wherever her fate may lead,
May she think with gratitude of our deed—
Believe me, the time is here,
The golden liberty is very near,
Then we'll sail across the ocean
Who knows?
May you pass your day of honor with good cheer,
I'd better stop writing poems, my dear
. . .

It was only in July that Mrs. Baer told her about the difficulties of the situation. On 25 July 1943, when the coupons were two weeks overdue, she sent this telegram via the German *Reichspost*, special delivery: COME IMMEDIATELY, SUFFERED ACCIDENT = PAPA. The delivery had to be made in person. Two days later, the coupons arrived. Oh yes—those were bad times . . .

Neukölln, 17 September 1943

My dear Hannah and little Ruth!

Having arrived in Berlin without incident, I immediately looked up your friend Lissy. Unfortunately, you were right. I put the note in her mailbox. Hopefully she'll respond.

Now about the journey itself. We arrived in Stettin at a quarter to nine. The next train for Berlin was scheduled for 10:14 A.M., so I had plenty of time to have some coffee and boost my strength. Then came the surprise. The train for Berlin was reported to be thirty minutes late. After a ten-minute wait, the next announcement about the train came: ninety minutes delay. Meanwhile, the next local train for Berlin left at 10:45 A.M., and I was able to get off at Gesundbrunnen Station at 1 P.M. From there, I took the local train to Schönhauser Allee and the subway to Sonnenfelder Platz. At a quarter to three, I was at home. There I had the same experience as you did. Nothing to eat. Neither butter nor jelly. I had to eat bread with cheese. But I was already used to that. Now about the reception. Ursel came and asked: 'Well, how was it?'

Your insights are too late today. You know how I feel about you. It is for this reason that it is hard for me to write the following. I don't know what we should do now. For I am deeply sorry that I must inform you—not because of what happened between us—that you won't be able to come to me anymore after all. Your Baers have prepared everything all too well. Yesterday I met Mrs. Wodtke together with Mrs. Gruber. She told me that the NSDAP block leader had informed the NSV that I was sheltering two unregistered people. She was asked to find out where you are registered and to which district office you belong. As you can see, they really fixed it so that you can't stay with me. I simply don't know how to deal with all this. Under the circumstances, returning is unthinkable. My heart is bleeding not knowing what will become of you now. Please let me know immediately what I can do for you. Should I speak with Uncle Otto about it? We must find a solution that will not leave you to your fate.

If you had had more trust in me earlier, it needn't have come to this. I don't mean to reproach you, but I keep wondering, what now? I have no answers despite the sleepless night. You are one of those dearest to me, Hannah; you can be sure that I will always and at any time be there for the two of you, to help you get through these difficult times. Always, always . . .

Either the letter ends here abruptly or the other pages cannot be found, written in that Sütterling handwriting, which hardly anybody can read anymore. Of course, faded ink. Did you notice how concerned he was as well that German trains run on time?

All these last trains also ran according to schedule, had conductors, regulated railway switches. And then came back empty.

—H. R.—
In Sorau/Niederlausitz a girl is hiding, a woman, a mother.

'The sanctity of our peace will come /
The brutal force will succumb'
1942 'The Good, forward it does stride /
And evil madness, dashed, must abide'
1943 'As long as humans roam the earth /
Of justice there shall be no dearth'
1944 'And thus news of victory we can send /
And bring the devil's war to a timely end'

H. R. used paper with black borders like that used for death notices. As German soldiers are freezing to death in the Siberian winter, she has a dream: 'It was like a Te Deum! I saw Hitler on the gallows in the British Museum. His head stuffed with straw, his eyes empty. But it was only a dream . . . Oh, if only it were real!'

Do you know about [the] survivor's syndrome? No? Let me tell you about it. It's not your everyday pathology. Example 1:

'(A sailor—because of a ship's accident)

One day he was freed from the common lot of human life. It happened all of a sudden with a slash of a knife; from that day on, he existed beyond the pale of humanity; he lost his reality; he became a false pretense. Are these words too strong? Why—isn't he destroyed? Please just take another look at him. There is an unusual perfection in his emptiness, which is especially complete. The accident activated it, turned the former sailor into something that is nothing. He went under. His decline is a masterpiece. It has been incredibly well organized and carried out with special intent. — Since he is alive, he is not totally eliminated. He is a cripple who gets about on an artificial leg and crutches. He can be used to form a rune, a Hebrew letter. Why did death spare him? Ask divine providence! What was its purpose in doing this? Was this man supposed to be a failed experiment, a blueprint for destruction? He is a remnant. This remnant has remnants; come here and get some. One leg is left to him. He can speak. Once he was human.'

Would you like to hear the school essays on this? Yes?

'Indescribable energy for life—a man of the people—uses sleights of hand—fake, deception, deceptive images—in order to deceive himself about it, that is, in order to *live*!! With emphasis. Above all, the spirit of life!!!'

Jean Améry also took his own life. Late. Later. Did you know that this syndrome is sometimes hereditary?

I breathe a sigh of relief at the border. I made it, got through. My heartbeat quickens as I hold my passport, forcing my hands to be still. My ears are still waiting for the command to stop, feel the dogs at my back, see the customs barrier already opening, come to a halt.

Of course, my papers are valid, and I don't carry any contraband.

But if they should demand that I get undressed—why should they demand that—if they should demand that I get undressed, and I would get undressed. And they would see the star through the clothes—it can't be seen—through the clothes branded into my flesh—it isn't branded on; I was never there—branded into my flesh, and the dogs would come.

In a complete stupor, I greet the non-German uniform as if it were a harbinger of freedom. Just in case, I am learning many languages and other things.

This happens to me every time I cross a border, even on a quick jaunt across the Rhine into Alsace.

A school bench breathes life into tin cans. Bored fingers etch lines, boxes, people, aphorisms, answers to problems, sharpen pencil stumps in holes especially made for this purpose, a hiding place for snatches of popular songs as well as pencil shavings. The scene is repeated under the table, enclosed in darkness, hardened chewing gum on greasy wax paper; stuffed under the table, the corners hide comics about courageous heroes, bought at newsstands—or a sneaker, a glove, a scarf, or a book for next week's class work.

Above the tables, there is a loud noise, and the two spheres above and under the tables hardly come into contact with each other. It could be that the hardened chewing gum is needed, is no longer there, and had a quarter stuck to it.

When the noise has subsided, somebody says aloud that the money is gone. In the sudden silence, the Ten Commandments fall on the heads of the students, to no avail, since all of them allegedly own hardened chewing gum to which pennies are stuck, collateral for obtaining soda and candy in the future.[3]

Since the beginning of school, a year and a half ago, Walter has had greasy hair and has worn shirts from the discount department store. His palate rolls when he speaks. What does the child of a railroad worker want with Latin? Sure . . . anybody can. But seriously. What good does it do him? It's doing the child no favor—and besides, he should first learn German. Walter Schölzing looks like the ghost of Elvis Presley while the Ten Commandments are getting a subscription for a chamber music concert. Schölzing, hardened soul, admit it! During break you were nowhere to be seen. Nobody claims to have been with you anywhere. And your hands too were gliding under the bench where the chewing gum had been stuck. The eyes directed toward you singe the back of your head; they look at the coarse boots mercilessly. We made it.

We're in a first-class train car when we go on vacation, in those days, still, to either the North or the Baltic Sea. This journey is a bit sticky. We'll wash up later.

And Plato, Caesar, Cicero, they are all lying under the table. A quarter is stuck to the inside of their cover; we don't need it now.

Some faces are strictly High German.[4] Unimaginable that such a High German face would have messed up a bib.

Manfred doesn't have a High German face; he has a simple German face from Runkel. That's a disadvantage.

When heating oil is being delivered to the school, and the thick black hose is laid down, it gets slashed. What does a German face from Runkel have to do with a slashed hose? Isn't that an open and shut case? Because it is an open and shut case, I get up and say that I was in the classroom the entire time. I say I saw Manfred's German face reading. My High German face turns red, but I remain firm even when confronted by the principal. Manfred's German face from Runkel was terribly clever, crafty, wasn't it?

After the final exams for high school graduation, I learn that Manfred really was the . . . I'm the only one who didn't know it. A High German face can be useful for all sorts of things. Manfred would have been expelled from school. But he wasn't—department chief at Buderus.

I am the only asset of a poor woman. Eleven years of marriage and financial support that, according to the salary guidelines for the promotion of government employees, can be claimed retroactively, stayed like dregs on the bottom of your coffee cup. My father's name becomes unpronounceable. Mr. F. too prefers the bureaucratic way. Thus no modern single parenting here—the disgrace of being employed. Adding to the disgrace is the inability to make a living. Or the other way around. Makes no difference.

Let me create a picture of this time for you—with candy. Imagine the arrival of a guest. The guest of that time brings a box of chocolates. As soon as he is gone, we open the present. Why not right away? Well, listen—don't you understand? I'll explain it to you: as a rule, we are at the opera by about eight o'clock in the evening, leaning nonchalantly over the railing and casually picking over some chocolates . . . Well, all right, so we open the present. For two, three days we take out one little piece after another until about half of its contents is eaten up. Then the box is carefully sealed and stored in an old refrigerator in the basement. After some time, the chocolate glazing discolors. The candy turns whitish.

We wrap the box according to postal regulations, fill out the enclosed warranty, and send the package to the manufacturer. Within a few days, we receive a new box and a few candy bars to boot, as consolation.

I might as well have taken the example of bananas or apples. What—you've already eaten an apple today? Then you have to leave the others. You know this very well. An egg—sunny side up? My dear, it was swimming in the soup at lunch today. A slice of some cold cut handed over the counter by the butcher . . . Furtive bending down for a lost handkerchief. It'll get washed at home. My eyes remained happy about the penny or dime that was lost in the asphalt. They continue walking down the street.

Back to the topic of discussion: After several years, she entered into a liaison—yes, that was the expression then—with Wolf; of course, he was not Jewish, and, of course, he was also married. But tall and athletic, a broad, good face. Compared to our circumstances, Wolf, whom I took to be a business owner, had a lot of money. For example, money for the children to go to the movies, five-pound boxes of candy—imagine all the stuff that one could store in the basement—for the mother. To this very day I never got one. At the time, we acquired an almost limitless acquaintance with Laurel and Hardy, who filled the Sunday morning movie program. Once, I went to the town where Wolf supposedly had a business. I saw a little store where he sold all kinds of housewares.

Again, I am the only asset: Do you know the concerti for cello and flute? Rhythm, style, morale, esprit, irrepressible charm—my God, there was so much to learn. Which student of this school, with a close connection to the spirit of Goethe, would have known his own father's income. The parents' contribution rose before me as an almost insurmountable obstacle toward attaining this exalted spirit. I am sent home with an envelope that bears my name. I return this envelope, empty but sealed, the same way. And, you know, I don't enjoy the class trip either.

An enlightened school. Under the keywords *modern philosophy* we learn about Communism.

We continue to be tolerated by the bourgeoisie. The thesis of collective guilt enforces caution in their dealings with us.

Her unlived life is supposed to live on in me. A famous intellectual woman, holding discussions with prominent representatives of politics and business. Of course, for such a life there is no particular profession, let alone a training course. This is the education of a Varnhagen and a Henriette Herz.

The mother's heart may have secretly been filled with doubt: four years later she walks into city hall with an attorney and notary. He wears black-rimmed glasses. His hands feel like the pages of his files, which fill up cabinets locked with roller doors. The notary doesn't eat noodles with tomatoes, nor tomatoes with noodles, and definitely does not need to make the sliced sausage last longer.

Unfortunately, the lawyer's household money remains in his private account. So she continues to collect her Jewish disability.

Before the wedding, she didn't dare let him move in. He disgusts her and us. Every jacket button represents a son who wasted twenty years living with his mother-in-law—another way of wasting one's life—and, of course, then there's being a notary.

Dismissed by the Latin teacher who recites Sappho's odes in her spare time, I come home from school. She is sitting at the kitchen table. It's the kind of table with a built-in washbowl. She is holding her head with her hands. I see her crying. I have never before seen her cry.

Four weeks later, she dies on the autobahn between Karlsruhe and Rüppur. At her graveside, much crying and screaming. My hair cut, I don't know by whom. And for a long time, I didn't cry anymore.

She came from Königsberg. Hair dyed black. An average forty-fifty-year-old face. She fights against the use of so many foreign words in a German that she pronounces with a coarse accent.

Standing in front of her class, she begins to talk one day. Even though she was a teacher, she had to wash stairs. That's the way it was because the Russians came. I am sitting far away in the back row near the door. My skirt is tight and gray, a crease in the middle. I don't like getting up because the skirt hugs my hips too closely. My mother had picked it out. The dark blue sweater too will last a long time. At the beginning of the school year, I was standing in front of four hundred students—playing in a chamber orchestra. Recess.

Ludwig Uhland. Believes in the transformation of all pain in the springtime. While Mörike's blue ribbons rustle in the lecture hall . . . 'We slaughtered a little pig today, according to ancient tradition; must be a Jewish, finicky fool to despise such tasty vittles.' I shouldn't write this into the albums of the newly admitted sixth graders, an early, later, middle Uhland? Yes—Agnes Miegel is our teacher's favorite. So, there she was kneeling in the living quarters of a Russian.

School benches are very useful for drawing circles. BDM, she was there too. She jumped through the solstice bonfire, my mother from the train. In a flight through unknown buildings. The soldier whom she had shaved ran after her. She sees him turn the corner hastily, hides pressed against the wall of the entrance to a house, rings the bell somewhere on the upper floor. The buzzer opens the door. She walks up the stairs.

A gentleman is there, elderly, friendly. With glowing red face and drenched in sweat, she asks for one night, only one.

He pushes her inside the room. Tells her to sit down, drink a glass of water. The vested, light brownish suit leads a thumb to a side pocket. Neatly ordered flowerpots are lined up in front of a window through which the SA patrol can be seen down in the street.

A faded light cascades through the gathered curtains into the room. The man sits down on the plush green furniture cover. He places a hand with an opal ring on his left knee, leans his face toward hers. With the back of his hand he gently lifts her chin. Her lowered eyelids smell his breath. Between the waist of his pants and the couch cover, his belly hides his genitalia. He keeps his legs spread while sitting. He speaks in a kind of bureaucratic German, quite nice, talks about the prices life demands. And surely not the first. She keeps her arms and legs pressed together. Her wrists tighten. The man gets up, walks broadly to the window. She could get washed in the bathroom. She gets up, passes the kitchen. The paint of the table legs is chipping. Leftover cabbage and potatoes remain in a bowl. She opens a door, a bathroom, a toilet. Mechanically, her hands turn the key. The windowsill is wide. It abuts a ledge that leads to the roof. Rust rubs into her hands, while her feet flee.

The woman in a pleated skirt stands in front of the clean blackboard and explains how to wash the stairs. The bell rings, signaling recess. An apple from the bag. I don't feel at all like eating. But one has to do something.

'Back then, between Strasbourg and Metz, it was all very different. The Germans had attacked the French from behind and set up the front. The things that can still be found in these fields today!'

Back through Alsace.

Here I encountered it for the first time. Everywhere these festivities in the mountains. At home, it was the Boy Scouts who started it. Kolping journeymen keep it going.

'I think it's funny; it's a lot of fun. We are jumping again through the bonfire. What's the big deal?'

When the Russians come, they [the women] put on white dresses. They meet them with flags and glowing faces, crawling out of the cellars of Berlin.

The ruffle of Senta's skirt makes it billow. Now they are grown up and beautiful. They love the liberators without looking closely. The stars have been torn from their coats. The girlfriends survived his headquarters; they no longer know how. Arms and legs, pale as the crumbled walls, the peels from the garbage can. And yet, they are as beautiful as the month of May, when the trees flower, their bodies, with which they now meet the Russians.

The German girls are pulling their scarves low over their foreheads. Not she and her girlfriend. They had 'Sarahs' in their papers—Hey Russian, do you want to see?

The Russian doesn't want to see anything. In front of him is the billowing ruffle. A wooden shed in the midst of the rubble is near the street. Soldiers have brutish hands. Red and yellow stars crisscross Senta's head. If she were to scream now, she would be heard by an SS or SA man or a home guard or a BDM with pinned-up braids. The girlfriend's hair lies in undone plaits on the floor. When the liberators are done, they drop the two off at their lodging.

As the devil would have it, one of them got stuck in the ruffle. He came back to her, meaning to be human and fatherly. And since God moves in mysterious ways, this thin pale girl wants it too. So instead of the Sarah, the Russians stamped a *Kunigunde* into her passport. Thus the kiss had the whiff of counterrevolution. And was forbidden to the Russian as fraternization with the enemy.

The man wrapped the ruffle around his neck and tied it to a frame. Together, they kicked over the chairs with their feet.

Outside, it was only September.

What do you want, Jew, soap or a warm room? The Jew says, I want warmth. The chimneys are smoking, and there is plenty of soap. — The blond, short-cropped hair bends over backward with laughter. He's had his job for six years; he was trained here, stayed here. Three times a week in the evening, he practices. Soccer. He's a little chubby already, drinks too much beer.

He wants to talk, especially about the night before. And how it all went downhill. Abruptly he stops, distrustful, when the son of the supervisor comes in. 'Here, take this—deadline at 3 P.M.' The doors falls shut. The matter of the night before ended early this morning. Puffy red eyes I can show you, my colleague. He picks up the paper; it's all written down. He can't even read it. He is exhaling the odor of cough drops on the supervisor's vest and turns slowly toward his typesetting machine. Some time ago, he went on educational leave. The boss was amazed. Then he came back and as always talked a lot. He thought it was all about soccer, but they also had social studies and stuff like that. The man impressed him very much, said something about Jews. Tell me, have I ever met one of them? What do they look like?

I am standing there, listening to him. What do these Jews look like? In the old days you had to show your ear for the passport and at the border crossing. You there, colleague, want to see my ear now? I finally say it.

He is all excited. He'll tell his teacher. He's actually met one, probably the only one in his class. Next time he cracks a joke, he stops abruptly. 'Sorry about that.' We'll have hamburgers for lunch. Can you eat that at all?

Maybe next time, I too could go on educational leave. Then they would have me, the real thing, close by, and they could touch me as a living piece of history.

'Nowadays we are more enlightened, you know . . . actually I don't know any . . . Jews, I mean. They are somehow, you know, they were even then in separate schools, sometimes in the yard, yes . . . pale . . . it's the foreignness, I really can't say exactly. Just no opportunity to get to know them.'

His wife had told me on the phone that he was already taking his second trip to Israel. He felt truly connected there—maybe that's not the right word. Oh—this Promised Land. In his day, the promised people were pale and suffering from consumption.

He claims to be deeply touched by this people and its fate, especially in Germany.

. . .

'The identity, could this identity—somehow get in the way of performance . . .' he didn't want to say exactly that, 'but you understand—a case where this identity might conflict with performance . . .' So, a genuine, racially healthy Jewish conflict at work—please, the man is doing his best—or not? One could have said no, right away . . . Somehow this Judaism is archaic—the Anti-Christ lives, doesn't live. Of course, the Sermon on the Mount. Nevertheless, Paul's writings doubtlessly open the possibility of working with Jews. God, how grateful I am to Paul.

His eyes smile impersonally behind the eyeglasses. It's certainly not his fault.

From time to time he looks up. An angel is mirrored in the tasteful tabletop, probably an archangel. Jesus lives in the annunciation.

'Would you like another cup of coffee? You know, these long meetings—actually much too much coffee. My wife has already adjusted herself to it, fewer calories—one isn't used to this at all anymore. Yes, in the old days, we were really grateful for every piece of bread. You know, the other day we were invited, my wife and I, it was a really sumptuous meal—more than sumptuous . . .' Before my eyes appear salmon fillets and coq au vin, vanilla ice cream with hot raspberry sauce, cream truffles . . . 'I said to my wife—you know, somehow it is macabre—in the old days, in town our main concern was bread, dry bread. My earliest memory of the train station back then. September 1945. A policeman takes this piece of bread from his pocket.

'Well now, back to you. Thank you for your effort. I was now able to form a personal picture. Please, don't misunderstand me.' 'Good bye.' 'Good bye.'

A fine rain falls softly on the paths in front of the big house. Educational institutions usually offer a fine rain in the evening—or Ping-Pong. Did you know that he was really well preserved—I mean for his age.

'What I must ask you confidentially, do you know any details about . . . a certain Jew—I mean, how shall I say, his conscience . . .'

What about the conscience of a Jew?

'Please understand me, I didn't mean to say that . . .'

What did he mean to say?

'What do you think?'

I am thinking Dreyfus and thank Emile Zola. The affair goes back a long time now, and yet it had caught up with me. What's so special about this story? Really? My friends don't understand it.

Weren't we all at some time, somewhere, thrown out. We are always being thrown out from somewhere, my friends and I, because we pick up stones. But this time—this time I don't have a stone in my hand. The stone around my neck the others can't throw.

‘I must make a confession. You don’t know me. I am meeting you, how shall I say, with a sense of uneasiness. You know, you look like Ruth Deretz. She was in the same class with me then. And somehow also a bit—well, attractive like you, a tall beautiful girl, you understand. She was then . . . I was born in 1921. Was with the Hitler Youth—by my own choice, I volunteered. Then I was on a U-boat off the coast of Africa and Spain. Don’t misunderstand me, I regret all of this today. I had to watch executions—some of my companions didn’t want to take part in that anymore . . . And I’ll tell you right away: Heddernheim, VDM, there was a satellite camp. Those who say today they didn’t know. That’s simply not true. Not the whole extent, of course not. But still—we did know. The other day we had a class reunion. I suggested we take a trip to Auschwitz. You should have seen how they jumped on me—I was really shaken. No, they still haven’t learned anything. Well, I can’t even begin to tell you enough.

I know, you really came only to apply for admission. Yes, we’ll get to the point momentarily. Please excuse me. Could you repeat your name, I mean, spell it. Your address please, ah yes, ah up there, oh I have it already, naturally. Your age is missing: thirty. Really, wouldn’t have guessed. Now, I’ll read the whole thing to you once more to make sure that everything is correct. Spelling mistakes? I don’t understand that.

The first rays of the sun blink through the dusty office window and catch a corner of my application. I, Ruth Deretz—I am hungry.

The landlord is a Sudeten German. Sudeten German—one can say that, no? Of course, you are allowed to say that. The landlord from the Sudetenland now owns two houses—through the work of his hands—and a government subsidy, as I later hear. In our house, nobody works with his hands, because my mother's hands are trembling. They tremble completely senselessly. There's no reason why they shouldn't stop trembling already. But they tremble. For this trembling she gets reparation. In her defense, she can say that she has no vocation, no school diploma, no parents, no brothers and sisters—her life and this trembling.

When she applies for a rent subsidy, this trembling is again deducted from the compensation. Even though she went early in the morning so that she would have the trembling still under control.

What if the landlord should find out that he has leased an apartment to us. Hard to know.

Above us lives an elderly man, supposedly a clergyman, and his wife was very angry when the children were making music with their flutes in the afternoon. Jews always want to become something better. Violinists, pianists, all that is no accident.

How shall I explain this flute? I had no special Christmas wish. What's a tree of lights like that doing at the home of a yid anyway?

When Hannah comes to the city from the village, is divorced from her husband, the goy, she again has the courage to wear the Magen David, not on top of her underclothes, of course not. But still.

I see the lighted trees of the people in the street and of the other girls in school. If I had at least a decorated bouquet at home, what shall I say? That my mother doesn't love me? Christmas is at least a custom. At Hannah's, there is a second one, that is, Hanukkah—but that is in the Jewish community. So Hannah asks her daughter what she would like for Christmas. And now back to matter of the flute.

Hannah's daughter says, nothing. And again nothing the following year, and also nothing for her birthday, only a beautiful flute of her own, a silver shimmering concert flute. Two years before, she had answered this question with nothing, and nothing again the following year. She wanted Hannah to make up with her divorced husband, her father. Hannah remained silent. That was two years ago, and now the daughter wishes for a flute. The heavy flute of ebony wood was the first instrument she was allowed to learn on, borrowed from the music school. She was the big exception, says Hannah, the only one who had no sense for music, who heard nothing and couldn't sing any songs. That's why Hannah's daughter wants this flute.

And since Hannah doesn't remarry her father, Hannah's daughter plays the flute.

And plays until her bent arms are exhausted.

Mrs. Rau stops and waits on the landing as our door opens. After all, she said, her husband and she belonged to the Confessing Church. I look at her. Bitterness has disfigured her mouth. It's attached to her neck. Sensible shoes, woolen suit, gray tinge like her hair. I didn't understand that, this business with the flute and the church.

Our next-door neighbors, I know nothing about them. And since I don't know anything, I bring in our laundry at night. I suspect that they are our landlord's countrymen. I am sure they too will one day be just as hardworking.

'We are from Wullachen in the Bohemian Forest. You know, all Germans were expelled, as it were. We were told that we had to be in Gilowitz the next day at ten. With a hundred pounds of luggage. Not much. There we were put in a collection camp and then taken to Hohenfurt, the Kaplitz train station, and loaded onto cattle cars.'

My ears repeat it: Hannah loaded onto a cattle car.

'I was twelve years old then, I should add. At that age, it was even a bit adventurous.'

She was six years old.

'Until we were confronted with raw reality and had to stand in line for food in the camp.'

. . .

'The only thing I haven't forgotten. It was a beautiful day in May. We had a big dog at home, and he ran after us.'

Her sister ran after her . . . and stumbled in the process.

'. . . when we had to get on that truck.'

. . .

'We had to leave everything behind. In Butzbach we were split up and assigned to different families. There were people there who took in refugees.'

Where were the people then who took in refugees? In England? Germany? Where?

'We were incredibly well received . . . in 1956–57 the church community gave us this piece of land. It was all accomplished through hard labor—yes—there was also a government subsidy.'

Restitution, isn't it?

'After all, most of us had farms back home, large farms. The subsidy was calculated accordingly.'

Tremendous pain, numbers etched into the arms, according to which the sum was calculated.

'Somehow I settled in very well.'

Have I settled in?

'It's possible to tell the children about the homeland. But the connection, that's missing.'

She said nothing, said almost nothing. Oh—I wish I were missing the connection!

'Somehow it's all in the past.'

Somehow, that's true; it's all in the past.

To ask the loaded question . . . yes, a combination of acne and a skirt that's too short. Luckily, the acne goes away later on. When things need to be taken care of, shopping is to be done, other things to be taken away, calls to be made, a child to be raised. Imagine this unanswered loaded question, a growing girl whose hair falls in black braids over her shoulder. When she passes a construction site, a young worker whistles at her—he seems stuck in the ground up to his hips. His eyes pierce her knees. Saint Bernadette—passes by. When an angel blushes. She doesn't have fair skin. Blood doesn't fill her cheeks.

World or non-world—a god who abandoned us. Why did that goddamn God permit this to happen? Who broke the laws so that you punish us so? Is God the Angel of Death from the land of Mitzrayim? Does it mean you exist since you abandoned us? If we have to do penance, then it would be best to do it the Catholic way—or would it? To be allowed to be a victim, the fascination of renunciation. If the eternal life is the better one, why not right away . . . A little bit of death perhaps? Bernadette began to love the masculine death that was unknown to her, to the fatherless child. Anyway, without a doubt, it is a masculine type. Otherwise, men would die female deaths.

In any case, Bernadette caressed her unknown death. In her family, dying was not done. Not anymore. That was long before she was born. The dead just don't die. She takes death's pulse, runs her fingers over knife blades.

An apron with a colorful pattern. —Wearing an apron later went out of style. Somehow this must have had something to do with washing machines. —She knotted the ties of the apron together, wound them around the top post of a bunk bed—into the drama of the situation I must interject: public housing project. The post is not high enough. Her feet graze the floor. Her neck bears the marks of the ties for a while. From a psychiatric standpoint: a completely normal suicide attempt.

Can't an empty heart find consolation in God, the Father, the Son, and the Holy Ghost? Certainly, says Reverend Becker, even if not immediately. In about four or five years at the latest. But how is that with the Holy Ghost? The spirit remains incomprehensible to her, and Jesus wants her to be only human anyway. And yet, the Reverend Becker wants her to take the oath even if the soul should hold back. Do you know the picture of the pious Helen by Wilhelm Busch, the last scene when the spirit vanishes?

The host tastes like paper. She never took communion again. For the second time she failed to escape the Jew in her.

There's one thing I've still forgotten. One day it was there. Fat and bold, traced in ink, etched with the tip of a pencil.

The bell rings. I sit down at my school desk. There it is in front of me; it stutters at me the whole long hour. We are having math class, maybe the fractions and then divided by life. All day long, I think, we are in math class, and I'm staring at the desk.

Finally, past this nude Bauhaus statue, along the fence, on the left, the ruins of a church. Ringing the doorbell, the buzzer sounds, up the stairs, school bag into the corner. 'Well, how was it?' – 'Well, okay.' I hide my face behind my farina—my old face doesn't fit behind farina—in which the raspberry syrup dissolves into paths. I do my homework when Hannah sleeps. I chew on my pencil, look through the curtain. In the house across from us lives Annette, who sits next to me. What did I do to her? Did I do something to her? Her mother is leaning out of the window, yells something down into the yard.

When Hannah gets up, I have to tell her. Is it my fault? 'What's the matter with your seat?' When I finish the story, Hannah goes into the kitchen to the cabinet with the medicine. Then she picks up the telephone. She talks for a long time into the mouthpiece '. . . if necessary, take her out of school . . . won't put up with it, won't take it . . . enough . . .'

The next morning after the bell, the math teacher leads me into an empty classroom. For the other students, the class is on hold for the time being. I am the worst in his subject, I know. No, I should tell him.

Why didn't I come to him right away? I should have done that. When the hour is up, I go back to class. Whispers, what did she have to discuss out there . . . My neighbor turns her back on me. In the end, the teacher changed her seat, the daughter of the Inferior Court judge . . . I am sure she didn't think anything of it. When you're bored, you draw a lot of things on school desks.

Did you know there is a laundry service in Dublin called the Swastika Laundry—they drive through the streets with their logo on the vans—no kidding. Not that I want to defend her . . . the child after all thought nothing of it. And in the end, the parents too . . . Yes, that's it, in the end the parents too.

Today I want to talk with you about labor unions. 'Collective labor union': as I read the other day, this concept is very vague. I can only confirm this much. The term derives from all the suffering in history. In their ritual litanies—for other people, these are cleansings—Christians, Communists, Social Democrats all line up one grave next to the other.

Jews, what do they have to do with it. First of all, their graves are elsewhere, and second, it's not a concept of struggle. Here, after all, it's a matter of the workers' movement.

And as far as Jewish workers are concerned, they too will be remembered under the rubrics of Communists and Socialists. Christian is probably excluded here. As is well known, the collective union draws lessons—from the victims—the Christians, Communists, and Socialists. We are not liable for other victims. In the end, even the gypsies might get after us. No, we want to keep to the truth. For that I take personal responsibility as district chairman.

Only this one fellow up front, typical journalist, makes a motion to include the Jews. Is it possible to take a vote on that? The Jews are voted in as victims. I am against it. All in favor raise your hands?

Only a few raise their hands; even fewer leave the hall. So, as far as I can see, the Jews have been voted down in this motion.

People jump from their chairs and applaud.

All the way up front are the old and the new communists. 'I'm in a mood to smack the guy who made this motion.' The factory foreman rolls his bald head toward him. 'Not with me,' hollers the proletarian fist.

This vague concept of community unleashed a real storm in this battle-tested hall—at least this time.

I happen to come across an essay by the Korean philosopher and writer Ham Sok Han: 'The history of the Jews and the Koreans seems to me to have certain similarities. Both are regarded as enigmas of world history.' When confronted with enigmas, humankind reacts emotionally, sees the enigmatic as threatening. 'Like the Jews, the Koreans live a drama of suffering.' Like the Germans, the Germans would prefer to say, in a divided country. And now they too are even using the Jews . . .

'Always threatened by their environment and impoverished, they survived a history of suffering for six to seven thousand years.' Did they really survive? Am I surviving the not-I [*nicht-ich*]? 'Threatened but not defeated, rather determined . . . Unlike the Jews, the Koreans have hardly had any political power or wealth. All they have is people . . .' Oh, would that I had more people! We are searching the ashcans of history for our culture; we are caricatures of ourselves; we are standing knock-kneed between Judaism and Israel. And yet, it's hard to believe, a philosophy that speaks positively about these Jews. Dementia not excluded either. And yet imagine: Minjung, a culture of resistance. One shouldn't forget, this damn Han. Han too belongs to Minjung. Han is suffering—suffering from life, a real, conscious kind of suffering. I am sick and tired of carrying suffering incarnate in my face.

I'll sing you a song. A different one? I don't know any other:

'Miriam, be strong,
A rebbe enters through the door,
Miriam, come today for the first kaddish.
Kaddish for what, my God.
Miriam your husband is dead.
She doesn't cry, she doesn't scream,
too great is her pain.
She just presses her child,
his child, against her heart and says:
My child, go pray
for your Taten,

A bullet hit him,
A soldier.
Kneel with me.
For he'll never return.
And great is our Adonai.
And great is our Adonai.'

Just imagine, this was my lullaby. A voice like Zarah Leander.

Oh yes—Ham Sok Han, he is reputed to be the 'Korean Gandhi.' Our people too sang to the very end.

'Churchill—of course, Churchill.' The soldier sitting across from me has a young bearded face. His knee-high motorcycle boots are in the wall. He twirls the tip of his goatee with his left hand, undoes it again, smoothes the reddish ends.

'Can I be of help?' While he continues to cut the little cubes, he talks about who had started the war, the second. That stuff with all that money, restitution going to Israel, he thinks is nonsense. 'There has to be an end sometime. What do I have to do with this. Absolutely nothing.' The little pieces are spilling over the edge of the wooden cutting board. 'And what are they doing with the money, Lebanon and the like—easy to see, no—I don't see that. Think about what could be done around here with that kind of money.'

The woman at the stove thinks: Don't revive dead Jews. Nobody wants that either. Sinti who are alive and forced laborers . . . nobody wants that either.

'All that unemployment and the like,' says the soldier. The woman thinks of her sister's oldest son. If morality were to be had free or at least at reduced prices . . . 'That stuff with the tanks, that too is nonsense. If we don't sell them to the Saudis then others will; it's business.' The woman remembers the child's voice on a radio program Thursday evening—topic: Iran, a martyr's letter, written and read by this child's voice.

'Collective responsibility—what does that mean, collective responsibility for the creation of Israel, I reject that notion—I really reject that.'

The soldier sits up, straightening his back. 'Nobody else wanted to take them either.' 'Who's "them"?' —'Well, the Jews of course.' The woman ponders whether the soldier is able to pronounce the word fluently. Or was there a slight hesitation, a lowering of the voice as with foreign words that first have to be practiced. Is there something impure or unfamiliar in the word that, after having been pronounced inadvertently, might fall on the speaker vengefully? 'People in concentration camps, that's clear, was an injustice and so on. But now, there has to be an end.'

'Was an injustice and so on.' Was an injustice and so on. Was an injustice and so on. Is injustice and so on. Injustice can be avenged. Then the avenger is right. The dead are lousy avengers. Others besides the avengers can meet injustice with justice. It is also possible to meet injustice with injustice. A double negative makes a positive, said my German teacher.

'Gypsies—well, all right, Sinti, they're called, I guess, so they too and the forced laborers—that's going too far, there's no end to it. It wasn't much fun either being a Russian prisoner of war. And the others, what did they do. Napoleon—and the Russians and so on.' 'And so on?' 'Yes, Churchill, what business did he have getting mixed up in it. There was Austria, Czechoslovakia, and Poland, and that would have been the end. And Roosevelt too refused it—the peace offer on the western front. The Russians, the things that were going on there, wherever they went . . . Germans didn't do things like that. Plunder and rape was condemned. But among them . . .' 'But among them,' the woman thinks. Yes—under the Germans it was different. Every last railway car was registered, checked off—and declared ready to go again. Maybe today they would have gotten rid of the smoking chimneys.

The woman sits down across from the soldier. Her hands rest on the table, on the other end of which he has piled up the cheese cubes.

'The *Amis* near Hammelburg, do you know that, a column of women, communications assistants, all unarmed, they mowed them down—just like that . . .'

In the camp, they were all just like that, weren't they. Just like that, as a Jew. Imagine, I would tell you that in the camp you were just like that, just like that, as a man. That, you could get through your skull, soldier. But just like that as a Jew, Shylock or Nathan understands that, but you?! 'Once the documents are made accessible . . .' What if the documents are made accessible? Then we will find out that they all have their corpses in their cellars? How comforting.

Just you, German, you no longer have a cellar. Simply too full. And the material from the camp smells sweet and heavy.[5]

'My grandmother only began to believe in 1978 that that is how it was for the Jews. I went to Dachau with her. You could see everything. The hair, the fingernails, the gas chamber. I know a fellow who to this day has a sack of soap in his basement. Asked if I wanted some.'

'And—did you want some?'

'What am I supposed to do with it? Why don't you leave me alone. I've no use for it. Can't do anything with it after all.'

'Simply doesn't go for anything. Those SS caps, they bring something. They are being traded now for three hundred German marks. Or the round insignia, original, those are good for five hundred German marks. And all that stuff that's still to be found in Leningrad: flags, Reich eagles, everything taken away, or Göring's art treasures, who knows who ripped those off.'

The soldier's cheekbones are covered with fine soft hair. His fingers are stroking his goatee. He looks toward one end of the table—past the woman who is sitting there—while he untwirls the ends. The woman wants to see his eyes. 'Why don't you want any soap?'

'What do you want with me, for god's sake.'

The soldier is in the service of a democratic institution, he says. A tank in the back is better than one in front of the chest. He is a trainer, is not interested in politics. He was no slave driver. Why not let these things be.

'Oh, yes—soap, I find that disgusting; a piece is made maybe of two dead bodies. No, what should I do with it.'

'Lamp shades too?'

'So—I didn't even know that. They really made use of everything.'

'To Dachau?'

'I went to Dachau alone. Just interested. Bergen-Belsen too. Well, yes—Shoah. Saw that. It's all right, suffering and all. But it doesn't concern me. I wasn't part of it. I don't think it could happen again. After all, the citizens are enlightened. I knew a few guys who were in a paramilitary group Hoffmann—with live ammunition and the like. But it would never have gotten that far had they not been outlawed.

'To my mind, this is nonsense. Is this now a democracy or not. They wouldn't have stood a chance anyway.'

'Outlawing what?'

'Offering soap for sale?'

'Why that? There's nothing in it. They could make better use of the time, drug dealers, for example.'

'How popular do you think medals are again today? How many people would have to be prosecuted. Nope, I'm against that.'

'What do you want—what do you mean: twenty Jewish children at the Bullenhuser Dam, right before the end of the war—SS doctor went unpunished? Do you know at all whether he knew anything about the end of the war—my uncle was hidden in the manure ditch, a whole week. And do you know what his orders were?'

The woman wants to consider whether the order was right. She says this in a colorless tone, with cool fingers.

'I go there in the morning and home in the evening. Of course, I try to do well. Especially in war command and the like.' 'Chemical warfare?' 'That leads to nothing. We really learned that lesson from Vietnam. Yes . . . and atomic blitzkrieg . . . I tell my people, put your radiation suit on, bury the food supply.' And then? 'Why—and then? After all, the combat mission continues.'

'Meta, Meta,' calls the child, who is supposed to be staying with some people. 'It won't be long, and you'll see, I'll bring you something nice.' The boy wipes his cheeks and swallows with big eyes and black curved eyelashes. He's becoming as beautiful as his father, Meta thinks as she jumps down. She is riding in a taxi. She is not accustomed to this, but this big strange town . . . She rummages through her pocket for a piece of paper: Richmond Street, in German gothic lettering. Who can still read that.

That's it. Paying clumsily—by the way, on such occasions paying is always done clumsily—getting out, she comes closer. (Don't ask whether this exists—it does exist.) A front garden, like many others. On the gate in big legible letters: Freundlich. A Freundlich, which—you know where—doesn't exist anymore. The man who opens the door is her grandfather and gives her innumerable kisses. And asks whether she left him at home. 'You know,' says the grandfather, 'this is a white neighborhood. I can't afford that.'

She had left him at home—you know that already—his brown color cleaves to her hand.

She says nothing and thinks of the lollipops her grandfather gave her as a child, as if nothing else had ever been in his pocket.

'. . . this is a white neighborhood . . .' People from the South. But here, the Freundlich with the German Bert in front of it. Can he be a normal racist? Again this creeping normalcy.

A picture of Hannah is in the armoire. Come get me, Meta, says the boy behind this photo. She turns and leaves. The grandfather wants to give her a hug. She doesn't permit it. Rushes through the streets, looking for house numbers.

Or she permits it. Doesn't rush, goes very slowly—if at all. Grandfather is grandfather, a man with quite normal faults . . . Perhaps time will heal him or other such stupid words will soften his horror that she chose a colored. And stays seated with tea and homemade cookies.

When he pulled out a dollar note from his wallet, as he had been doing all those years, to hand it to me secretly behind the back of his new wife, he was so excited he grabbed the wrong piece of paper. At home I noticed between the banknotes, folded together, he had given me his last will. The note read that he wanted to be buried with Röschen.

I was burrowing underground in Berlin
lived like a rat
from people's refuse
who were sitting around the table
startled by the ringing of the bells
we held our Jewish ears

When the summoning call faded
milk and bread flowed from the stairs
that once creaked under us
My face hungered for the sun
The draft between the floorboards
told me about the August heat
so it seemed to me after three-times June in March
Lying crumbled up on our beds
dressed in suits and yellow knit vests
and were ready for conversations with books
Stomping, harsh steps
were running over our heads and hands
we were hiding
behind His eyelids

One day we stole up the stairs
my racing heart
in the last years
had been beating ever louder
chased after me to other countries
until I returned home to my cellar
resolved.

Again and again he visited Berlin.

'If Hitler had won the war, we would have been treated like the Jews. You can read up on all this in his *Mein Kampf*.'

Then you did know? Have I met somebody who knew?

'Not the details. That I can only say in retrospect. Honestly, I must say, actually I didn't know anything about the numbers of transports of Jews here in Bockenheim.'

How did you find out about the persecution of Jews in Bockenheim?

'Actually for me—you know, the thing about the Jews' star and similar things—I only know about my hometown, what my sister once wrote to me, that the Jews had been loaded onto a furniture truck. They drove through the streets and picked them up, that the Jews, who had a rather good relationship with their neighbors, weren't all that frightened yet, they . . . said goodbye . . . that they were led to believe. As a junior priest I didn't really know any Jews here in the community. Sure, we had a synagogue down here. I was asked once before whether I had been aware of this—the synagogue, that it was set on fire. I can't say whether I noticed this or not. It is on the other side of town, but if somebody had pointed it out to me, then I would probably have noticed it. Well I must, to be completely honest, I must say, the fact that this happened to the Jews, I just wasn't aware of this during the war.'

But it must have been quite noticeable that they were deported. After all, they didn't come back.

'That's what I am saying. I hardly knew any Jews around here, and the wealthy Jews, they weren't around any longer. After all, they left in good time. Apparently this was all done secretly, under cover of night, so that we, if I'm speaking now only for myself, didn't notice much at the time.'

There was no one in your community who lived next door to a Jew—where the furniture was tossed into the street—or who said, he won't be coming back, who may have had a problem with all this from a religious standpoint?

'Now that's fifty years ago—so all I know is that we had a Negro here. That was a Catholic family. They were under a lot of pressure. And we did help them, supported them. And under cover of night that Negro was badly beaten, and the family—whether they are still alive, I don't know—was kicked out of their apartment . . . This Jewish star and so on—those were, of course, pitiful people. We have, we were helpless; we couldn't do anything—and a few Jews did get support. I can't tell you offhand whether somebody here in Bockenheim hid a Jew. Here and there it did happen, people like Anne Frank who for years . . . or Hans Rosenthal who lived in a garden shed—I believe—it's not as if—yes, the quiz show host on television—and as much as I can remember, we didn't notice it that much since here in the community—I must say quite honestly—we hardly knew any Jews. At any rate, one thing is certain: we didn't know to what extent and to what degree—we didn't know that then. The whole thing became clear to us only when the concentration camps were discovered. We were more conscious then of the burning of those left behind in Hadamar, against which the Bishop of Limburg launched a protest, and Count von Galen as well. Now and then we would receive an urn with the remains of one of the sick people, as they were called; relatives received an urn with someone's ashes. I was actually present once in Praunheim, I believe, or maybe even twice: 'Your relative died on such and such a date in Hadamar, or some other place, of pneumonia. We are sending you herewith his mortal remains.' Then, as spiritual leaders, we were present at the burial of the urn. Neither did I know anybody of this kind; I was here in this community until 1939, from 1929 to 1939. I don't know anybody personally who would have been picked up here as mentally disturbed or not normal. Not in Praunheim either, those were mostly people who, people who were already institutionalized and sent then from those institutions to Hadamar. Afterward—I believe—the bishop's protest did have results. That was with tremendous evil cleverness, that the public was kept as ignorant as possible. This isn't just a lie. If we say today that we didn't know anything. Although we knew that Jews were taken away, the extent, the extent of what happened in each case, about that I can say with certainty that I didn't know.'

Where did people think they were being taken when they were deported?

'Well, now you are really asking me too much—about that, I can't say anymore. It's more than fifty years ago. We were completely helpless, you know. We stood helplessly by. We didn't stand by, didn't watch either, rather we had to bear it helplessly. It was the kind of a system that had a grip on everything down to the lowest level. All it took was one word spoke out loud against the system, and it would have cost a person's freedom—under certain circumstances, his life. I believe that the Nazi hold was much more severe, much more powerful, than today's Bolshevism or Communism. Even better organized through and through.

'How this was possible, puzzles me to this day. How can a people let itself be tyrannized like that and be led into a dictatorship. The German people was also seized with hysteria then. It was simply a national hysteria. Such things have always happened; from time to time they break out in history. The whole history of the crusades was a form of hysteria. The French Revolution too was to some degree hysteria.

'I don't know if this is a particularly German characteristic, this disposition toward hysteria. After all, we have been the cause of all kinds of things in the course of world history—whether this is essentially different from other peoples, I don't think so, but with us, it's especially noticeable since we find ourselves right in the middle of it.'

1986

The parsonage is equipped with built-in double windows dating from 1923. This is where he lives, right next to his church, and where he ministers, now mostly to Spaniards. The faith of all the others has largely eroded; Saturday, Sunday they're on the soccer field, he says. He tirelessly performs his rounds, and there might be none to succeed him. Jasmine bushes sway in the summer breeze around him. The care of birds is part of the budget. Yes, in the old days they cleared the rubble from the church by hand.

The bell rings. There is a woman, ugly Madonna-like hair, around the mouth an expression like that of the wife of the pastor from a Sudeten German home. Well-manicured hands hold a handbag. Her sweater is white and expensive. The mother of two grown sons has come for confession as I am leaving.

The times have become godless and democratic, people unhealthily obese. Reverend Kondermann has had the same housekeeper for twenty years and has remained agile even though annoyed at the moment: he still wanted to edit the interview. I took it with me on the tape recorder and certainly won't write him anymore.

Teenage girls practice dancing in front of mirrors to the soul rhythms on the radio. When she was fifteen, she was allowed to go on her first date. 'Before then it was not allowed. That was because of my mother. And then, of all things, with an American. First of all, we were brought up with the notion that a girl shouldn't have to spend anything when she goes on a date. So I never had any pocket money. Especially with Americans who as soldiers made money, who took us on dates to clubs and paid for the cover charge, the drinks, and the meal. That made us really proud. I was in Darmstadt, and at that time there were the Red Scarves—well, I don't remember it that clearly. I know later in Frankfurt there were not only soldiers' clubs but also discotheques; most of the guests were Americans—for example, the Storyville, and I know that the Mexicana burnt down. There were a lot of them. Dancing was really nice. I had a passion for dancing. Yes, this was actually what made us go again and again . . . and added to that, the foreign atmosphere that, of course, always attracted us. My girlfriend always went to the clubs, and so I went along. And she said too: She would never consider a German, only blacks. Later, I also married a black man.

What I always admired a bit about Americans was their carefree attitude. They didn't give a damn whether somebody ate a roast chicken with his fingers or held the knife and fork the wrong way. They absolutely didn't care, and it tasted good and felt good.

They dressed differently. The black man always, or almost always, takes care of how he looks. It's always a bit crass, a bit too bright, but the latest fashion.

It was primarily due to my mother that we met this young man at all—that is, at the German-American carnival. On the other hand, she felt somewhat embarrassed about the neighbors. How could she permit this, what kind of home is this, the daughter runs around like a slut with a black guy.

This was something, my mother . . . that was something that pained my mother, this pigeonholing and degradation because one was dating a soldier.

My mother, after all, was a victim of the Nazis, and the Americans came back then, at the end of the war, so to speak, as saviors, and my mother also worked for the Americans later, after the war, and somehow they were the liberators. And from this point of view, she had nothing against it.'

A thirty-six-year-old woman is standing in the bathroom mirror. A housedress tied in the back, big red roses printed on a black background. Darkness still pushes at the windows. She brushes her hair in front of the massive postwar furniture. A child is buried under a feather-light white comforter in the heavy twin beds. From behind the child's closed eyelashes, the pliable wall balloons. The light of an elongated metal lamp radiates from the edge of the bathroom mirror. Slightly open eyes cast a shadow on the lashes. The light breaks through the lashes—deflected by the woman who is brushing her hair. Thus the child lies bathed in her glow.

When the woman in the room puts away the brush and gets ready to leave, the child's eyelids open hastily. In a moment the woman will lean over the child and give her a kiss. She'll tell the child to get up. She'll be making breakfast. She always makes breakfast for him, the only one whose place setting has a soft-boiled egg, which he eats hastily after complaining that the woman didn't shell it properly. This is how long the child had sat behind a mug of milk. When the door of the apartment shuts, the child gives a sigh of relief and asks the woman for the rest of the roll.

The day passed, while the child lay in the crevices of the carpet, ran fingernails over it, and dreamed that the mother would read to her. Some days she would read 'The Red Mittens,' written in English. The child imagined its meaning. The reader intoned with suspense and compassion—with great love for the language.

At her feet too an American soldier, surely he was an officer, had once placed his love. In the end, she rejected him. Wanted to stay in Germany, married a student who spent his days singing Viennese songs—also not drafted. Now she reads from 'The Red Mittens.' For the bedroom, they chose German oak. Yeah, yeah—a cliché, true enough but nevertheless, lasts to this day, at least in an attic.

Down the hallway, creaking with linoleum, through a swinging door, then second room to the right. Knocking. Louder.

'Come in.' She is a character from an Andersen fairy tale. White hair pinned up in a knot, over her shoulders a large shawl with fringes to the floor. Lulu has a magnifying glass in front of her, on a huge pile of newspapers. A cabinet with jammed doors, a mirror above the dresser. On the cabinet are two round tin cans.

'Get up on the chair, my child, and get down the one on the left.' It bears the picture of a carousel and children on a seesaw. Balloons soar above their heads. 'Now, why don't you open it.' A warm aroma emanates from the spiced biscuits. They were baked, a perfect match for this tin. 'No, don't be shy, take two. Then, be good enough to put the tin back on the cabinet.' On tiptoe, given a push with the fingers, the tin is back next to that other tin, about whose contents I know nothing. On it is the picture of a woman in a long gown and loose flowing hair. Her gaze is directed into the distance; next to her is a small naked child.

Aunt Lulu's bed comes from the hospital. She has covered the comforter with blankets. On the table is a glass sphere. To look into it is to look at heaven and hell. Aunt Lulu, don't you want to be my grandmother? Or at least an aunt as real as an aunt can be? Why don't you look at my thumb under the magnifying glass; it's furrowed and huge. I wonder if it can cry too?

A glass of milk in the kitchen. During the night she looked into the living room through the crack in the door. He was on top of Hannah and was slapping her. Her dress with the washed-out dots was torn at the top.

She crawled back into her bed. Slivers on the tiles.

The man's strength blocks the door to the apartment. Hannah reaches for the kitchen table and picks up the bread knife, brandishing it. She will go through the door, and she does. Hannah's daughter is left behind with the man. She wants to run down the stairs after her. 'Stay.'

He had often beat her, pillow over the head, a cane from the closet, the cord from the electric razor. Hannah later applied cool compresses.

She presses against the wall, keeps the apartment door in view. The man goes to the telephone.

'Making an effort . . . cracked up . . . yes? No, no problem.' Puts the receiver back.

The police didn't believe Hannah's story. Her steps on the stairs. Hannah's daughter rushes toward her. They move to a different town. It didn't matter which one. But it was this one.

Hannah and her daughter are newcomers, as the saying goes. This is how it was for seven years, until she died.

The daughter draws circles in the dust on a shiny table. She is surrounded by Hannah's furniture. Witnesses of other voices. Hideous trees outside the window turn dark. She flicks on the radio and turns off the volume. This is the quantum of light her head can bear.

Finally, God, why, oh why, did you kill her? And with her, you flung my guilt onto this autobahn. What am I to do here. We never know what to do when left alone.

She knitted a long cardigan for her mother, white with a braided pattern. For her sister, a yellow one. On a November day—nobody can imagine that it could have been a day in April—they threw a piano from the fifth floor onto the street. The piano did not wear a star, and it smashed to pieces on the asphalt. Hannah wore it on her coat, removable, so she had figured it out. But removing it still won't get you any coupons. Young and beautiful, why not beautiful, beautiful in spite of everything, she rushes along the walls of the houses. A 'Heil' resounds in her ears, extended lower arm. There she is with her nylons and long black hair. The mouth with the cherry red lipstick now has to mumble the word. Her heart is throbbing in her throat. And the heel of the boot moves on. She takes the streetcar, uses the platform—again two. They look at her so strangely. If she only had been wearing a headscarf! The missing star begins to shine. When this old Berlin streetcar slows its pace, Hannah jumps off, walks on, farther and farther away, and walks farther.

At some point, her daughter lies down in this big double bed, doesn't want to see colors, eats something or other with no taste, then goes to the bus stop from where the school bus will transport her just like the others. She doesn't learn French. For Hannah never learned it either, this language of the enemy at Verdun. Her father had an Iron Cross First Class.

Not German Jews, they said, no, Jewish-German, with the accent on the last word.

One day she has a visitor at her table. The man has a beat-up face, a little flower in his hand. He comes from Munich, out of prison, off the street. He was a student of buildings and other structures—a writer and Dadaist—he was from her other world, and he had kissed her. With this first heavy kiss in old cars and a kitschy, expansive, white star-studded sky. Now he is standing here and comes from a totally different place. He had protested loudly on boulevards against the newspapers of the now-dead Tsar, and he was beaten for it. Hannah's daughter says nothing about the still fresh blood. A white fog penetrates her dark hair until she too is caught in it. She thinks of her prison of trees, leaves, and sunshine. His tongue burns with questions that society takes seriously. Hannah's daughter is not society; she is only one, 1—as in the final analysis all Jews are only one. The writer forgets for a moment the burning of his tongue and leads her into a wet murky meadow. Delights in her eyes, her hair. Hannah's daughter is wearing thin shoes, and she is cold to his touch.

He returns to his streets with a daily agenda and debates—writes long letters to the end of her world. Hannah's daughter looks at these things and puts them aside at night by the glow of the radio light.

Only later, much later, does she run down the same noisy streets. Is terribly startled when Krahl and his friends sing the Internationale late at night under her window. This is not allowed, Hannah had mumbled to herself some time ago. In general, it would be better not to talk about this. As for herself, she goes several times to the polling place so that her name in the file has a government-recognized check mark. Heuss seemed to her to have integrity. SPD, absolutely not. They have Günther Metzger, the proletarians, as well as her now-divorced husband. He wouldn't give up his socialism. In 1931 they had voluntarily hung the national-socialist flag in their homes. And after the war, Oh! everyone had been a doctor. And everyone's wife had been persecuted.

When the wife was gone and divorced, a rumor made the rounds of the small-town magistracy. The husband disentangled himself now from her impetuous embrace and went, as the saying goes, socialist.

But Heuss too was dead now. So she goes to make an appearance. Determined, she approaches the ballot box to drop in her decision.

That it isn't valid, only she knows, and thank God not those assistants, who by virtue of their honorable résumés—whatever that may mean in such a time—are standing around her. As a reward for showing up, she receives an assertive check mark on the voting list, enough for her to nervously hide her deficient loyalty. The weeks that follow again pass much too slowly. Gradually, the horror over the shrill sound of the unexpected ringing of the bell begins to fade.

The entrance hall is reflected by its bright yellow flagstones. The man walks in the middle, his head drooping, his brown hair falling over his forehead. His hands are bound together in front. The policeman to the right speaks to the receptionist through the opening in the window of the railway ticket counter. The other one holds the man by the shackles. A jolt from those tied-up fists. Let me go—free . . . The one who had just been speaking at the window jumps back, yanks the man's right arm, the other one twists the left one.

The man's head hits the bright yellow flagstones with a thud. Hair is covering his face. Both arms are above his head, pressed to the ground; the policemen are kneeling on his wrists. The man is crying. A long drawn out scream: 'Mama.'

Hannah's daughter has been watching this man from the end of the spiral staircase, far away, from above. A doctor with a syringe enters from the side of the reception office, moving quickly. The syringe is prepared. He tests the tube, holding it in the air until two or three drops of liquid run down the needle. Hannah's daughter leaves her place at the railing, without a sound, and positions herself in the dark hallway.

Otto, where are you? Give me your hands, your dear bicycle-thief hands with the radio on an unpaid installment plan. I know you are not allowed to hold me on your lap. Please, do it anyway. Otto, I am scared. Don't leave me, Otto. What do you mean—dismissed?

In order to exist, the master class needs to have a servant, and he is Otto. Who is he exactly? Maybe Rudolf Platte playing the Captain of Köpenick or the oldest son of a tobacco worker from Lampertheim?

She is lying in a bed on the floor. The three mattress parts are barely held together with string. A yellow rug from Hannah's apartment, a clothes closet from the first years of marriage, a radio on the built-in shelf. A backing board, an orange crate serves as a table. Political posters decorate the entrance door. The inhabitants tried to be imaginative with the kitchen shelves.

There is tomato soup thickened with flour—no little lumps—and plenty of pepper. Two people brought somebody's address from Hamburg. Pink Floyd resounds through the apartment. The bowl of a pipe makes the rounds, raising consciousness. Marx and Balint are flung about the beds. Hannah's daughter lies in one and listens to them. But she doesn't want to learn anything.

Sometimes she flees to the children, who are presumably still good human beings. She lets them make a mess with paint, splash it around, and be unruly—until the parents can't stand it, or themselves, or anything any longer and separate.

Then she sleeps until her head proclaims 'too much sleep.' Just you try to find the purpose of life in bed . . . She sleeps and lies awake, opens doors for people—Margie sleeps on the couch in the kitchen. She comes from a home; sometimes she foams at the mouth; sometimes she has a boyfriend who has a gun in a shopping bag.

Another room overflows with comic books, which are being read by thin, very thin people who drink Coke. Don't you want to try? Hannah's daughter is not fearful; she keeps that possibility in mind. Conversation about Turkey, drugs, clean and off. Hannah doesn't like the comics. Perhaps that's why it didn't work.

Of course, she provided the spoon, heated it over a fire, the arm tied—hey girl, haven't you left yet.

When Adorno dies, there are speeches, tears, more speeches—only no one seems capable of silence, how terrible. She had thought of philosophy as a quiet matter. Wrong. In German philology there is Middle High German instead of Frisch and Dürrenmatt. Hannah goes back to bed. The man whose room she is using takes her to a big lecture hall. Afterward, they look for people to put up posters in the city.

She goes with him to a filthy dive and puts posters up with him all night. They meet the other two at a corner. She wants to say a quick hello when the man holds her back by the sleeve, and, kissing, they pass by. That was the police. Later, it wasn't all that nice between them—but that's not important now.

Mr. Krahl, by the way, went up the stairs and with his thick skull said that she had a nice ass and spilled coffee on the rug.

The wide sleeves of her friend's green jacket are too long on her. Discolored pants, black shoes—in the side pocket, a quarter for a phone call. Just in case. On the back of her hand is a number, written with a pen. Her hair is long and unpinned, her face without makeup.

From the railroad station they walked up the tree-lined street. Masses of people meet them coming from the other direction. Legs and faces, feet and washed-out jeans. Her boyfriend pushes her quickly into one of those lines. Left and right and everywhere faces, all looking straight ahead. She doesn't feel well at all as she is supposed to link arms. So many people goose-stepping. Well, yes—it's a different matter now. A thousand throats are blaring VIETNAM—Amis go home and USA-SA-SS. She is cold inside her jacket; next to her, unfamiliar fists are being clenched. Uniform, one big mass. Her boyfriend yells too, very loudly. His fist too is raised very high.

'Do you want this?' the question rings from the Sportpalast. 'Yes!' the response thunders a thousandfold and goose-steps down an endless road, past the One, hand raised high.

In time, she repressed this feeling, practiced, mumbled, and then she too yelled—louder than the rest. She'll also read again, attend a seminar. Thirty, thirty-five serious faces. Somebody sets the papers on fire in the ashtray; another looks inward, his head on the table. The foot of the speaker taps incessantly. After two hours, the black one, whose head had been resting on the table, lifts to his elbows and explains what was wrong with it all. The session is over. We were all carrying the same book under our arms. It is blue with a hard cover.

It stays that way for a while until those who were first begin to carry different books, brown ones—also with hard covers; some, no books at all; others, all kinds.

Hannah's daughter belongs to the blue-brown group. She now has a table and a chair. She is hard at work. Gradually, she too is permitted to lead something. Small groups listen to her; phrases are sometimes chanted in the hall.

A lecture has been scheduled this evening in this cellar that is much too large. What do the Communists have to say about 8 May 1945.[6] Only a few people are present, exactly two, who don't belong. Nevertheless—the lectern is decorated with the obligatory red flags. Within this group, nothing touches us. We are accustomed to the fact that, besides the police and the capitalists, the janitor too is our enemy. The cell leaders are counting their cells. Who didn't declare his absence. After all, we could exchange the night shift. The girl with thick glasses, sitting next to me, holds her notebook on her knees. Her pencil races to keep up with the words of the lecture so that she can study it once more later with her cell.

The lecture follows a directive that had been delivered nationwide. The speaker, a former electrician, has of late been growing a slight mustache, too short to be a real mustache. You know, I wouldn't be able to kiss a man with a little mustache like that. Strange, even then I already thought that they're not ashamed. The wearers probably thought nothing of it—at least not the old people, or did they? Anyway, the former electrician . . . stumbles over his dead from the Third Reich. Of course, the communists had more. About those six million, he says nothing. This rubs me the wrong way—even if nothing else touches me. This rubs me in a strange way. The chairs are squeaking. The girl next to me continues to scribble some of the words hastily. Otherwise, people's legs are already stretching out. I must say something now. During a lecture, there is no discussion. The choir will sing to finish off the evening. Those six million, aren't they my problem? Their contribution to the class struggle was minimal after all, wasn't it. They were part of it too but only because they existed. What shall I say about that?

Slowly, Hannah's daughter packs her bag. Quietly. She can't think of anyone now with whom she could talk about this—and Judas takes me home again.

Hannah's daughter stands in the office door in a shiny pink dress, long enough to reach the floor. 'My Mom wants to know if I can buy the matzo.' Mom doesn't ask herself. She had her children baptized, had picked for them a second Aryan name. The man who distributes the round brittle bread in the community knows that. Mom dips it in well-beaten egg and bakes it in hot fat. Or, for breakfast, spreads it with butter and honey, making the brittle bread crumble at the edges. Back then it couldn't be found on supermarket shelves. Again this stupid notice: a merchant in Pitigliano offers her Seder wine. What business does a merchant in Pitigliano have offering Seder wine? In the wine, a bit of life is unexpectedly reflected—where, if necessary, a home could be found.

The rehearsals for Purim have begun. Hannah's daughter strides in. Once more, once more. Pause. The small freckled woman supports her head with her hands, crinkles her nose, laughs a little. 'Once more. From there, yes. And please, slowly. Lightly. The dress, gathered on the side—yes, take it up a bit. Better. That's better.' Hannah's daughter strides and strides, and strides again.

Dignified, she is supposed to approach her king; silently, she is to serve a drink; and mute, she is to tell her suffering with her eyes. For she will be put to death should she address him without being commanded. And again she is supposed to practice her stride, proud but not provocative. How terrified everybody is when Hannah's daughter appears in the middle of the play with her hair cut short.

As the opening act, Ritula is dancing on points with Bella. Mordechai is really too fat. But finally, the presentation has been gotten through, and it ends with Carmel fruits and holding hands while dancing in a tight circle. In the office next door hangs a map with the heading *PALESTINE*. Twice a week Hebrew classes are offered for Erez Israel.

He is there too—Roni with the red hair and the light skin. Seizes her around the waist and places her in the middle of the circle. He is going back, wants to become an aviator. Throwing bombs on

Mughira's house. That's the desert that blooms there. Miracles begin to grow there in the springtime, really, except that their language is Arabic. Hannah's daughter's name is not on any travel list, even once, to see the Promised Land. Doesn't she want to see her country?

A country is not a country. Sand, desert, stones—dumped in front of Palestine's door, razed with bulldozers, water siphoned off. Houses blown up. Have you gone crazy; that suffering robs you of your senses . . . *Felafel, falafel, fellahin, falashas,* ashes, rubble and ashes, barbed wire.

Roni's airmail letter speaks of a completely normal war. Sabra and Shatila. Again he breathes normalcy. Roni writes that he is an aviator like any other—in Vietnam, Iran, Iraq. There, just look at this. She is sitting at this dumb shiny table covered with dust and writes on it with her finger *Amalekites.*

Sabras are fruits that push their thorns into your fingers and don't let go.

To what god are you praying now, the one whose mouth spits stones?

'My child, girl, you didn't have it easy. I know. You were a little worm, in the middle of the war. I don't like to see you go. Who will there be to help me around the house? Who will take care of your brothers? Aunt Helga's little ones too are very attached to you. Every day, so much fresh laundry . . .'

Martha Elisabeth is sitting on the chair in the kitchen across from her mother, her hands twisted together. Her round face is looking at the floor through her eyeglasses. Her classmates are all married by now—except for Else. She still wore thick long braids, had sickly parents at home, and carried the smell of cooked cabbage into school. It is true; her mother wasn't well either. Oh, she liked going to school—and what beautiful handwriting she had. The teacher sometimes praised her for it. Actually, she wanted to become an assistant to Mr. Rosenzweig, the attorney across the street. But then she developed these headaches, terrible headaches, and she needed glasses. How is she to read all those files? Her mother agreed. So she got a job as a salesgirl. At first, her boss was a nasty woman. Oh, was she ever nasty! She didn't even dare say she had to go to the bathroom. Always held it in. At times, she had such a bad headache she couldn't see. The doctor ordered her not to carry anything heavy. But she couldn't let her mother carry those baskets through the streets.

'On the other hand, my darling'—the mother leaned forward to make a difficult stitch in the white cloth . . . did you notice that on such occasions there were always stitches that needed to be made in white pieces of cloth . . . —'Franz is, of course, not a bad match. They have it here, you know.' Do you dislike this hand gesture too? Martha Elisabeth lets her eyes run along the rectangular tiles. Franz was the top athlete in town. He has been in the army for two and a half years. He is apparently doing very well there, she heard, advanced quickly to a supervisory position even though he is not a member. Yes, of the party, of course. He didn't talk to her about it. She feels his cross around her neck. He gave it to her in a velvet case for their engagement; for her mother, flowers. And as often happens in many stories, it all went very quickly. Franz had to return to the front.

At this point, I always remember the soldier who, in his Pan-Germanic uniform, used the entrance of Paris to call on Picasso. And imagine, Picasso opened the door.

So Franz had to return to the front. She had met him at an athletic event. She was a good runner—couldn't show any weakness at that time—until the matter with the headaches began. He appeared very strong to her in his white shirt and black pants. Did you know that there was a sports club called Maccabee? She noticed right away that he was from a well-to-do home and, at any rate, also a good Catholic. He walked her home, put her arm in his. At first, she was thinking of bleaching her hair. The drug store sold stuff for that. Her mother——no, with the Maccabee it was this way: there once was a top player, who had a friend; after they had won a game, he took off his shirt, that's what they do, and underneath he wore another one. Two entwined triangles glistened on the white background; you know what I mean. The audience in the stadium held its breath.—— Her mother had beautiful blond curls, all natural. Once, after having spent hours with the curling iron——this was really from a very different story——a strand of hair fell from under her headscarf. His hand pushed it back. Kissing before confession. Her heart was beating, terrified, no, better not, and besides, what if a baby came of it——no shit, that's what she was thinking then—— So his hand just pushed this long singed curl back under the scarf—and then he had to go to war. She wrote to him at the front every day. Really—every day, usually in the evening when the laundry had all been ironed.

Martha Elisabeth is a petite person. An hourglass figure—Scarlett O'Hara—deeply wrapped in a woolen cape. Only her hands are red——Sterntaler was cold too——She can't get used to the rubber gloves. On 10 August everything was ready. Instead of an organ, air raid alarm——I really don't care about that.——Nevertheless, the bride was very beautiful, white with a lace veil reaching the ground and a wreath in her hair. Franz had put on all his medals; in the background, both pillars and leaves camouflaged the trench. The mother-in-law did not embrace her. Franz was her only son——that much was clear——. They had a room for the night at her house where they were to live together later on. She wore a bleached, richly embroidered nightgown——Josef Čapek wrote an entire story about such a nightgown; later, he too was in a concentration camp——she was lying in the feather bed with Mama's richly embroidered gown. The summer outside was warm. Then she turned her face toward the wall. What Franz looked like, she never knew either, then or later. She keeps her eyelids tightly shut. 'Oh, Franz, my dear.' In reality, she doesn't say a word. His hands are now clumsy. Franz didn't know exactly what to do either. When he was an altar boy, he turned a deaf ear to such things—not the others, not that altar boys in general . . . that is, turn a deaf ear. Franz is sweating. The featherbed is getting in the way, heavy. Besides, the bed is squeaking, and in the next room, his parents. He tells her.

He is a good supervisor of the communications company, say his companions, doesn't put anybody through the grind. Martha Elisabeth secretly smoothes her slipped-up nightgown. Only in the morning do they realize what had happened. Franz had fallen asleep. Martha Elisabeth looks at him now. This is Franz, her husband. Surely, she's lucky. He's a good person, says even her aunt, will take care of her and perhaps a child. Wonders whether the child will come now.

With a heavy heart and still in the heat of battle, I must bring myself to write you this letter. In the course of our struggle for southern France, your dear husband, our comrade, who was held in the highest esteem and respect, met a hero's death on 29 August 1944. He died, faithful to his oath for Germany's future, for his people, and his family. He gave his life in faithful fulfillment of his duty, surrounded by his comrades in arms . . .

Death occurred instantly. His comrades gave him a dignified soldier's burial, and soon I hope to be able to send you a photograph of the grave. None of us could believe it . . . However, no eternal bond can be woven with destiny's hand. We don't know who among us will be next. All we know is that we are called upon to protect and defend our home- and fatherland so that our people and our dear ones back home can lead a life of peace worth living. We also know that our sacrifice for this lofty goal cannot be too high . . . Bear it, please, as a courageous German soldier's wife, with your gaze on your boy, in whom his blood and character live on . . . All of us urge you not to be discouraged, for he gave his life, the highest price, for you and for all of us. With our eyes directed toward the future, we shall never cease to hope. Yours, Ernst Spark, First Lieutenant and Company Commander O.U. September 1944.

The Führer's birthday is printed in red capital letters in Martha Elisabeth's notebook; next to it, she writes the weight of the child, every day; and later, the teeth. After this letter, her notes cease.

Ruthi's father was not among the fallen. Fallen, how strange that sounds. My father, he is dead. How would that be? No, the warrior widows—warrior sounds like Homer—the warrior widows and their sons explain the condition of the men, fathers, as fallen. My father, he was shot—in the back—he himself had been shooting around for peace in foreign countries; so they just shot him down. He met his end in a radio patrol car like an animal. No, my father fell. Do you hear.

Ruth's father did not fall. He was burnt and reduced to ashes. Her brother also doesn't have a dignified soldier's grave—always on top of each other—he climbed on the dead, naked, because it is easier to remove the clothing from the living. When the bullet finally hit him, his body fell on the other bodies. His hands grasped the already cold flesh.

Martha Elisabeth ordered Icelandic moss for the soldiers' cemetery—it was the most expensive of three choices. Yes—actually—I wanted to talk about Ruth. As mentioned, Ruth had a father and a brother who didn't fall. Later Ruth became a teacher, speaks fluent French. Martha Elisabeth talks with her sometimes in the evening when she is leaning out of the window. The poor thing, didn't have it easy. Ruth is going to France, just imagine. To France. 'But I can't,' says Martha, 'don't know French, and then the little one.'

Ruth will travel in this direction for Martha Elisabeth. South of Valence. Ruth takes the piece of paper from her pocket. This is where it must have happened—twenty-five to thirty kilometers left of the road—this is what she did—in a southerly direction from the factory grounds. Ruth tries to remember. 'As he was driving along this road a bullet hit your husband from the right so that he collapsed onto the steering wheel.'

Along the Drôme river. Why is that mentioned here? Ruth drives along the entire road, gets out; do you see an honorable soldier's grave? There is no grave; that's what she'll tell Mrs. Steder. She has done her best.

Just imagine her asking Mrs. Steder to accompany her to her father and brother's mass grave to look for them. In that case, there would be no language problems. Perhaps the earth, a piece of tooth or jaw, that's how one is supposed to recognize most of them . . .

Ruth described everything to Martha Elisabeth, what it looked like on the road near the factory grounds. She took notes of Ruth's description and put them with the other things. The November Revolution, she gave an ardent speech about class struggle in front of his little bed. This had frightened the child very much. Now his wife had it printed in black and white with an insignia. Oh, do not weep, my dear ones——new line——That I parted so soon from you.——God's will is done——new line——We'll meet again. On the reverse side, a coffin sinks slowly into the ground facing the cross, on which the words *Greater Germany* are written over the letters *INRI*. That's how Franz Steder is presented for the last time, enveloped and mailed. Martha Elisabeth is a courageous woman.

She started an album for my daughter. From her first attempts at crawling, walking, grasping, laughing. One day she says she has a surprise. Takes out a second expensively bound book from her bag. She had duplicates made of the family photos of Franz and herself. They are for the child. She will always know who her grandfather was, right. Martha is happy—this wasn't cheap. I freeze. What's a swastika doing in my house. Of course, it's on the uniform, naturally. I never noticed that before. I don't have such pictures in my photo box. Of anybody. Martha Elisabeth continues to flip the pages. On every page those damned insignias. 'Just look at this face,' she points at it—I see the insignia. 'Please, ' I finally tell her, 'keep it out of the album—why don't you make a separate one, please. Here are the old ones, all together.' 'Well, if you think so,' she says, 'doesn't matter. I haven't pasted in all of them yet anyway. So it makes no difference . . . But it's nice, isn't it?!'

When Hannah's daughter was little—I already told this story—she played queen and came with her wise Uncle Mordechai to the Persian court.

As Esther, she saved her people from Haman, the murderer. Haman was strung up on the gallows, the gallows he had prepared for her.

The children rattle their noisemakers and eat hamantaschen on Purim. Now she wants to show her daughter Purim.

She stopped at many bakeries. She is forced to flee, to run when a Persian in a white cap asks about her uncle—the traitor—and she, a traitor too? Guilty of his misfortune? Isn't there anything for which she can claim innocence?

She is still looking for somebody who will bake hamantaschen for her daughter. Then they would eat a whole lot of them.

Glossary of Terms

Pages 119–20

'Cheerfully plant little trees' is a play on Tu b'Shvat, the New Year of Trees. It's a custom that Jewish children of the Diaspora receive as a special gift a tree planted in Israel. The child receives the gift, but it is also considered to be a gift of the child to Israel. Seedlings are planted at Tu b'Shvat.

Page 120

The hajj is the pilgrimage to Mecca, one of the five essential duties of Muslims (also known as the Five Pillars of Islam).

Page 121

Fes is one of the four 'imperial cities' of Morocco. 'One knows of no other city as ancient as Fes that is so full of the religion and science of Islam, a city that would have been founded by the true descendents of the house of the Prophet.' (Al Kettani) The mellah—the Jewish city—is located in the al Gadid section of Fes. Unlike other cities like Taourirt, the Kasbah of Quarzazate, for example, the mellah of Fes has not been deserted through emigration to Israel. There exists a lively Jewish community life with several rabbis and synagogues.

Pages 121, 161

Kaddish, here, refers to a mourner's prayer. Actually, it is a creed, a hymn of praise to God.

Page 121

Allah akbar is the beginning of the *adhan*, a call to prayer, which the muezzin sings or recites.

Page 121

Hammam is an Arabic bathhouse.

Page 121

The hand of Fatima is considered to be an amulet. Her five spread fingers symbolize the five duties of Islam. Fatima was the daughter of Mohammed, married to Ali, the fourth caliph and first imam of the Shiites. In Christianity, the symbol is of Mary's hand, whereas in Judaism it symbolizes the hand of God.

Page 122

Damascus was the center of power for the caliphate of the Umayyads (661–750). The caliphate achieved its greatest influence as a centralized power after great conquests made by the Arab armies in the West and East.

In Andalusian Córdoba the emirate of the Umayyads continued to exist after the decline of the central power in Damascus. The emirate and caliphate of Córdoba achieved the height of its power in the tenth century. It had to defend itself against the Berbers and the Egyptian Fatimids. In Córdoba there existed conciliatory, tolerant policies towards non-Muslims. The Jewish communities, in particular, experienced a golden age that ended only in the twelfth century with the persecutions of the Almohads.

In the sixteenth century, when the Christian clerics decided that the mosque of Córdoba would be the location for a cathedral, the city authorities protested. They threatened that any builders who profaned the mosque would be punished by death. It was only through Emperor Karl V that the clerics prevailed, whereby sixty-three columns of the mosque were destroyed, and it was concealed by a Renaissance-style cathedral.

Page 122

Isabella is a reference to the Catholic queen, Isabella of Castile, married to Ferdinand of Aragon, who, during the period of her reign, intensified the climate of intolerance against non-believers, both Muslims and Jews. Since the mid-fifteenth century, many had converted to Christianity because of persecution. In 1481 the Inquisition was introduced in Castile so as to maintain control over these newly converted Christians. With the approval of the Christian masses, converted Jews and Muslims were condemned and expropriated. The traditional occupations of the Jews, such as merchants, bankers, and scholars, were reviled as un-Spanish and unchristian. The Jews were exiled from Spain in 1492, the Muslims between 1609 and 1614. During the Inquisition those who had converted were persecuted with the greatest severity.

Page 122

Rambam, Rambam, Maimonides refers to Moses ben Maimon (1135–1204), who is considered one of the most influential Hebrew scholars of the Middle Ages. According to the beginning letters of his name, Rabbi Moses ben Maimon, RMBM, is also known as Rambam.

Page 123

The Rif is a mountain range in North Africa. The inhabitants of the Rif belong to the tribe of Zanata Berbers, who came from Tunisia and Tripoli and first settled in the northern and eastern regions of Morocco between the eighth and twelfth centuries. Northern Morocco—mainly the Rif mountain range—has not enjoyed the same economic advantage that other regions attained during the colonial period. While the number of emigrants from the Rif mountain region is especially high, its inhabitants feel ignored by the central government. Their main source of income comes from the cultivation of hemp (cannabis). During the early 1920s the Berbers of the Rif fought a war of independence against the French and Spanish. Thus, the Islamic Republic of the Rif was established by the legendary Abd al-Karim. The republic was ultimately destroyed by an allied campaign by the tribe of Guela'ia Berbers (from the High Atlas Mountains) and the colonial powers. In the Rif there still exists a fundamental attitude that is critical and anti-monarchical, especially since Hassan II carried out brutal retaliation against the Rifian Berbers for a short time after independence had been won.

In earlier times, both Jews and Berbers wore the same traditional clothing. For every male Berber, this included carrying a dagger. The government prohibited this traditional carrying of arms by the Berbers in certain regions.

Page 125

The candleholder here is a Sabbath candleholder. Normally two separate candleholders are used. These candles may not be lit during the week. Sabbath, or *Schabbes* (in Yiddish), begins on Friday evening at sundown, according to the Orthodox tradition; therefore, each Sabbath begins at a different time. No work should be done, and many other activities such as smoking, using the telephone, coming into contact with money, etc., are also forbidden. Sabbath candleholders are to be used exclusively for religious purposes.

Page 127

A dreydel (Yiddish) is a cube-shaped top.

Page 132

Joseph Schmidt (1904–42), born in the Bukovina, was an internationally known Jewish singer in the field of operetta and light music. He died in a refugee camp in Switzerland of a throat ailment for which he had refused treatment.

Page 136

Number of Jews in Germany:

1933	515,000
17 May 1939	213,930
10 May 1941	168,972
1 January 1942	131,823
1 January 1944	14,544

17 August 1938: Beginning 1 January 1939, Jews must add the name Sarah or Israel to their non-Jewish names.

5 October 1938: Jews are ordered to give up their passports within fourteen days.

15 November 1938: Jews may no longer attend non-Jewish schools.

1940: Denial of clothing ration cards and termination of telephone service. Since the beginning of the war: curfews are established, and all radio sets are required to be delivered to the authorities.

1 September 1941: All Jews over six years of age are required to wear a yellow star on their clothing.

3 October 1941: Jews must receive special permission to leave their homes and to use public transportation.

1 July 1942: Formal education in schools is discontinued for Jewish children 'in light of the unfolding evacuation of Jews.'

Page 151

Alfred Dreyfus was a Jewish general staff officer in France. In 1894 he was found guilty by a military court of spying for the German empire and condemned to lifelong exile on Devil's Island. In 1898 Major Esterházy, who in the meantime had been dismissed from the French army, admitted to writing the letter to the German military attaché that had been used as evidence for the successful prosecution of Dreyfus. Another member of army intelligence admitted falsifying this letter. Clemenceau took up Dreyfus's cause in 1897. Émile Zola published his famous article 'J'accuse' in 1898. Zola was indicted on grounds of libel against the army. The judgment against Dreyfus was dismissed by the appellate court in 1899.

It was only after Clemenceau took over the government in 1906, however, that it was possible to carry out the appeals process. Despite the proven innocence of Dreyfus, a new trial could take place only in military court and not within the civilian justice system. In 1908 Dreyfus was the victim of an assassination attempt. The assassin's trial ended in a declaration of his innocence.

The Dreyfus case represents the emancipation—and decline—of European Jews within bourgeois society. For the first time, a Jew had achieved a high-ranking position in the military. And yet the anti-Dreyfusards carried the day: one can see this in everything from the prevalent anti-republicanism, anti-democraticism, and anti-Semitism to the monarchists of the Action Française to the National Bolshevism of Jacques Doriot.

'What made France fall was the fact that she had no more true Dreyfusards, no one who believed that democracy and freedom, equality and justice, could any longer be defended or realized under the republic.' (Hannah Arendt, *Elemente and Ursprünge totaler Herrschaft*, Band 1, Antisemitismus [Frankfurt/M: Europ.Verl-Anst., 1955]; Hannah Arendt, *The*

Origins of Totalitarianism [Part One: Antisemitism], new edition with added prefaces. New York: Harcourt Brace & Co., 1976, 93).

When Dreyfus died in 1935, only the socialist press recalled his proven innocence.

Page 153

The Magen David, Star of David, is the shield that David carried in his battle against Goliath.

Page 153

Reparations: After 1945 Jews laid claim to the following: restitution of all Aryanized and confiscated Jewish property, and damages for survivors who had suffered harm and injustice as well as compensatory payments for displaced persons. In exchange for the acceptance and integration of five hundred thousand victims, the state of Israel also demanded a guarantee from the occupational powers against its reparation claims.

Twenty Jewish organizations demanded compensation in the amount of $500 million in October 1951 for the re-integration of Jewish victims outside of Israel. Hermann Abs offered the delivery of goods valued up to DM 1 billion over three years. Eventually, a payment of $715 million was agreed upon.

In comparison, simultaneous negotiations with more than thirty nations on the payment of Germany's foreign debt were conducted efficiently.

On the other hand, the laws governing restitution were passed only in 1953 on the initiative of the Americans. The Adenauer administration certainly did not, however, accept the claims of all surviving victims within its jurisdiction. There were also never any plans to make full restitution. No damages could be claimed for emotional and physical injury, while forced labor was also not compensated, etc.

Page 153

Hanukkah (holy day) recalls the rededication of the temple in Jerusalem. The purification of the temple, which had been desecrated by Antiochus IV (167 B.C.E.), is commemorated for eight days. A new candle on a nine-candle holder (menorah) is lit each day in memory of a small vial of oil whose contents lasted for eight days until new oil provisions could be supplied.

Page 157

Mitzrayim is a name for Egypt.

Page 161

In Yiddish, *Tate(n)* is the word for papa.

Page 166

'Twenty Jewish children' were killed by the SS during the night of 20

April and the early morning hours of 21 April 1945 near the Bullenhuser Dam in a school in Hamburg. The children ranged in age from four to twelve years. Arnold Strippel, the officer in charge, who was a one-time SS Obersturmführer (colonel of an SS assault troop) and head of a guard unit at the concentration camp Neuengamme, has still not been convicted. The children had been victims of tuberculosis experiments that lasted five months. Arnold Strippel, who was head of the security guard at the time of the murders, has evaded criminal prosecution by laying claim to authoritative testimony of his inability to stand trial. He lives in Kalbach, near the city of Frankfurt/Main. (G[ünther] Schwarberg, *Der SS Arzt und die Kinder [von Bullenhuser Damm]* [The SS doctor and the children from Bullenhuser Damm], [Göttingen: Steidl, 1988]; there is also a film on this subject by Lea Rosh).

Page 170

Hadamar was the death sanitarium where the Nazis carried out their program of euthanasia. Until 1 September 1942, as many as 10,072 human lives were destroyed because they were considered 'useless' and 'worthless.'

Page 170

Graf Galen, Bishop of Munster, protested against the power of the Gestapo and their arbitrary methods of arrest. He also protested vehemently against euthanasia. Alfred Grosser comments: 'Would the vehement protest of the Bishop Cardinal Galen of Munster against euthanasia have been so forceful if there hadn't been Catholics involved? His protest ought certainly be considered successful since a type of mass murder under Hitler was discontinued. One doesn't want to believe this, were it not for the nontactical distinction continuously made between baptized Jews, i.e., those converted to Catholicism, and nonbaptized Jews. And if the German Catholic Church protected the Catholics first, then it seems that the protection of German Catholics was a particular concern of the pope. He was paralyzed in the protection of other people because of his fear of reprisals against the flock over which he considered himself its special shepherd.' (Alfred Grosser, review of *Geschichte Deutschlands seit* 1945 [The history of Germany since 1945], *Eine Bilanz*, Munich: Dtv Taschenbuch, 1981, 332).

Page 186

Matzo and Seder wine are required for the celebration of Pesach (Passover). Seders are celebrated on the first two evenings by family and friends, where bitters (in memory of slavery in Egypt), matzah (the unleavened bread that was the provision for the exodus), a hard-boiled egg (symbol of fertility), ground nuts mixed with red wine, apples, and cinnamon (symbol of the mortar that the Jews had to mix for the Pharaoh) are consumed, as well as four glasses of wine. During the Seder meal, stories from the Talmud (the Haggadah) are read out loud.

Pages 186, 194

The Feast of Purim: The legend for the holiday of Purim is found in the Book of Esther. The Persian king Ahasuerus (Xerxes) banishes his wife Vashti as punishment for her disobedience. In her stead, the Jewish Esther is made queen. Her foster-father and uncle, Mordecai, who has a minor position at court, reveals a palace conspiracy in which Haman, the king's courtier, takes part. Mordecai attracts the hateful revenge of Haman, who then plans a large-scale pogrom of Jews throughout the entire Persian Empire.

Haman is often called the Agagite, among other names. Agag was the king of the Amalekites.

Mordecai turns to Esther for help, who hesitates because of the danger to her. She does support the Jews of the Persian Empire, however, with her three-day fast. Haman orders a gallows constructed in order to carry out Mordecai's execution. Esther develops a plan in order to save her people. The king wishes to honor Mordecai for his exposure of the palace conspiracy. While Haman is required to bestow the honor, Esther reveals his plan to destroy the Jews. The king hangs Haman upon the gallows that had been intended for Mordecai. Mordecai then takes over the position held by Haman at court. A proclamation is issued throughout the empire guaranteeing all privileges to Jews, who were then free to gather and defend themselves against their enemies. They enjoy a joyful feast. Mordecai issues a decree, establishing the dates and rites for Purim.

Pur means 'fate' (which Haman declared over the Jews). The story stems from the Persian Diaspora. Purim is celebrated with unrestrained joy with pranks, costume balls, and the presentation of Purim skits.

Page 186

Erez Israel means 'the land of Israel.' This is a Zionist term that elucidates the claim for the Holy Land by the Jewish people as a historical right. When Israeli troops marched into Lebanon in 1982, there were those who sought to prove that the southern part of Lebanon was a traditional part of Erez Israel. Originally, however, the term was used as another name for the land of Canaan.

Page 187

In the long period in which the Israelites wandered through the desert, the Amalekites ruled the Middle East. Their exploitation of Palestine is depicted in the books of the Bible. Throughout their exile, plagued by exhaustion and thirst, the Israelites were mercilessly plundered. At a later point, the cattle herds of the Amalekites, who overran the land, destroyed the harvests.

King Saul, the first king of the Israelites, brought an end to the Amalekites' reign and took their king, Agag, prisoner.

The Further Books of History: 'Thus saith the Lord of hosts, I remember that which Amalek did to Israel . . .' (1 Sam. 15:2).[7] 'I will utterly put out the remembrance of Amalek from under heaven' (Exod. 17:14). Thus did Saul, the king of the Israelites, defeat the Amalekites, yet spared their king, Agag, disobeying the voice of the Lord, and took their possessions for himself. Samuel had Agag brought before him and said: ''As thy sword hath made women childless, so shall thy mother be made childless among women.' And Samuel hewed Agag in pieces before the Lord in Gilgal' (1 Sam. 15:33).

The Fourth Book of Moses: God punished the Israelites for their murmuring against him. 'But as for you, your carcases [*sic*], they shall fall in this wilderness. [. . .] until your carcases be wasted in the wilderness. After the number of the days in which ye searched the land, even forty days, each day for a year, shall ye bear your iniquities, even forty years, and ye shall know my breach of promise' (Num. 14:32–34).

The Fifth Book of Moses, the 'Addresses': 'The stranger that is within thee shall get up above thee very high; and thou shalt come down very low. He shall lend to thee, and thou shalt not lend to him; he shall be the head, and thou shalt be the tail. Moreover all these curses shall come upon thee, and shall pursue thee, and overtake thee, till thou be destroyed; because thou hearkenedst not unto the voice of the LORD thy God, to keep his commandments and his statutes which he commanded thee' (Deut. 28:43-45).

Page 189

Maccabee is mentioned in a story by Sally Grosshut, *Schiedsrichter Rissing leitet ein Spiel* ([Referee Rissing officiates at a game], Wiesbaden, 1984). Maccabee was used as a name for Jewish sports clubs, a name that refers to the rebellious Jews who rose up against the Seleucidic reign of Antiochus. They were led by the son of Mattathias, who had the force of a hammer, thus he was known as 'the hammer,' the Maccabee. He created a regular battle troop.

Page 190

Josef Čapek, 'Das Märchen vom stolzen Nachthemd' [The fairy tale of the proud nightshirt], in *Geschichten vom Hündchen und vom Kätzchen* [Stories of the little dog and little cat] (Hanau, 1982). Josef Čapek died in 1945 in the Bergen-Belsen camp.

Norbert Mattes
Translated by Karin Obermeier

Editors' Notes

1. A glossary of terms is provided, referring to the page number of the the term's first occurrence.
2. *Graue Kloster* refers to a well-known Berlin school. Originally a Franciscan monastery, it recently celebrated its 425th anniversary.
3. In the original text, 'The Ten Commandments' are ambiguous and conceivably personify a figure of authority.
4. Dischereit uses the term '*hochdeutsche Gesichter*' to describe these faces. Dischereit's use of this linguistic term to describe faces suggests differences in class standing and in degrees of urbanity and provincialism, of which Runkel is emblematic.
5. The word 'camp' (*Lager*) in the original contains a double meaning that is nearly impossible to capture in translation. In German, *Lager* means camp as well as warehouse.
6. The day 8 May 1945 marks the end of World War II in Western Europe.
7. Translator's Note: There currently exists no English version of Martin Buber's German translation of the Bible, *Die Schrift*, because of the difficulties in translating Buber's unique and creative use of the German language. Karen Obermeier, has, therefore, used the King James Version when directly quoting passages from the Bible. *The Fifth Book of Moses*, the 'Addresses' (Deuteronomy), also contains similar passages on Amalek (Deut. 25:17, 19).

Maxim Biller

Harlem Holocaust

As on almost every Saturday afternoon, we sat at the Club Maon; and Warszawski, who always acted as if he had narrowly escaped from being deported, dropped his hand onto Ina's knee. It was the knee of the woman who a few years ago had made his novels known in Germany. That their content was exclusively concerned with Warszawski's survivor guilt, she would mention only in passing in her now defunct newspaper column 'Review from Abroad.' From the beginning, Ina enthusiastically and primarily valued the complex narrative structures of this New York writer and professor of linguistics, who, for his part, now placed even greater value on her legs. His hand slid higher along her stockings; his fingers got briefly entangled in the seam of her silk skirt and soon disappeared completely under it. Despairing, I turned away; my head felt light and hot like a helium-filled balloon—but I stood no chance against Warszawski; the very next moment his hand left Ina's thigh and fell onto mine. He pressed hard, his grip made me heave a sigh of surprise, and he said: 'German flesh is good flesh . . .' I held my breath. The word *flesh* still evokes in me frightful associations. 'Of course, it also has,' said Warszawski, as if in defiance, 'such a sweet taste and burnt smell.' And then he smacked his lips, practically wallowing in this allusion, which is why I replied, as unperturbed as possible: 'How do you know this, Gary, I mean that human flesh tastes and smells sweet?' 'How do you know this . . . how do you know this, Gary,' he imitated me promptly in a loud voice and said, laughing: 'Not from Friday and Robinson; that you can believe!' Then he pinched me once more, and his hand flew back under Ina's skirt. 'May I present Ina Teutonia Polarker, my muse and my cunt,' said the great Warszawski. He pulled out his hand, sniffed it with an unfocused look, and while something died in me again, and the helium balloon gained in height, he hissed: 'Don't be such a spoil sport, Fritz!' Although he had some trouble with it, he pressed out the r threefold, fourfold, his Americanized tongue turning it into a stupid pseudo-Prussian 'Frrritz!' like the Hollywood Nazis—and the i too came out flat, as in a caricature of Kyffhäuser drawn from below. 'Don't be such a spoil sport, Frrritz!' He held his finger under my nose, but, of course, it smelled of nothing.

Ina Polarker's name is not Teutonia, and my name is not Fritz. My parents had long fights when they were naming me, and my mother won out in the end; she called me, against my father's will, Ephraim. After all, she comes from a family with a spirit of opposition: grandfather Glückler thought Hitler vulgar and kept a sizeable collection of Expressionist works out of Göring's hands. However, the resistance did not extend any further; no Jews were hidden or flyers circulated, but when I begin to have my doubts about the glorious Glücklers, I turn my thoughts simply to the Rosenhains: My father's father wrote, alternating with Werner Höfer, in the *Twelve O'Clock News* against Jewish-American cultural bolshevism and penned stiff superman oratorios, which he produced himself. His brother, Georg, who, in contrast to my grandfather, was not known for his artistic talent, enjoyed making communists, homos, and Jews sing at the Prinz-Albrecht Palace in Berlin. It would be a mistake, however, to regard it merely as an irony of fate that I, the grandson and grandnephew of such types, am named Ephraim Rosenhain, of all things. This was, as I said, my mother's idea, and, after all, one of the guys strung up at Nuremberg was called Alfred Rosenberg. This too was no coincidence but predestination—I am absolutely certain of it.

What a clan! Once, years ago, I brought my then girlfriend Eve—Eve Lurie—home for a memorable dinner. That was long before our separation, which Eve, in her hysterical way, declared one day out of the blue, because, as she said, she couldn't for any length of time live, sleep, and eat with an incarnation of German history like me. She was, of course, right. It was around this time that I became aware for the first time that the dizzy spells and hallucinations that had visited me ever more frequently since I entered puberty were by no means due to some physical illness. This system of phantasmagorias was probably a congenital trait, present since birth, and it took a while before my sensitivity, my hunger for guilt and atonement could fully unfold . . . So Eve, the beautiful daughter of Jud Süss, left me, and, promptly, my air pillow brain became bigger than before, shrouded in this hazy veil of nothingness, transparent and ephemeral as a tear. The migraines too returned after Eve left me, whereupon I started to take a certain kind of pill that on the one hand alleviated my pain but on the other intensified the dizziness and the associated hallucinations. All in all, I actually enjoyed this desperate game, which prompted me to imagine a different, better, and more credible life, which worked every time and even went so far as to make me, merely to pass the time, twist the faces of passers-by into a surrealistic shape—a block of concrete, the dial of a clock, a hideous animal face, an apple or tangerine . . . For a while I lived as Ephraim in a wonderland, which made it easier to forget, and at some point everything was as before; everybody looked normal, and all that remained of this time was a better knowledge of medication and the recognition that I had been a tightrope walker who had learned not to interpret and not to suffer a few strange psychic spells as frightful symptoms of an illness but, on the contrary, to make them serve as a sort of therapy.

Of course, I was hurt by the separation from Eve. But I didn't blame her for it, since I knew from the beginning what kind of woman I was dealing with. After graduating from high school in Paris, Eve had moved to Israel, where she served in the army for two long years, getting herself deflowered over and over again by Israeli soldiers; it took that many times, in Eve's words, since this kind of thing never works right away with a princess. Eve's stories . . . her mother, she told me, was in a concentration camp as a child, and since concentration camp always sounds so martial, and yet anonymous, I asked her about the exact name of the place. In Theresienstadt, she replied, reticently, since she knew as well as I that Theresienstadt, the Nazis' show camp, was anything but a concentration camp, was almost a paradise on earth compared to the extermination camps of Sobibor, Auschwitz, and Maidanek.

Eve, the blabbermouth, was also a chameleon: in some photographs she had the natural coloring of an Israeli, in others she was a busy Parisian socialist in a tweed suit, and in others, dressed in an

Indian flower-print dress, and with black marks around the eyes, she looked like a malnourished, German culture groupie, and then again, in this one incredible photo, which her first and only husband, Chaim, had taken of her in Florence, like a very wealthy, heavily made-up, upper-class German Jew in a light, almost white, mink coat, smiling stiffly under a newly fixed nose. The time she spent with Chaim, who apparently made more money in ten years with three jeans stores than the Rosenhains did with a construction machine factory in a hundred years, was very depressing for Eve. For a while, she had played the innocent game of ingénue to his nouveau riche friends and relatives in the community. Then she remembered that her socialization derived from an educated, cosmopolitan, Jewish bourgeoisie of leftist leaning rather than the cryptofascist, matzo ball fantasies of a gang of Polish Jews, who had learned to read and write in Adenauer's Germany. At least this is how she described it to me, repeatedly, and always in the same way. I was often infected with Eve's hatred for these people, who, so she said, stole three years of her life. Once, when I dared to agree with her out of a sense of solidarity, she slapped me in the face and grumbled: 'Only I can do that!' The slap made me dizzy. Instead of setting her straight, I choked and was seized with a cough to clear my throat. What could I reply to somebody like her? After all, this Eve, a petite, neurotic figure, told me three times a day that she had immediately sensed the horror as soon as she came to Germany, and when she saw a street sign or an inscription at a store containing the capital letter K, she would immediately add the letter Z in her mind . . .

And why did Eve leave the narrow-minded Chaim and flee to the suffering German son of wrongdoers, Ephraim Rosenhain? He loved her with all his heart and took her home that evening for dinner without thinking—Saturdays were usually the great family gathering. Thus Ephraim was forced to introduce his Jewish girlfriend to the unrepentant Rosenhains, and it was, of course, the grandmother who, jokingly, started to talk about marriage and seriously quoted Bismarck: 'It is good to refresh our blood with a Jewish mare . . .' I said nothing, and nobody else bothered about this comment, and when Eve, whose German was not yet very good, asked me later what a 'mare' was and reproached me, saying that I should have defended her, I explained reticently that, due to my family background, only half of me was a resister, and that evening it was the bad half that had called the shots.

This asshole Warszawski! He was still waving his fingers in front of my face, describing spirals and circles in the air, which only intensified my dizziness and that flat elevator-feeling. He breathed and grinned; he shook his short round torso, and I noticed clearly how he purposely poked the tall Ina in the side several times with his shoulder. She swayed and trembled, but even though one of those violent blows almost knocked her off the chair, she did not move away from him; while he, like a human steam piston, rotated farther and farther in his chair, and she slipped ever closer toward him . . . Then the waitress arrived, and he finally left us alone.

I ordered my usual chopped eggs and roast veal with kasha. Ina wanted only a salad, and Warszawski ordered soup with rice and cholent. 'The crown of our cuisine,' he said loudly, 'the brown jewel of Ashkenazic gastronomy.' The waitress smiled politely while the department store glasses, with light blue tinted frames, moved back and forth on her nose like a surfer. 'What's in it today?' he asked her. He leaned forward, extending his neck so his head was only a few inches away from her flat stomach. 'Kishke, beans, farina, boiled meat, and potatoes,' she said, bashfully. But then she pushed the glasses back on her nose and puffed: 'What kind of question is this . . .' 'A test question,' said Warszawski. 'One never knows if one is dealing with decent Amchu or some filthy Khazars.' He burst into autistic laughter, and the waitress looked at him with frightened eyes.

Warszawski's mouth was filled with air; his cheeks had turned into bellows, and I spotted the caramel-colored false teeth of the sixty-year-old mounted in a straight chalk line without spaces, which always remind me of the worst. Since the time of the Fassbinder scandal, I have never forgotten the picture of the chairman of the Frankfurt Jewish community in a daily newspaper: from that man too there protruded, all too evidently, an ugly amorphous balustrade of artificial teeth. The photograph was, of course, accompanied by a report. I read it at the time with great interest and did not forget how effectively the martyr detail was mentioned, that the chairman of the community, who was fighting against the play, had not only survived several extermination camps but also, during this ordeal, had lost all his teeth as a result of a vigorous German kick. Of course, so it occurred to me, he now has enough money to replace his conspicuously poor, makeshift dentures, with which he had been fitted a few months after the war by American military dentists, with an expensive beautiful piece. That, of course, he didn't want to do . . . The worst, the very worst, had taken place in the East at another time, but I was so naive that a Jewish tooth prosthesis reminded me, without fail, of the Himmler or Mengele in me.

By the same token, my Warszawski has probably had more problems with cavities than with the Nazis. He came to America as a child in the early thirties; his parents had assessed the situation long before 30 January 1933. His father had been an anesthesiologist at the Charité hospital in Berlin; his mother had been a set designer for the UFA film studios. The Warszawskis quickly found work in New York; both were able to practice their former professions. He was employed at a clinic on the Upper East Side; she worked freelance for small theaters. Present and future were thus secured, but the memory remained: Warszawski's parents spoke only German with their son; they socialized mostly with immigrants in Yorkville and Washington Heights; and they got all gushy every time Germany came up in conversation. Warszawski couldn't stand 'this blind, backward-directed brouhaha'; he hated 'their Rilke volumes, their Heine quotes, and their Georg Grosz reproductions, their weekly get-togethers at the "Kleine Konditorei" on Eighty-sixth Street, where the quiet and mediocre gathered around the loud mouthed and conceited, the foot soldiers of the third Diaspora around the goyim Graf and Brecht, where narcissistic, romantic Enlightenment intellectualism reigned supreme, memories and only memories, but never a plan.' This is how Warszawski described it in his autobiographical sketch, 'This Is My Life,' which appeared in *Merkur*. It was also in this work that he disclosed how he had fled from his parents' world of feelings into the more pathetic, but more honest, world of his black New York friends, a beatnik long before Cassady, Orlovsky, and Kerouac, liberated from 'this numb, Central European stuff. At least for a while.'

Warszawski, the Kissinger of literature: he liked nothing more than to rub the glorious American ideas of freedom under the noses of his new West German friends, people who, as he maintained, were all hopelessly convinced that Europe, on the one hand, shed a whole lot of blood and shit over the whole world, but who, on the other hand, were culturally superior to those whom they had enslaved and defeated. 'I, the most American of Americans, if there ever was one,' Warszawski would say, his eyes wide open, probably to shake up his audience even more. 'I always know, in contrast to you, what is good and what is bad, and it gives me direction. In my country, straightforwardness reigns both in theory and in practice. We Americans always know exactly what decision we have made. When we are bad, we are bad. When we are good, we are good. We don't know anything about abysses of degeneration, nor about stubbornness or hesitancy. The Second World War was a good war, and that made us proud. The war in Vietnam was a bad war; we had fun, and then it hurt, and then we defeated ourselves.' Warszawski turned away from his audience, falling silent for a long time, until they could no longer bear the menacing, unctuous, artificial pause the great man had created, and one of them would say, for example: 'Didn't we?' Warszawski was suddenly terribly tired. He slowly raised his huge eyelids, with long gray lashes, and let them drop again. 'No, not you. You are aesthetes. You are inflexible; you ruminate. You die, and you want to know why. You don't even believe what's in the books you have on your shelves.' Warszawski nodded. 'You discovered America, but we invented it,' he said to the somber silent audience. 'We can tell you the greatest shit, and you believe us anyway . . .' He pronounced this sentence with all the seriousness he was still able to muster, but then he could no longer hold back, and he burst into his sardonic filthy laughter; he howled and moaned, knocked his legs together, and turned his fat red cheeks into a balloon.

Warszawski frequently gave such performances, and as I knew from experience, he unfurled the same text every time. Earlier, before the matter with Ina, I even liked it when Warszawski put us down, us 'late-born ignoramuses,' as he used to call us, his German groupies. Who could deny it? During one of his early visits to Germany—to sign a book deal and to discuss the translation—

Warszawski, in my presence, threw the following brief monologue in the face of the German publisher of his *Romagna Antica*, a Holocaust novel that was hardly noticed in America: ‘Why me? I know why. You are a dreaming liar; you like to have me because I have experienced death by escaping it and now am writing about it. What do you want? Absolution? We Jews put Christian blood in our matzo, and we Americans want to be paid when we redeem others.’ Pause. Warszawski turned away, as always. The publisher furrowed his brow above his apathetic face. ‘I thought,’ he said, as in a trance, ‘that we had clarified this.’ Warszawski answered slowly: ‘Am I talking about money? Did I talk about percentages?’ His eyelids went up and down in slow motion like the wings of a huge moth. He put one arm around the publisher’s shoulder and the other one around me, the translator, and said in a mellow tone: ‘How I love you, you late-born ignoramuses. Your thinking is pure, your souls petty.’ And while he spoke, he blinked his eyes at Eve, who had taken a seat across from him.

Eve, who at that time didn’t have anything against the way I’d learned about history, was present because the publisher wanted to make his guest feel that he was not alone. He asked me to ‘bring my Jewess,’ and so I brought her; she was an asset for us that evening; she soothed the writer with her Middle Eastern glances and movements; she conversed politely with the publisher, hinted in the course of the conversation at her origin, in a fresh unassuming tone—unfortunately, Warszawski’s blinking at Eve, at the same time as he let his leaden arms sink on us German idiots, was not a lecherous blinking; he sent out no horny signals, as was his usual custom with women, and it is, of course, quite clear why. For this short moment, these two people, who had known each other for less than half an hour, were among themselves, in a world to which other people had no access. The feeling that came over me then, for the eternity of the batting of an eye, resembled a revelation; suddenly I understood why Jews and Christians would forever have to live as adversaries and why this could never be changed. But I am not thinking of that now; I prefer to imagine Warszawski snatching Eve from me—he never did, never even tried—and how grateful I would be to him for it, because I would be able to say: You took Eve from me, leave me Ina, and don’t kill my child.

The waitress at the Maon stared at Warszawski in disbelief. At some point he stopped laughing and caught her frightened look, and for a while it seemed as if the two were trying to hypnotize each other. I can't say what went on in Warszawski's head, but I believe the waitress considered him with intensity. Almost every Saturday she had to put up with this man who played games; she was uncertain what it was he wanted, what he wanted from her; she understood neither his language nor his way of thinking. She pushed her sweaty hair away from her forehead, and still regarding Warszawski with dread, she spoke softly to herself: 'Decent Amchu, dirty Khazars, decent Amchu . . .' Then she raised her voice: 'You are meshuga, you know that?' Warszawski opened his mouth and then closed it again without having said a word. Everything about him was serious now, and he looked at the floor. 'Well what is it,' the waitress said, in a harsh tone, 'do you want your cholent now or not?' 'Of course I want my cholent,' said Warszawski, 'and while we are waiting for it, I'll explain to my friends here what it is.' 'No, Gary,' said Ina, 'not again.' And she gave me a look that was both so pained and so distant that I understood once again how definitive our separation was.

Warszawski paid no attention to her, neither did he notice the glance Ina and I exchanged. Again, he was only preoccupied with himself. 'Cholent,' he said, with pathos and a schoolmasterly undertone, 'cholent, my dear Fritz, my dear Teutonia, is a typical Eastern European Jewish dish, which our housewives prepare every week for Shabbat. By noon on Friday, they are already standing in their primitive kitchens, cutting carrots, celery, and parsley, crumbling bay leaves, washing barley and beans, and lining the heavy iron pots with goose fat. Then the pots are filled with peeled vegetables and pieces of beef and marrowbone mark, and from then on our divinely ordained stew cooks by itself on the tiniest flame all night and half a day. But when the children and husbands of the housewives finally, shortly before the second Shabbat meal, sneak into the kitchen, lured by the sweet smell of the cholent, and lift the lid of the pot, in order to get a taste of the divinely ordained stew ahead of time, they are surprised every time how a dish that looks like shit can taste that good. It is more than physics; it's alchemy that makes pure healthy products that, under the lowest heat, spend twenty-four hours together in one container and take on the same color, a deep friendly brown, a brown of life, a brown of hope and of mutability . . .' He sent a theatrical Hasidic glance toward the ceiling, toward the heavens; he held his fanned-out, open hands vertically in front of his face like a Chagall figure and said: 'Whether in Galicia, Bohemia, or Ukraine, whether in Brooklyn, Buenos Aires, or Mea Shearim—where there is civilization, there are Jews, and wherever there are Jews, cholent will be served at the table, the most abhorrent, archaic sacrifice of which people are still capable . . . Yes, this is the legendary mosaic tradition, which defies aesthetics and glitter, negates images, but which in word and in devotion hears the voice of the God of the desert!' He lowered his eyes. 'Do you think I don't notice how the two of you have been leering at each other the whole time?!'

We had been meeting at the Maon on Theresienstrasse for several months, every Saturday at two. The Maon, the meeting place of the Jewish sporting club Makkabi Munich, was located in one of the many atriums of a gigantic futuristic building of the sixties, which is held together by countless stairs, horizontal glass hallways, and open staircases. The contrast couldn't have been any greater, for our restaurant was located in the third inner courtyard in a flat, one-story extension that looked as if it had been glued on in the haphazard way of temporary structures that were erected right after the war. Inside, pennants, little flags, and a lot of posters with Hebrew lettering and stars of David were everywhere, but the decor itself was what one would find in any Bavarian pub: chairs with light-colored, round, wooden backs, a simple counter, and everywhere white and blue tablecloths. In the front room, enclosed on three sides by glass walls, shimmering whenever the weather was good, in faded broken sunlight, food was being served; in the back, separated and hidden from view by a high Spanish wall, were the card and chess players. Most of the people who came there were old; they were people with terribly thin hair, hoarse voices, and knobby noses, with watery eyes and big earlobes covered with peach fuzz. The women had serious yellow faces; the men moved about slowly, but—once they were seated—they were capable of quick and energetic gestures and facial expressions. A cabinet of horror, a real witches' kitchen, besides, the language spoken between those walls was almost exclusively Polish or Yiddish, a fact that was especially hard for me in the beginning because—this is how I had come to feel about it recently—in these two languages murder and death were leering at each other. I had made the acquaintance of both only a few years before through Claude Lanzmann's *Shoah*, and although I was not less critical of this film than of *Holocaust*, because it was—only in a different, intellectual way—straining just as much for effect, I was never able to get the melody and music of that Polish-Yiddish language symphony out of my head. Oh yes, Claude Lanzmann . . . His only true historical service was to have given Simone de Beauvoir all the orgasms that Sartre still owed her. At least this is how Warszawski explained it to me once, and I was unable, for a long time, to get this comment out of my head, and I never found out whether Warszawski was poking fun or whether he was somehow serious about really either despising, or envying, Lanzmann. He could have had reason enough since, after all, at that time he was still waiting for that innocent halo of fame and wisdom with which we goyim had long crowned Lanzmann . . .

Of course, at some point, I did get used to the macabre anachronistic ambience at the Maon, this mixture of casual everyday and demonstrative mummification of history. And yet, it was absolute madness that I should be sitting down here regularly for lunch with this scoundrel and with Ina. It had, of course, been his idea, shortly after his last return from America. For a wonderful six months before that, in connection with his first German reading tour, he had visited me in Munich for a few weeks, had met Ina, the German who had discovered him, seduced her, and afterward introduced her to me, and then returned to his family in New York, where he taught linguistics at Columbia University, only to suddenly, a mere six months later, pull out of a hat a writer's grant that provided him with the means to spend a whole year without financial worries in Germany, in Munich at the *Literaturhaus* on Leopoldstrasse.

Ina and I no longer counted on him; we loved each other so much that I forgot everything, Eve, the dizziness, the headaches, the hallucinations, and the great Warszawski; I felt physically and mentally better than I ever had since childhood, when life was still one cheerful diversion, and I simply didn't have time and brains enough to ruminate and to work on my *locus minoris resistentiae*. But when Warszawski called unexpectedly and said he was coming, alone, without family, our elation turned into confusion; we started watching each other, and I suddenly realized that I would never really have control over myself since it was—considering my fate—impossible and that I really didn't want to. Soon thereafter we calmed down again; suddenly Warszawski's return seemed to us completely without problems; we now laughed about ourselves, about our fear of the writer, who really was nothing more than a little evil man with a big head full of muddled ideas and malice, whose books one had to value but never the man, who was much too obvious and obstinate. And then the day came, and when Ina said she would have to do Warszawski the courtesy of picking him up at the airport, I still thought everything was okay. A few weeks later, our child was dead, and my madness was back: Warszawski and Ina saw each other daily, and soon he moved from the guest room of the *Literaturhaus* into her apartment on Arcisstrasse. There he slept with her again, and for me she had time only during the day, time for melodramatic meetings in a coffeehouse near the Technical University. Sometimes we had lunch in the cafeteria of the conservatory at Königsplatz, and in that very place, the former Gestapo headquarters in Munich, Ina explained why she had surrendered so quickly when she was confronted with this American Jewish writer of German descent, Gerhard 'Gary' Warszawski. Again and again I had to listen to a litany in which words like *fear* and *repentance* and *death eroticism* occurred, and once I even started to cry over my tray of apple juice and tortellini in tomato sauce, not out of sadness but because so much nonsense was driving me to despair, a nonsense that projected from history directly into my present contemporary life. 'I don't have anything to do with the thousand-year Reich!' my screams filled the cafeteria. 'And you don't either! It's crushing me,' I screamed, but none of the entranced music students with their carefully combed hair and washed-out business shirts, who sat around humming scales and intoning arias, took notice of my outburst, and I quickly fell silent again: I lost all desire to scream when Ina crowned the whole thing with a tale about Warszawski's last reading at the *Amerika-Haus*. First he lectured, in a good mood and an entertaining manner, about his convoluted narrative style that he himself dubbed *surfiction* and traced his spiritual ties to the French *nouveau roman* and American cyberpunk, and then he began to read—at first with a clear, matter-of-fact voice that, however, grew visibly darker and veiled—the central passage from *Harlem Holocaust*, that is, the most successful part of his closet tetralogy. In the end, he took, as in a trance, the poignant questions of his German audience, each time painfully contorting his face when somebody pronounced the word *Holocaust* overly carefully and with effort. This clown! Later, they went to a restaurant with a few people, where he very quickly regained his aggressive buoyancy. At some point, when he was drunk, he had Ina drive him home, and in the middle of the night, he woke up, stepped onto the balcony, and alternated singing the 'Star-Spangled Banner' and the song of the Hitler youth from *Cabaret*. Afterward, he stumbled back into bed and fell asleep with the words: 'I don't know how I will be able to bear staying here another eleven months.'

I shuddered. 'You don't understand him,' said Ina and pressed my hand, which she had grasped impulsively. Startled, she let go of it. 'You don't understand Gary at all.' 'When are you coming back?' I said. Silently, she stroked the back of my hand. 'Stop, it tickles,' I said, impatiently. 'I'm sorry.' 'When are you coming back?' She did not answer. 'In eleven months?' 'Not even in eleven years,' she said, softly, and I knew that she was right, and we fell silent, and suddenly one of the idiots at our table began to sing something that sounded like an especially melancholy Wagnerian passage, whereupon I turned toward him and scolded: 'Stop already, you showoff!' He stopped immediately, and I pictured then how I was going to tell Warszawski, who was always late, with the same determined straight face: 'You can go now, you lousy victor of the war. Ina belongs to me!'

I loved her so much it hurt. She was less striking, less splendid in appearance, than that marvelous Jewish Eve, but then she had much less body hair and, despite her height, had softer and more charming movements. I understood her; I knew exactly where she was coming from, what she represented, and why she did what she was doing. She was tall, pale, and had dark curls; she was one of those women with ambition and education who still goes to the hairdresser once a month and who buys English and Japanese designer clothes on sale. In the old days, before we knew each other, Ina had a careless relation to social norms; she was a torn spiritual child of the seventies. In the beginning, she was equipped only with a few Velvet Underground recordings and a Warhol book. She became—after this short-lived brush with camp—one of the youngest members of the Marxist Group, which had a Jesuit way of thinking and an SS-like organization. Being schooled by this group was for her, for a while, the greatest, most exciting experience. Ina also had old photos of herself, and one of them, from her sophist phase, shows her with naked upper torso in a frazzled wing chair, her hair falling, glistening, straight over her shoulders as she gazes past the camera with a melancholy and, at the same time, coquettish look . . . And what came after that? As a student of philosophy and German studies, it was more difficult for her to adjust to the new, goal-oriented tone of the time, which had emerged by the end of the decade, but she still managed the ideological leap without effort. This was most likely due to the fact that Ina—whose hair, after an Iroquois intermezzo, became long again, although layered and permed—was endowed with an effortless curiosity and versatility that enabled her to gather with equal energy data about the Weimar Republic, Heidegger, and the Structuralists as well as punk, Malcolm McLaren, or Neville Brody. Yet, despite her sporting sense for current trends, Ina undertook her first journalistic steps (after receiving a Ph.D. in philosophy with a dissertation on Spinoza's excommunication) in the arts pages, where she could, this was her unshakable opinion, work more systematically and seriously than in one of the new youth magazines. Her decision paid off; Ina quickly became a permanent contributor at a big daily newspaper, with her own regular column in the weekend insert, which she gave up only a few months ago. Ina's reviews were always fair, inspired by her great love for literature, and what impressed me the most was the incredible fact that she refused, on principle, to engage in trashing, since—this was her view—destruction did not further anybody, neither the reader nor the author nor the critic; on the contrary, she said, trashing is the most dangerous entropy, part—if you will—of a subconscious human program of self-destruction. However, she would add, I shouldn't take this literally; she only exaggerated what she was saying in order for me to be able to grasp her position in all its dimensions. No, this wasn't hubris, nor was it academic know-it-all cleverness; this was empathy; this was serious regard for the object, which bespoke respect and sensitivity. How could a woman of her caliber put up with a fellow like Warszawski, who thought, worked, and argued exactly the other way around? And how could she, a person who used her head, let herself be mutated by him into that reprehensible type of woman with whom intellectuals, especially Americans, like to surround themselves? Suddenly Ina was Arthur Miller's Marilyn Monroe; she was Nancy Kissinger, a physical display object, a long-legged flesh profile with protruding breasts, there to be touched, to be pawed; a life-partner of the little comments à la 'Please, Gary, don't!' or 'That's so sweet of you!' And this is the reason why it was fitting that Ina, since she was back together with Warszawski, hardly participated anymore in conversations and discussions that took place in her presence—and if she did, then only monosyllabically. Nor was it a coincidence that she hadn't published anything for a long time, that she confessed to me every once in a while that reading had become a terrible bore for her lately, and she didn't know where this was coming from exactly; at any rate, she was at the moment so totally incapable of concentrating that she couldn't even manage to watch television quietly and relax or, at the movies, to make it through a serious film without fidgeting and writhing in her seat. 'I know what you mean,' I said, triumphantly. 'You needn't say anymore.' 'You know nothing . . .' she replied. I said: 'He made a fool out of you; you are now like the secretaries in Cary Grant and Rock Hudson movies who at first always looked so smart with their black-rimmed glasses. At one point, however, they take them off for a kiss and never put them back on again.' We were sitting—it was for the last time—in the cafeteria of the conservatory; it was already late afternoon, and we were alone in the huge hall with the low ceiling, except for the Italian concessionaire and his teenage son. 'That's enough, Ephraim,' said Ina. She was serious; the two lines that run in a half circle from her nose to the corner of her mouth looked motionless and deep, as if they had been etched into her white face. 'You won't get anywhere with this,' she said then, and it sounded as if she were lecturing me, as if she were scolding a strange child without really caring.

An impenetrable dead end? By no means! How chaotic and contradictory the whole thing still was became clear when, by the end of this same meeting, which had started in such an aggressive way, we were able to engage in a regular conversation. Even if we didn't talk about us, about our love, for a few moments, at least we were again like soul mates who had a common belief, and it didn't matter whether we were talking about our daily lives, the new edition of Klaus Mann's diaries, the first general meeting of the newly elected Soviet parliament, or the latest issue of a literary journal. In parting, Ina told me that she could no longer meet with me; she didn't have the strength to be alone with me, but we would have an opportunity to see each other again since Warszawski had finally realized his plan for a regulars' table. He now gathered a group of people around him every Saturday, and, of course, she was to let me know expressly that I too was more than welcome. As if in a trance, I agreed to the Maon meetings, those meetings that I anticipated every time with a mixture of fear, joyous tension, and doubts and that were, from a social standpoint, almost always a flop. I went anyway because of Ina and also because of Warszawski. By the way, I was the only one of his German friends who attended regularly, since the few Jewish intellectuals who existed in Munich, and whom Warszawski probably knew, didn't come anyway—I think they were afraid of Warszawski; they were in mind and temperament much too reserved and refined for his table. 'They are all nothing but collaborators!' was Warszawski's usual phrase when he had to come to the conclusion after half an hour that once again he would be left alone with Ina and me. 'These birds from the Varnhagen Association and Shalom Germania are pulling the same hypocritical trick as the great Nachmann, only these airheads don't make nearly as much as he did with the right half of his big *yekke* ass. Pathetic petty collaborators! The lowest of the low! First they blow the shofar with a bang, and then they piss together with the Romans on the arc of the covenant and hold barbecues at the Temple. And in the end, they have their foreskins sewn back on. Haman's host! Greek whores! Fraternizing with the pig priests!' He caught his breath and said slowly: 'Anti-Maccabees!' And then, even more slowly, savoring it, with the emphasis on the second word: 'Yehuda kill!' Confused, but visibly gloating, I followed Warszawski's hate tirades; I kept my mouth shut; I didn't want, as back then with Eve, to arouse his Jewish self-glorification with a misunderstood comment. Ina didn't say anything; she always had to put up with Warszawski's constant squeezing and poking, and sometimes, when Warszawski was especially happy or irate, he grabbed her, without regard for the other guest, by the breast, whereupon she laughed and tried, for her part, to touch his belly. This developed every time into a mini struggle; for a few short moments, the two turned into a whirling autarkic tangle, and I just sat there, senselessly letting the last drops of mineral water from the long-empty glass run down my throat.

The waitress had listened to Warszawski's cholent discourse, shrugging her shoulders. She alternated between sighing and grinning, but since nobody paid any attention to her, she disappeared into the kitchen. A while later she served us chopped egg, the salad, and the soup, but rather than putting the plate down, she simply dropped it from a height of a few inches. The artistically designed white and yellow egg pyramid collapsed; the pieces of tomato and the salad leaves of Ina's brimming bowl slipped onto the table; the broth, naturally, also spilled; and within a few seconds, the clean tablecloth turned into a food-stained, unappetizing rag.

We were just having hors d'oeuvres when the door swung open, and Eve entered, accompanied by a short, thin-faced man, who had pushed his rectangular pilot's sunglasses up above his forehead. Without hesitating, Eve came to our table with a friendly dispassionate greeting for me, exchanged a few words with Warszawski, whereby they winked knowingly at each other, and even though she didn't wish to sit with us, she introduced her companion. He was Israeli, an IBM man from Haifa, half brother of Chaim, her first husband; his name was Udi Something, and he was quite obviously Eve's latest crush. I recognized this especially by her clothing. She wore a simple, brightly colored dress, sandals, and silver earrings with turquoise stones—everything about her was light, uncomplicated, and firm, and all in all she had something summerlike about her. Eve and Udi sat down at the neighboring table, cooing and moaning with abandon, in Hebrew of course, and Eve was completely submerged in her new world. How she nodded at him! How she turned the cleavage of her dress with its heavy dark folds toward him! How she strained to lift her chest and let it sink again!

It was only after a while that I realized I was staring like a lunatic at the two of them. Since they were sitting behind Ina and Warszawski, I was able to watch them effortlessly, without having to overtly turn around and twist my body. At some point, Eve leaned forward, her profile appearing next to Ina's; I compared the noses, the lips; I saw the dusky tense shimmering around Ina's eyes; I saw Eve's bright forehead; my pupils wandered back and forth as at a tennis game; I contemplated what was different here and what they had in common, but the comparison resulted in nothing, not a hint or insight, perhaps only the feeling that in some distant time, when I was a young man, I had lost myself, that I was no longer capable of following the tracks along which my life was supposed to move, that my alienation from the rest of the world began within myself.

And then suddenly my gaze came to a halt on Warszawski's big red skull. Framed by a light, milky patch of fog, it looked like a bleeding piece of meat that had only recently been hanging on a hook in a cold storage room, a spectral thinking instrument. He had the skull of a man who, completely different from me, has always been hard and ambitious enough never to stray from his path. Warszawski had one single idea, and he chiseled and worked on this idea as on a monolith, until it penetrated ever more clearly and unambiguously the heads of the public and the critics, lodging itself there, probably forever. This idea had occurred to the young Warszawski while the war was still on, in America, in New York, when he began to listen to Jazz with enthusiasm for black culture, black everyday life, black people. For some time, Jazz music was everything for him, and his subway rides to East Harlem were part of a constant attempt to free himself from all that self-pitying melancholy that was spreading more and more over his home, in proportion to the constantly increasing news reports about the conflagration of European Jewry that followed the earlier deprivation of their rights. Warszawski's bebop euphoria had a Savonarola-like pubescent charm about it; it was enthusiasm and gesture of protest in one; the seventeen-year-old regarded American blacks as his Jews; Europe remained as invisible and submerged for him as Atlantis, and all he wanted to see was not this distant natural disaster, glorified and turned into kitsch in the conversations of his parents and their friends, but the concrete oppression of a race that lived ten subway stations away from where he himself was living, working, and singing and making music in order to live. This is how Warszawski later described the frame of mind in which he found himself at that time and which impressed him as much as ever, as he conceitedly gave people to understand on almost every occasion.

But all this came to an end one night. In almost every one of his novels, Warszawski retells the scene in the winter of 1944 when he came home at three o'clock in the morning, after a night of dancing at the Apollo Theater. He unlocked the door without a sound, so as not to awaken anybody; his 'blood was full of syncopations, and his heart was filled with participation and sex' (from *Harlem Holocaust*); he was all wound up and hungry and had the feeling that he would never in his life be able to sleep again, and thus he stole quietly along the walls where the wooden floorboards made the least noise, through the dark apartment to the kitchen, and only in retrospect did he remember how strangely sacred and idyllic the white light looked as it came streaming from under the kitchen door, an uncontained diffused light, whose magic impressed itself on him forever. 'It must have been,' Warszawski said a few years ago in an interview, 'a light that a human being really sees only once in his entire life, namely at the moment of death, when the first cherubim have already begun to dance triumphantly around his head.' Don't make me laugh. Warszawski opened the kitchen door slowly, and he saw his father in a bathrobe, his gray hair slightly ruffled and falling forward in the style of an ancient Roman senator; he saw his mother in striped men's pajamas; then he saw the stranger, whose thin nose, bent to the left, was the first thing he noticed about him. Otherwise, the man had an empty, two-dimensional face with wide-open eyes that seemed painted on and cracked blue lips. Even though he was wearing Warszawski's father's tweed coat over a dark brown jacket, his shoulders were also covered with a checkered wool blanket, a fact Warszawski noticed immediately because, as always when the oven was on, the kitchen was terribly hot and sticky. And when he heard the stranger's apathetic statement: 'I'm shivering with cold,' he saw something that actually didn't exist: the steamed-up windows flew open, and the crystal-clear New York winter wind charged into the overheated room. 'Gerhard,' said Warszawski's mother, 'this is my cousin Leo Schneider. Leo, this is my son, Gerhard, and if you want to please him, you'll call him 'Gary' as everybody here calls him, and we sometimes too when we don't forget.' But her cousin did not react, even though she was smiling at him. His cut-up mouth remained small and didn't move. 'Hello, Leo,' said Warszawski, but Leo remained silent. 'He's been having a lot of trouble,' said Warszawski's father. 'With whom?' 'I don't know what they're all called, and you wouldn't know them anyway, my friend. Come to think of it, maybe the name of their boss means something to you . . .' 'Which boss, Papa?' 'But no, I don't think that they talk about him among your people in Harlem,' said Max Warszawski, and, as was so often the case, he had an inexplicably reticent tone of voice, which his son, Gary, hated because he never knew whether his father was joking or moralizing. 'Papa, the Negroes cleared their jungle yesterday and made trumpets out of coconuts and skirts and pants out of palm leaves so they wouldn't have to run around naked anymore, and then they worked and worked on cut-down trees until they made paper out of them; they took the paper to the printer, and they printed the latest news from Europe on it and called the whole thing a newspaper,' said Warszawski, impatiently, and added: 'What do you want from my life, Papa? What do you want? Am I supposed to listen all the time to your Nazi nonsense and commemorate our thousand-year history of suffering? Am I supposed to say kaddish every day for my people? Am I supposed to stop living because others are dying?' Warszawski burst into a sudden outcry; his huge eyelids trembled; he felt the rush that seized him, the rush of truth and honesty and of hatred against all those who do nothing but play act. 'I'm shivering with the cold,' said Leo. They all turned toward him. At the same time, an enraged Max Warszawski hit the table with the flat of his hand; the big bread knife leaped up and fell on the floor, landing just a few inches from his foot. The big bang was followed by another bang; the kitchen window was actually ripped open from the outside, and at that moment Max Warszawski said: 'You are a precocious shit head, Gerhard!' the shutters opened and closed in the wind, banging and cracking; this was the sound of a storm, of collapsing ship masts, tumbling sails, and splitting wood, which normally only happens in pirate movies; huge dirty snowflakes blew inside; Warszawski's mother said: 'He didn't mean it that way, Max, and one day he'll be able to understand everything even better than we do,' whereupon Warszawski moaned in torment, but then Leo said again: 'Shivering with cold . . .' and then the snowflakes began to melt on the gray table and on the green tile floor, and the stains that remained were red, dark red . . .

This is how Warszawski described in *Harlem Holocaust* his first encounter with someone who had escaped the Nazis, and it was to this witching hour that he later pinpointed his initiation as a writer. It also turned into a Road to Damascus experience, for Warszawski was to learn, in the days and weeks that followed, bit by bit, Leo Schneider's entire story, absorbing and internalizing it like an addict. Of course, the new inspiration he received from the concentration camp survivor by no means diminished the intensity and enthusiasm of his passion for Negroes. Warszawski had simply discovered a second, in all likelihood more profound, layer of his inner life; he suddenly felt an archaic painful fermenting and simmering inside. His Jewishness was now everything to him: a combination of despair, deriving from a sense of desire and duty, as he said, from which there was no escape, because the tradition and the enemies always remain all powerful. Seen this way, his mother's prediction—if these were really her words—that her son would one day come to understand the shameless stigmatization of his people would very soon come true. And indeed, the know-it-all, hard-hearted Warszawski, the self-appointed enlightener, soon began to take notes—at first only on single loose pieces of paper—of Leo's stories, which the latter, after he had regained his strength, willingly dictated to him without the secretiveness and taboos that always surrounded such stories later on, and here I am quoting Warszawski himself, who once commented about this: 'Those who escaped from being exterminated are, of course, in a state of a lifelong shock, a condition of confusion and of underlying apathy. These are people who live among us like zombies, but it is not a bad conscience that plagues them so much as the fact that they, instead of those near them, survived the destruction. Rather, they had simply come to understand that life is death no matter whether in times of peace, of war, or, in this case, the Shoah, and thus they form a club that crosses the borders of the countries of the world where they had ended up after the war. A gigantic silent club of wise men weary of life, who know—through a foreign murderous intervention—what we, the children of order, will never comprehend: namely that human existence is no more than a moist drop of rot on the creator's collar. They feel the exclusivity of that knowledge; it depresses them and makes them proud at the same time, and this is the reason why most survivors never talk about the camps, not even to their sons and daughters. One has to understand this, really understand.'

I don't remember the occasion on which Warszawski said this. I rarely heard him speak about anything this quietly and without affectation. I understood that it was the Holocaust heretic in him who was speaking and that this must have been the reason why he chose a soft voice to speak about it. What fascinated me about this speech was its sophomoric skepticism. But Warszawski knew this himself, of course, which was the reason why, as far as I know, he never spoke about it in public again. And yet it was exactly this thought, this unique view of life after death and the memory of it, that was the basic premise of Warszawski's monolith of ideas, of his stylistic literary hook: for what Gary Warszawski told in his novels and short stories, over and over again, was the story of Leo Schneider, who had escaped being deported to Poland because he was hiding in a very ordinary clothes closet while his family was being rounded up. 'It was,' writes Warszawski in *The Voices of the Others*, 'fate's crafty sleight of hand that I was not discovered. I leaned against my sister's clothes, a hanger pressing against my neck, and suddenly there was the familiar smell of my sister, a smell that reminded me of the time, as a young boy, when I watched her taking a bath, when I later stole her underwear, put it on, and played with myself. I was stuck in this idiotic closet, unable to stand upright; I bent my back away toward the left; my face was pressing against a heap of laundry, and everything was black. Outside was the hum of the hectic voices of the others, but I pictured Ilse's bra and how she slowly took it off and her long rosy nipples appeared, driving me to such distraction that I got an erection. I was unable to move for fear and arousal, and then I heard them searching the rooms one more time, and when the door finally fell shut and was being locked and sealed from outside, I struggled out of the closet, fell on the floor, tore open my pants, and satisfied myself. From then on I knew that I was on the lam, and I was gripped by a sense of fear and terror. But had I known then how much heavier the nightmare of survival would weigh on me in years to come, I would have calmed down immediately and probably would have done it again.'

The clothes closet metaphor is clear. Warszawski used Leo's concrete experiences and alienated and magnified them for his purposes. But he also considered himself an escapee: America, New York, Jazz clubs—this was his hiding place where he amused himself while the 'white Polish sky turned black.' Warszawski employed this construction, convincing and catchy as it was, again and again with pathological single-mindedness: The Nazis had covered themselves with practical guilt, but the guilt of the Jews who survived was a metaphysical one. 'And this is the reason,' I have heard Warszawski say on several occasions, 'why—crazy world!—the children of the perpetrators have a much easier time coming to terms with the whole monstrosity of extermination than do the offspring of the victims. Shitty, isn't it? But rather than being unjust, it's truly and typically Yahweh . . . What an asshole!'

Warszawski's books dealt exclusively with himself—though at first glance it was all about Leo Schneider, about his flight from Hamburg via the Netherlands, the south of France, Spain, the Pyrenees, and Lisbon, which Warszawski reworked just as frequently in ever new variations, as well as his first years in America. However, Warszawski loved mendacious obviousness and the metaconfusion of his *surfiction*. The hero's name was always Leo, an intelligent poetic fellow but without the need for literary expression. That's why he had to get along with an antagonist whose name was Warszawski and who wrote down Leo's experiences and who was a pre-beatnik, yet had nothing to do with the real Warszawski, and why he had to bow to an unnamed authorial narrator who, in turn, was nothing but the invention of the genuine living Gerhard 'Gary' Warszawski.

Why these loops and encapsulations? At times I thought that Warszawski was serious about it, that it was a method to encode the actual physical terror in a welter of poetics and theory, and at other times I thought it was all nothing but boasting, grasping for effect, and undisciplined excess of a talkative author.

We spoke about this once in exactly the same spot where, a few years later, he first met that woman who had written and talked about him extensively until somebody came up with the idea of giving him a major publicity campaign in our country. By the way, it won't surprise anybody to know how well Warszawski's books sell in the land of Goethe, Beethoven, and Himmler. The reviews all had the breath of historical empathy and a penitent redemptive enthusiasm, and thus it wasn't long before Warszawski, whose mixture of Jewish seriousness, grotesque sense of humor, and genial shrugging of the shoulders nobody could really deny, was hoisted in Germany onto the pedestal where Roth, Heller, Malamud, and Bellow were already leading an enchanted life of restitution. That bastard! He knew very well that by rights he didn't belong in this pantheon; in America he was read only by a small coterie of friends and colleagues; he was one of countless writers who had to make a living by teaching English and writing an occasional article in the *New York Times Book Review;* the public over there took no notice of him; as an experimental writer, he vegetated on the sidelines of publicity. In Germany it was a totally different matter. His voice quickly became more prominent here; he was frequently invited to appear on television and was interviewed at length, for his exalted bearing and penetrating look provided the kind of high-class entertainment that we normally had to get from Zadek, Gysi, Reich-Ranicki, and all those other guys. I call it the Alfred-Kerr syndrome.

Warszawski knew whom he had to thank for his late fame, and his first encounter with Ina ended—I know it exactly, even if I wasn't there—after dinner at the Roma restaurant on Maximilianstrasse, in the house diagonally across the street, above the offices of the English House, somewhere between the second and third floor, in an elevator they had stopped in order to have sex with each other standing up. That asshole Warszawski, that old repulsive hypochondriac, I am sure he carried condoms with him, naturally he didn't want to do without, and I can imagine pretty well his mad mendacious show of justification. I imagine he bit and nibbled and tore lecherously at my Ina and let his pants drop without being asked, while he was ripping her blouse; she fought a little but not really; without a word she pushed the wild gnome away and pulled him toward her again; torn-off buttons were flying around; her bracelet and earrings, and here and there whole bushels of hair, were being sacrificed. I guess it was this mixture of love game and wrestling match, common among adventurers of this sort; their bodies were flying back and forth in the small space of the elevator, crashing noisily against the walls, banging and cracking through the whole stairwell, and in the midst of this mute battle clatter, Warszawski, halting for a moment, suddenly said: 'My people survived the Babylonian Exile, both destructions of the Temple, the Inquisition, the Dreyfus Affair, as well as the Stalinist Trials of the Physicians, and the Final Solution too passed our ass by a hair.' He could barely catch his breath, excited and taxed as he was, and while he spoke, he covered his long penis with one hand. 'So far we have always found a way out of any *shlimazel*,' he continued, 'because we have, even if some would deny it, a clever strategy for survival. And that is why I wonder, as I am asking you: Why should I deny myself a ridiculous unobtrusive protective measure? Why should I, after all that collective diabolical suffering, risk the weakening of my immune system? I ask: Should a Jew be permitted to die such a banal death?' Naturally, Ina did not answer. On the one hand, she felt terribly sick, standing there half naked, her bra pushed up and her panties torn, finding herself in this low narrow elevator with a stranger who, instead of screwing her, gave lectures. On the other hand, she was fascinated by this man's effortless way of bridging history and hygiene, of combining Aids with the Holocaust, and this was probably the first time that my Ina, dumb little Ina, truly understood why the hatred of the Jews is such a metaphysical matter. Don't make me laugh . . . How much she must have been moved by Warszawski's race for the finish, the finale of his little performance: 'You may think,' he probably said in the end, 'that I'm joking. Of course not. If Leo, my doomed Leo Schneider, sits in the closet and thinks about fucking, then that is Holocaust blasphemy devoted to the truth, which you, the goyim, hate even more than my Jews. But when the two of us, also in the narrowest space, forgotten by the rest of the world, wildly and impetuously rub against each other, then *this* is a lie—like Adenauer's reparations, Brandt's Masada visit, and Springer's four principles.' He spoke softly, thoughtfully, with the cheap pathos of a speaker in his voice. Yet, suddenly, he revved up and yelled out, in his short staccato phrases: 'And it is a struggle! It is fear! It is a wild lewd strangeness! Do I know who you really are? No, of course not!' He placed his free hand on Ina's right breast and began to squeeze. She screamed, but he berated her: 'Keep your mouth shut! You are a German miscreant, Miss Polarker; don't try to trade in sympathy! I know what to think of the likes of you. You are as little done with us as we are with you, and so anything goes for you. Not a chance! As I said, we have survival strategies at our disposal.' He took out a huge condom with black knobs, adorned with a half dozen white-blue stars of David, and rolled it slowly over his giant swelling penis. Then he said, and this time again calmly and almost whimpering a little: 'You must understand . . .' 'Yes, of course,' replied Ina. 'You want to understand me?' 'Yes.' 'But you are not capable of that.' 'No . . .' 'Did you ever sleep with a Jew?' 'No.' 'Do you regret this?' 'Yes.' 'What is there to regret?' 'I . . . don't know.' 'You will shortly sleep with me.' 'Yes.' 'But before that,' said Warszawski, cold and emotionless, 'I'll lick your fascist shiksa pussy a little.' 'Yes, of course,' said Ina; she was absent-minded, not knowing what was happening to her. The next moment she saw this Jewish devil kneeling in front of her and submerging his raw red head in her lap; his furry tongue swished against her labia; he pulled with his teeth on her clitoris; he bit her thighs; and it wasn't long before she totally forgot to think, and thus she suddenly heard herself say, with a foreign accent: 'Oy, az ikh hob dir lib, reb Warszawski! ' And then, still in a trance, she added a wild, unconscious, archaic scream in High German: 'I feel so terribly sorry for your people!' Whereupon she ejaculated into his hungry Jewish throat.

How disgusting! How repulsive! This sounds like *Portnoy's Complaint*! And therefore, enough of it; I got carried away; my fantasy took me into fields where a Rosenhain really has no business going.

Of course, I don't know the when and how of Ina's first tryst with Warszawski . . . I only know that I met him years before for the first time, also at the Roma. There and only there! We had gotten together to talk about the translation of his clothes closet epilogue in *Darkness*, which was supposed to appear as a separate volume in the

German Warszawski edition. I hadn't met the great writer before; I was his new translator; I was excited and nervous; I had prepared myself for days for this rendezvous, and since I had to ask all the questions I had on that day, I immediately took out my notes after we had sat down together and started to unleash a storm on Warszawski. I felt miserable, but, as it was, I had stumbled in *Darkness* over a mass of idioms and metaphors that lacked clarity for which, in my naiveté, I had blamed myself, thought them to be the fault of my uninspired translator school English and what I took to be my own modest mental capacity. This is how it actually was. Arrogant, but with gusto, Warszawski discussed all my questions. I felt like a schoolboy in detention; there was this pressure from above; I took hectic notes, wrote down every word he said, until I suddenly realized that Warszawski's explanations and reflections all belonged together, like the molecules of a big complex chemical formula. Suddenly, I was entranced; I was a seer; I stopped writing, and while I was listening to Warszawski's explications—I no longer paid any attention to their true meaning because I lost myself solely in their linguistic melody—I saw before my inner eye something like the materialization of this system that I was just drawing up for myself; his poetic and philosophic strategy actually appeared to me as an object, as an act of making physical, as a thing. It looked like one of those science fiction spaceships that sped toward the audience too clearly, like special effects on the wide Cinemascope screen projected in front of a black, star-studded, universe background. And this is how Warszawski's concept of literature raced toward me, but suddenly the steel blue rump of this absurd spaceship fell apart, and another smaller rocket appeared, and the same happened again, and thus it continued and continued, all in an absorbing, magnetizing motion until a small space transporter emerged from this mess of steel and fire with a tiny inscription on the nose that read: *Zyklon D.*

'*Zyklon D*, my dear Mr. Rosenhain,' Warszawski said, courteously. I opened my eyes and stared at him in disbelief. 'This will be the title of my travel essay: A Jew in Germany in the Year **, as subtitle. One has to be unambiguous, egocentric, and ruthless. It's a reportage, that is, it will be; I've already begun writing it, and the punch line, the crux of the matter, is that everything I have so far hidden in my novels, in a shitty academic manner behind an overblown *tohuwabohu* of meta game playing and linguistic experiments, all that, I'll say completely openly and straight out. My prose, dear Rosenhain, is only for Boy Scouts, masturbators, and brain-amputated exegetes . . .'

A heavy rock was suddenly lowered onto my chest. 'I am,' Warszawski continued, 'a calculating rogue, a clever Yid, a literary Shylock like Kafka, that dirty swine!'

Another rock.

'The reportage, by contrast, I am writing for myself alone. All day and half the night I run around your childish country thinking about it, and the ideas and formulations tumble out of my head as though by themselves. Genial! There is nothing sharper and, at the same time, more senseless than purposeful clarity!' He lifted his shapeless skull theatrically and turned it slowly away from me, the chin pulled up, the gaze lost in a distant nowhere land. 'And this is about how the first paragraph will read: 'Everything for naught, but I couldn't help it, for what I saw during my summer ** in Berlin, Hamburg, and Munich did not create a new in-depth image but rather a blurred historical photograph, all too familiar to me already; the old, cowardly, narrow provincialism out of which had emerged the metaphysic of destruction is still everywhere apparent. This is exactly what I wanted to show, and it was, of course, not at all original. It was a mania, an illusion on my part, boring perhaps but not ridiculous." He broke off. 'I have to rephrase this; I guess it's too cryptic,' he said, seriously, and continued in a looser tone: 'And in the end come the shockers, the wake-up calls, the buzz words for you Republican cry babies: 'I shall return. Out of curiosity, out of sadism, and because the national division is a second Versailles, a national stimulant to incitement. I want to see the effect of the two halves coming together in this great battle of reunification; I want to see the Elbe, Saale, and Main rivers run red. For the next German war will be a civil war, the battle between Lessing and Jünger, Büchner and Benn, Stefan Heym and Martin Walser, a battle that, this time around, will be started by the good guys and won by the bad guys. A battle that I'll be sure not to miss. I am your dybbuk! An Ashkenazic zombie! A talking piece of soap!

The screaming, writing lampshade!" He turned back toward me, leaned forward, and said furiously: 'Do you think this is perhaps an exaggeration, Rosenberg?'

'Rosenhain,' I said, voicelessly.

'I know that,' he retorted, with a grin.

I had withdrawn more and more into myself under Warszawski's hail of stones and had slithered to the edge of the bench. I held my upper body in a tense, oblivious, sloping position, leaning on my left elbow, which was starting to tingle from having fallen asleep. While the numbness was dissipating only gradually, I was struggling to maintain a mannerly sitting position. Shaking the murmuring arm like a clown, I wondered whether this Warszawski was a liar, a braggart, or a Dionysian cynic, and therefore someone who actually deserved our respect, or even more, our hatred.

'So this was the end, an accusing, desperate staccato, if I may call it that, the expression of a diabolical, sentimental mood,' I said, in despair, but at that moment I noticed to my great relief that Warszawski suddenly nodded at me with a generous smile, whereupon I no longer felt the weight of rocks and of rubble on my chest but only, underneath it, good cheer and warmth in my heart. 'But what will happen? What will be the focus of the text?' I continued, inspired with hope.

'What do you mean?' said Warszawski, wistfully. 'The reportage?'

'Yes, sure.'

'You mean . . .' He paused, as if he were handing me a keyword, a common thought, a common phrase, which I only had to complete. And I sensed immediately, very clearly: We were of one mind, related in soul and spirit, two relay race runners at the moment of the passing of the staff. So I accepted his rules and said obligingly: ' . . . *Zyklon B* . . .'

'. . . D, my friend, it is the wonderful letter D that I have placed at the end of my title,' he interrupted me, running his tongue over his lips, which he then slowly pushed apart, and this was the first time that I got to see the row of his false teeth. 'You must have heard wrong, Rosenzweig,' he chuckled.

'Rosenhain,' I said, mechanically. Where was the runner's staff? Where was it?

'D as in dullness,' said Warszawski, '*D* as in dumbness, as in darkness, as in Dachau. *D* as in'—he hesitated and pondered, while I began again to cringe—'as in Deutschland.' He landed both hands on the table and said as if in a trance: 'This is unambiguous enough to my mind.'

End of the kindred spirits . . . It was, I mused—and now I felt surprisingly clear and collected—it was, seen from a narrower perspective, as much an illusion and a desperate escapist anchor as had been, from a broader perspective, the much touted German-Jewish symbiosis, the historical joining, shoulder to shoulder, of two people, which sometimes produced geniuses and sometimes corpses. Yes, and we idiots still believed in it, in the harmonious strength of George, Musil, and Egon Kisch, the insights of Freud and Schopenhauer, the common visions of Rilke, Fritz Lang, and Billy Wilder; we still believed in the whole romantic German-Hebraic idea of *Mitteleuropa*, in the metaphor of *Kultur* and *Kaffeehaus*. The Jews thought this ridiculous; they understood, perhaps better than we, the tragic entanglements of the Enlightenment, which is why they strictly rejected these efforts on behalf of a correction of history. Among them were people such as Lea Fleischmann, George Tabori, the indestructible Broder, or Warszawski, and the terrible thing about it was that despite everything, we ate out of their hands; yes, we had them explain the world to us, in the course of which the Nazi horror, when it seemed opportune, became as much a part of their argument as gefilte fish, Jewish humor, guilt feelings about the dead, or—they recoiled from nothing!—even Israeli complicity at Sabra and Shatila. Everything was oppression, so they intoned between New York, Frankfurt, and Jerusalem; everything was sociopsychological inevitability; everything was dispersion and reaction. Liars! Hypocrites and profiteers! They knew very well why they would, whenever there was no goy around, mischievously, conspiratorially amuse themselves with the expression: 'There's no business like shoah-business.' They knew it very well, and they granted us no respite; they didn't give a damn about the German-Jewish symbiosis, and sometimes I think I can't blame them for it . . .

Warszawski still told me this and that about his reportage; it was really to be the purest piece of agitprop, overflowing with his obser vations about daily life in Germany, which he naturally always steered in a way so that indeed not a single old-fascist marginalia or neo-Nazi monad in our country was left out: He wanted to hold forth about the radical-right soccer fans of the Dortmund-Borussia front, about the fascist aesthetes among our artists (Merz, Oehlen, Förg), about the Leni Riefenstahl mannerisms of German advertisers, about the power and the public influence of rightist publishers like Frey and Fleissner, about the radical-right skinheads in the German Democratic Republic, about the petit bourgeois opportunist xenophobia of the CDU, about the timid militant hatred of our poor and the perfidious dangerous social disinterest of the wealthy, about the swastikas and SS inscriptions on school walls and Heavy Metal leather jackets, about the pyrrhic victory of Habermas over Stürmer and Nolte, about Augstein's Hitler mania and Schönhuber's (justified, one must say) tirades against Galinsky—also about all that which, packaged and seen from afar, looks like a new abject writing on the wall, like the new, big, rising German Nazi thing. He wanted to write openly about all that; he wanted to put aside all literary distancing and encoding, all aesthetic suppressions; he wanted to put aside Leo and his clothes closet, Harlem and trumpets, symbols and imagery that went up in smoke in the future arsenals of literary history, however enduring they may be, because they do not grasp the here and now. For a moment, he wanted to divest himself of the mazes and mirror cabinets of his chiseled prose, of rigid survivor neuroses and of 'dried-out Jewish blood spilled long ago,' as he said himself; what he wanted was degrading, insulting candor.

And sure enough he got it: *Zyklon D* appeared six months after our Roma caucus, first in English in America, a 130-page diatribe published by a small Midwestern university press whose sand and dust, as expected, quickly settled on the small volume. But then the reportage appeared in Germany, in my translation. How I hated this job! And how I had to recognize once again Warszawski's greatness. *Zyklon D* was like a hammer, a shock, a new and different Warszawski monolith. Why? Because, leaving aside the promised Nazi horror stories, the writer—armed with his imperious Auschwitz bonus—systematically confronted us with a frightening, though true, idea: 'The Germans of today,' the end of the reportage stated expressly, 'are of course *not* guilty. But the defeat, the partition of the country, the painful reunification, and, above all, their perpetrator complex will force upon them again and again a new guilt. For what other nation in this world and in this historic region knows what it means to forever have to water the flowers on other people's graves . . .'

The conclusion, as Warszawski had told it to me at the Roma, had been completely different, and when I read this new, much more dramatic, ending for the first time in the English original, I was terribly moved and terribly insulted. I had spent a few momentous hours in the workshop of a writer and yet had seen nothing.

How could it have been otherwise? What did I know after all? What could I, what did I understand? Ephraim Rosenhain, the coward, the nobody, the fraud and narcissist, he too once reached for the stars, inspired by Warszawski, just to see how it would go, craving proof of his strength and of being an equally 'goyish' match—and all he was able to capture was passionless unsympathetic emptiness . . . This was during that summer Ina and I spent together in Cannes—just a few weeks before Warszawski's return—in that two-hundred-franc hotel with a white facade in colonial style, a palm tree in the yard, ceaseless traffic noise, and a low-ceilinged, airless room where we slept uncovered and naked in the big French bed, our limbs stretched out with exhaustion from the heat, like relaxed babies who don't know anything yet about the world. Every morning of that summer, while Ina was sleeping, I worked on a long story to which I gave the allusive title *Warschauer's Legacy*. The work progressed easily; there was so much I wanted to accomplish with this text and more issues that I wanted to raise. It was for this reason that I was never at a loss for associations and scenes and formulations, and if I had to pause for a few moments, then it was enough to turn my head: there she was, lying on her back, the blanket over her stomach moved lightly, a kind of trembling and yearning; her breasts lifted high and proud; even while lying down, they sloped only slightly on the sides above her rib cage; her legs, which she was clutching, were so close together that the knees touched. I looked at Ina and remembered immediately why I had spent days and weeks filling my spiral notebook, whereupon the strength in me was restored, the discipline to pull myself together, to concentrate, and to find the new phrase, the next word.

Miserable pathos of the dilettante! On the evening before the last, after we went swimming, I staged a private reading for Ina of my finished manuscript, and as I was reading, it became clear to me what a plodding, spiritless, and top-heavy text it was that had kept me in suspense for so long. How stupid I was! For weeks I had lived in a world of make-believe, I had been totally wrong in the assessment of my own work and effort; I thought A or even B, but what came out was a huge zero. Ina shared my self-criticism, which I didn't try to hide at all. 'Maybe you made mistakes,' she said, 'perhaps you have undertaken something that was wrong for you.' A puzzling remark . . . we were sitting on the huge bed, manuscript pages, which I had furiously torn from the writing pad, strewn everywhere, and outside, on the city ring of Cannes, the howling of motorcycles and trucks. I leaned with my back against the wall for support while Ina remained in her uncomfortable stiff position at the edge of the bed. 'Why wrong?' I asked, but Ina didn't answer, and suddenly she gave me a fearfully tame and humble look. 'Ephraim,' she said, softly, 'come to me . . .' I bent over and tried to kiss her, but she turned her face away. 'No,' she said, 'differently.' Again I didn't understand her. 'How differently?' 'I'll do it if you want to . . .' And now I understood. 'Come here,' she said. I slid over to her on my back and bent backward. I was incredibly happy. She pulled off my swim trunks, and then she undressed herself. Pale and dark, she bent over me. No, she had never done it before, and I lifted my head to see her face while she was doing it, her mouth and myself. It was a beautiful vision that made me forget everything, even my defeat; I gazed and gazed, and at some point I was no longer able to bear the sight, and while I relaxed my head and slowly closed my eyes, I caught a little angel flowing through Ina's violet-colored lips, rising into the air with two, three flaps of its wings and gliding out of the window.

I opened my eyes. I was sitting with Ina and Warszawski in the Maon in Munich staring obliviously at—again? still?—the purple fleshy skull of the writer. My head was a feather, a little breeze, and a whiff, and my thoughts suddenly swelled to hatred and insecurity; they carried me away; I sailed on a cloud of disgust, reverence, and muteness; I made my way through the most confusing state of dizziness that I ever had to bear, through an interminable, bluish patch of fog. The cruel haze spread over everything, and there, once again, was Warszawski's dull hand between Ina's legs; there were his quick, clutching movements with which he constantly pawed and felt up my girl; there were Ina's sighs, and there was her intelligent face with the dead eyes in it; there was his babbling and her silence; there was next to us the wonderful Eve with her Israeli, in a motionless apathetic embrace; there were, at the other tables, all the old Jewish women and men, whose cracked creased faces were now smoothing out under my eyes, arching like rising dough, and there were all their detailed concentration camp stories, which they whispered to each other in Polish or Yiddish. I nevertheless understood every word and also saw the monstrous images that went along with them, and this continued until they noticed that I was listening to them, but they didn't stop, on the contrary, as if on command they all looked at me at the same time and nodded their heads at me, whereupon I knew that from then on I too belonged to their secret club, and that made me by no means happy. Thin white patches of haze surrounded the old people and us, appearing like the artful rings blown by a boastful smoker, and though the restaurant was now beginning to stir, although the sunlight suddenly began to radiate through all three windows at the same time, and the walls and furnishings seemed to stretch like rubber, nothing remained hidden from me. For it was then that Ina, my Ina, began to unbutton her blouse; she took out her right breast and pulled Warszawski close to her; he didn't have to be asked twice and immediately began to suckle. He was hanging on her, an old lecherous baby, and while he pulled and sucked, sighed and gasped, Eve and Udi came over to tell us how sweet that little Warszawski was. Finally the old people also gathered around, and sitting in a circle, they too talked about this wonderful Jewish child, about his wonderful, intelligent little face, his delightful little eyes, and his dainty little fingers. Then they rolled up their sleeves and started a game with their tattoos in which the one with the higher number on the arm had to tell an especially juicy, informative Final Solution story, the gist of which was that only one survived in an entire family, while the others died anonymous deaths, a single survivor to whom it was clear that his life after their death could not be anything more than the mechanical maintenance of bodily functions combined with a diabolical defeatist knowledge . . . This is how it went back and forth between them, their taut cheeks glistening with terrible artificiality and youthfulness; they listened to each other with serious faces, while Warszawski was still suckling and suckling, and Eve was looking at her Udi with an affectionate gaze and said she wanted one like that too, and then one of the Auschwitz old men turned toward me and said with a high-pitched, girlish voice: 'My dear Mr. Rosenhain, it must be difficult for you to live . . . just as for us . . .'

Was it about to happen again? A new attack? I feverishly searched my brain. Or had they indeed all gone mad? It couldn't be that I was imagining all this, absolutely not . . . carefully I got up from my chair. Although the furnishings, the walls, and the trophies above the counter were still swaying lightly, the floor was again firm and secure. No more trembling, no more quivering. Without saying a word, I walked toward the exit. Slowly I put one foot in front of the other, and all I could think was: it'll all be all right. Suddenly I heard Warszawski's tormenting barracks voice behind me; I heard him hollering 'Frrritz! Frrritz! Heel!' and 'Atten-tion!' but I didn't react; I didn't even turn around when Ina called after me that I should stay. No, I never wanted to hear her voice again, never wanted to see her again. I squinted my eyes lightly in order to concentrate better; my sight was now much clearer than before, and I was therefore surprised when, the very next moment, I collided with the waitress. The tray in her hands jittered; I recognized the veal roast on it and Warszawski's brown disgusting cholent that looked like a steaming, fresh pile of manure; the plates were sliding to and fro, but the waitress was just able to keep her balance; she first said 'Oy vey iz mir!' and then 'where are you going . . .' but I paid no more attention to her either and especially not to Ina's desperate calls.

At last I was outside; I didn't close the door behind me; I could well imagine them watching me for a while longer from their tables; these lunatics, how they were watching me as I was quickly walking away, my body becoming smaller and smaller, until it had disappeared in the last inner courtyard at the exit ramp to the street.

I went to the English Garden. I often went there when I wanted to be alone. Anyone can get stirred up at times and need peace and quiet. I slipped past the Ludwig Church, past the university and the veterinary institute on Königinstrasse. I had a ghastly headache, but the dizziness was now gone; I could see the houses, streets, trees, and cars clearly. Only my eyes were still hurting, and since I knew the way very well, I closed them repeatedly for a few brief moments.

And there I saw us then: Ina and me, six months earlier, in the summer, after Cannes, in my bathroom, barefoot on the white tiles, she naked, I in my pajama pants. It was five o'clock in the morning; Ina was up early; she hadn't slept well during the night because the night before she had bought a pregnancy test for thirty marks. Now she fiddled impatiently with the little tube and the box mounted on it until I finally put my arms around her from behind so that she could hold still for a few minutes. In her distress, she might ruin the results, and then we would have had to repeat the whole thing the next morning. Our little baby lab was on the windowsill, and a bit to the left of it outside, behind the roofs, which were beginning to take on a reddish tinge, the sun was now rising; we could see it very well, we could also see how the light breeze was shaking the trees in the yard. Then, at one stroke, the birds began to chirp; two doves fluttered excitedly back and forth between the gutters and the windowsills; and from one of the lower floors, brass music could be heard . . . We were surrounded by a real summer backyard idyll, and if that weren't enough, the test tube with Ina's golden morning urine and this whitish test substance began to create a new color: it was the kind of red produced by the sun shining on the rooftops, the red that told us that it was clear we were expecting a child, a wonderful child. Four weeks later she had an abortion. Following Warszawski's pressure or plea or order, how do I know what it was, but I am sure he promised her another, more intelligent, more beautiful one in its stead.

I really don't remember how long I sat on the damp decaying base of the Monopteros, up there on the highest hill that King Ludwig had had piled up in the English Garden for his antique temple. Toward evening, light snow began to fall, but the snow quickly turned to rain; the air was unusually biting and wet, and since I was no longer able to fight against my tiredness, I leaned against one of the columns and tried to sleep. Then, suddenly, it was dark; I awoke; not a sound was to be heard in the entire park, neither a human nor an animal noise; it was as if somebody had turned off the sound. I rubbed my burning eyes, and when I finally put down my hands, I noticed a man also sitting on the base about three, four meters away and looking at me. He got up, came over, and sat down next to me. He was unshaven, smelled of sweat and alcohol, and the fly of his totally soiled pants was open. I didn't know him, and wondered why he had Warszawski's voice. He put his arm around me and said quietly: 'The core event of poetic writing, especially in my fictions, is not the Holocaust, nor is it the extermination of the Jews, but rather the erasure of this extermination as the core event from our consciousness.'

A madman, I thought at first, amazed but not frightened. I tried to shake off his arm, but although he was short and stubby, there was such strength in him that I was simply unable to free myself. I wiggled a few times back and forth until I finally understood why that sentence was so painfully familiar. Of course, this was almost verbatim the central passage of Leo Schneider's Union Square monologue in the dramatized version of *Harlem Holocaust*. What an incredible coincidence! What a miracle! I absolutely have to tell Warszawski about it, I thought contentedly, next time we meet . . . And then, since resistance was useless, I snuggled very tightly up to the stranger and fell asleep in his embrace.

Editor's Afterword

Friedrich Rosenhain's manuscript reached me via airmail six days after his death. The white envelope contained two writing pads bound in cardboard with 172 loose, and partially damaged, pages (handwritten and corrected by the author in green felt-tip pen) as well as a blank picture postcard with the outline of the Munich Frauenkirche on the reverse side. I have decided to publish Rosenhain's only known and accessible literary work—'Warschauer's Legacy' has been untraceable to date—because it is a document of a self-destructive talent and, at the same time, of the great German disease.

The text itself I have left unchanged. Only the title, which Rosenhain called

'Cholent with Warszawski,' is my contribution, since I think that it is far more reflective of the narrative. This is an intervention of which Fritz Rosenhain surely would approve.

*New York, 14 September 19***

Hermann Warschauer
(Columbia University)

Glossary

The story 'Joemi's Table: A Jewish Story' (chapter 6) is followed by its own glossary of terms. This glossary explains names and terms from throughout the volume.

Page 6

Kristallnacht refers to Reichskristallnacht, the pogrom by National Socialist organizations against the Jews that took place on 9 and 10 November 1938. Synagogues were burnt to the ground; approximately seven thousand Jewish-owned businesses and homes were destroyed; and nearly one hundred Jews were killed, while countless others were arrested, harassed, and threatened.

Page 7

Henryk Broder is a well-known journalist who frequently writes about current Jewish issues in Germany. Dan Diner is a historian who first gained prominence in his commentaries on the Historians' Debate in the mid-1980s. Marcel Reich-Ranicki is one of the most prominent, although controversial, literary critics and public intellectuals in Germany.

Page 8

Bitburg is the name of the soldier's cemetery in Germany, which President Reagen visited in 1985 to commemorate the German and American soldiers who lost their lives in World War II. The alleged presence of graves of SS soldiers ignited a debate among leading politicians and intellectuals in the United States, who urged Reagan not to go the cemetery. The play, *Garbage, the City, and Death*, written by the late Rainer Fassbinder, the prominent and often provocative German filmmaker, includes a male Jewish character whose demeanor and relation to money emulates typical anti-Semitic notions about Jewishness. The Historians' Debate, which involved some of the most prominent thinkers in contemporary German society, such as Jurgen Habermas and Hans Mommsen, focused on the relational causes for the 'Final Solution' and Hitler's role in the extermination of the Jews.

Page 9

Käthe Kollwitz (1867–1945) was a German graphic artist and sculptor best known for her depictions of figures suffering under poverty, war, and class inequality.

Pages 20, 153

Sudeten Germans were Germans who settled in the Sudeten, a mountainous region located in Central Europe in the Czech Republic.

Page 26

Daniel Libeskind is a contemporary architect best known for designing the highly controversial Jewish Museum in Berlin, which was built in the 1990s.

Pages 39, 145

SA (Sturmabteilung), the Sturm Troops, was the paramilitary wing of the National Socialist Party, founded in 1920, and largely responsible for carrying out the pogrom against the Jews on 9 and 10 November 1938.

Page 43

SS (Schutzstaffeln), the Protection Squad, was founded in 1925 as the personal protection force for Hitler. It later evolved into the elite troops of the National Socialist regime.

Pages 64, 145

The BDM refers to the Bund Deutscher Mädel, a National Socialist organization for girls ages 14–18.

Page 135

NSDAP is the Nationalsozialistische Deutsche Arbeiterpartei, or the National Socialist Workers Party of Germany, and NSV is the National Socialist Welfare Organization. The NSV was one of the largest mass organizations within the Nazi state.

Page 144

Rahel Varnhagen (1780–1832) was a German Jewish writer of the Romantic period, best known for holding a Salon that attracted prominent intellectuals, writers, politicians, and artists of the nobility and the emerging middle class. Varnhagen is also known for her collection of letters and diaries. Henrietta Herz (1764–1847) was a contemporary of Varnhagen's also known for her salon.

Page 145

Ludwig Uhland (1787–1862) was a German poet and professor for German philology and literature in Tübingen known for his adaptation of folk songs and ballads.

Page 145

Eduard Mörike (1804–1875) was a popular German poet whose claim to fame were poems depicting nature, love, and beauty.

Page 147

The Kolping-Leute refers to the Kolping Familie, a Catholic workers' organization.

Page 179

Theodor Heuss (1884–1963) was the first president of the newly established Federal Republic of Germany, and he served from 1949–59. A prolific writer as well as statesman, he received the coveted Peace Prize of the German Booksellers Association in 1959.

Page 152

Hitler-Jugend (Hitler Youth) was the youth organization of the National Socialist Party.

Page 181

Rudolph Platte (1904–1984) was a German actor best known for his roles in the theater of the 1920s and, after 1931, for roles in German film and television.

Page 182

Theodor W. Adorno (1903–1969) was one of the main proponents of Critical Theory. He lived in the United States in exile from 1934–49 and then returned to Germany to teach at the university in Frankfurt.

Page 182

Max Frisch (1911–1991) was a Swiss author and playwright

Page 182

Friedrich Dürrenmatt (1921–1990) was a Swiss author and playwright.

Page 206

Prinz-Albrecht Palace was the headquarters of the Gestapo in Berlin.

Acknowledgments

Grateful acknowledgment is given for permission to publish English-language translations of the stories in this volume.

Katja Behrens, 'Arthur Mayer, or The Silence' is a translation of 'Arthur Mayer oder Das Schweigen' in *Salomo und die anderen: Jüdische Geschichten* (Frankfurt am Main: S. Fischer Verlag GmbH, 1993), 67–152. Copyright © 1993 by S. Fischer Verlag. Translated by permission of the author.

Katja Behrens, 'Solomon and the Others' is a translation of 'Salomo und die anderen' in *Salomo und die anderen: Jüdische Geschichten* (Frankfurt am Main: S. Fischer Verlag GmbH, 1993), 43–53. Copyright © 1993 by S. Fischer Verlag. Translated by permission of the author.

Barbara Honigmann, 'Excerpt from Sohara's Journey' is a translation from *Soharas Reise* (Berlin: Rowohlt Berlin Verlag, 1996), 19–49. Copyright © 1996 by Rowohlt Berlin Verlag GmbH, Berlin. Translated by permission of Rowohlt Verlag.

Barbara Honigmann, 'Excerpts from On Sunday the Rabbi Plays Soccer' ('The Dead Men of the Donon,' 'Greetings from New York,' 'A Little Homage to MLK,' and 'On the Banks of the Mississippi') are a translation of 'Die toten Männer vom Donon,' 'Gruß aus New York,' 'Kleine Hommage an MLK,' and 'Am Mississippi' in *Am Sonntag spielt der Rabbi Fußball* (Heidelberg: Verlag Das Wunderhorn, 1998), 22–23, 49–51, 51–52, 53–54. Copyright © 1998 by Verlag Das Wunderhorn. Translated by permission of Verlag Das Wunderhorn.

Barbara Honigmann, 'Double Burial' from *Novel by a Child* is a translation of 'Doppeltes Grab' in *Roman von einem Kinde* (Frankfurt am Main: Luchterhand Literaturverlag GmbH, 1986), 87–97. Copyright © 1986 by Luchterhand Literaturverlag GmbH. Translated by permission of the author.

Esther Dischereit, 'Joemi's Table: A Jewish Story,' is a translation of *Joëmis Tisch* (Frankfurt am Main: Suhrkamp Verlag, 1988). Copyright © 1988 by Suhrkamp Verlag Frankfurt am Main. Translated by permission of Suhrkamp Verlag.

Maxim Biller, 'Harlem Holocaust' is a translation of *Harlem Holocaust* (Cologne: Verlag Kiepenheuer & Witsch, 1990, 1998). Copyright © 1990, 1998, by Kiepenheuer & Witsch. Translated by permission of the author.

In The *Jewish Writing in the Contemporary World* series

Contemporary Jewish Writing in Britain and Ireland
An Anthlogy
Edited by Bryan Cheyette

Contemporary Jewish Writing in Austria
An Anthology
Edited by Dagmar C. G. Lorenz

Contemporary Jewish Writing in Germany
An Anthology
Edited by Leslie Morris and Karen Remmler

Contemporary Jewish Writing in Poland
An Anthology
Edited by Antony Polonsky and Monika Adamczyk-Garbowska

Contemporary Jewish Writing in South Africa
An Anthology
Edited by Claudia Bathsheba Braude